THE
WAY
OF THE
PANDA

ALSO BY HENRY NICHOLLS

Lonesome George:
The Life and Loves of a Conservation Icon

THE
WAY
OF THE
PANDA

THE CURIOUS HISTORY
OF CHINA'S POLITICAL ANIMAL

HENRY NICHOLLS

PEGASUS BOOKS
NEW YORK

THE WAY OF THE PANDA

Pegasus Books LLC
80 Broad Street, 5th Floor
New York, NY 10004

First Pegasus Books cloth edition 2011

Library of Congress Cataloging-in-Publication Data is available.

ISBN: 978-1-60598-188-8

10 9 8 7 6 5 4 3 2 1

Printed in the United States of America
Distributed by W. W. Norton & Company, Inc.
www.pegasusbooks.us

Contents

To Edward

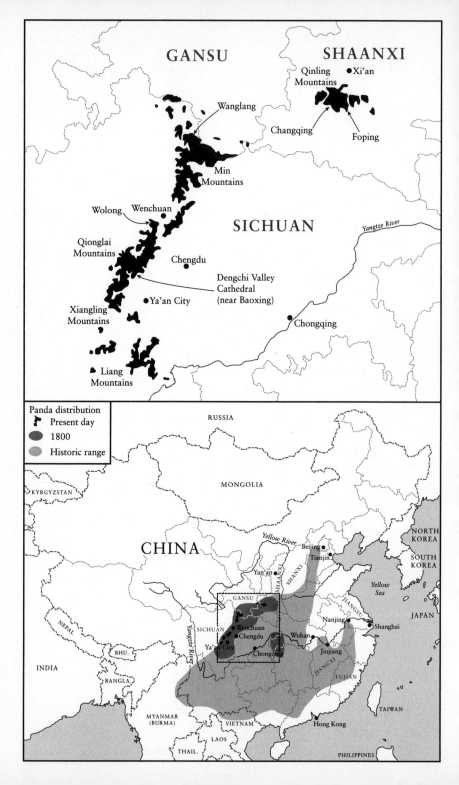

GANSU

SHAANXI

Qinling Mountains

Xi'an

Wanglang

Changqing

Foping

Min Mountains

Wolong

Wenchuan

SICHUAN

Yangtze River

Qionglai Mountains

Chengdu

Xiangling Mountains

Ya'an City

Dengchi Valley Cathedral (near Baoxing)

Chongqing

Liang Mountains

Panda distribution
Present day
1800
Historic range

RUSSIA

MONGOLIA

KYRGYZSTAN

CHINA

Yellow River

Beijing
Tianjin

Yan'an

NORTH KOREA

SOUTH KOREA

GANSU

SHANXI

Yellow Sea

JAPAN

NEPAL

SICHUAN

Wenchuan
Chengdu

Ya'an City

Chongqing

Wuhan

JIANGSU

Nanjing

Shanghai

BHU.

INDIA

BANGLA.

Yangtze River

Jiujiang

JIANGXI

FUJIAN

TAIWAN

MYANMAR (BURMA)

VIETNAM

LAOS

THAIL.

Hong Kong

PHILIPPINES

Prologue

Apart from its striking coat, there is very little that is black and white about the giant panda. Is it more like a bear or a raccoon? How come it's a carnivore when its diet is 99 per cent bamboo? How has the species survived for millions of years if (according to popular opinion) it doesn't like sex? How is it that an animal this rare and elusive has become so familiar?

This last conundrum is particularly surprising when you consider that the giant panda was not known outside China (and probably hardly known within China) until 1869. So this species has come from complete obscurity to achieve total global zoological domination in less than 150 years. In fact, it had probably achieved the current popular position it enjoys in human society in less than 100 years. To me, this is truly remarkable.

In a book entitled *Men and Pandas*, first published in 1966, renowned zoologist Desmond Morris and his wife Ramona speculated on the characteristics that may contribute to the panda's immense appeal. Many of them, like the panda's flattened face, its black eye markings and baby-like body proportions, certainly make intuitive sense. But what I want to understand is how and why the panda's indisputable appeal should have played out the way it did. I want to get to grips with the history of the giant panda – what I call 'the way of the panda' – in as much gritty detail as possible.

I do this for lots of reasons, but primarily because it's a super history, just a really good yarn. As a writer, that is pretty much my main concern. I want to write things that people want to read and I am hopeful – heck, quietly confident – that you will enjoy reading about the twists and turns of this extraordinary creature as much as I enjoyed researching and writing about them.

But I explore the way of the panda with other things in mind, too. Given the huge popular appeal of the giant panda, the symbolic role that we have found for this species, its ability to raise capital, the academic effort that's gone in to understanding its biology and the willingness of politicians to commit to its conservation, it is not that surprising that the way of the panda should also reveal a fascinating human history. Like the panda coming from nowhere to become one of the most recognised animal species on the planet, so China has struggled free from Western colonialism to become the self-sufficient, economic giant that it is today. So, rather wonderfully, thinking about pandas helps make sense of modern China's rise to global domination.

At the same time, the giant panda is a great muse for reflecting on changing attitudes towards animals and nature that occurred during the twentieth century. We humans have gone from hunting and skinning this animal, to seeking out live specimens to draw eager crowds to our zoos, to making serious efforts to protect it in its natural habitat. In spite of the relatively enlightened position we have reached, however, we still know surprisingly little about this species. There can be no better illustration of this ignorance than the attitude – most commonly encountered in Britain and the United States – that the giant panda is a maladapted species that deserves to become extinct. As Chris Catton noted in his excellent 1990 book *Pandas*, 'it has long been fashionable to regard the giant panda as an animal ill-suited to its environment, and incompetent in almost every function crucial to its survival'.

1. A captive giant panda munches away on ample bamboo provided by the staff at the Bifengxia Giant Panda Base just north of Ya'an City in Sichuan Province.

This sort of argument reached a low point in 2009, when BBC natural history broadcaster Chris Packham went public with his views about the panda. 'Here's a species that, of its own accord, has gone down an evolutionary cul-de-sac,' he told the *Radio Times*. 'It's not a strong species.' This is quite obviously silly because there have been pandas (or more properly, ancestors that looked very like the panda we know and love) that have been around for many millions of years: that's quite a bit longer than have modern humans. Bamboo, if you can eat it (which pandas have become remarkably good at), is a brilliant thing to settle on as a source of food because in a world without humans (as the world has been for most of the giant panda's evolutionary history), there was masses of this hardy plant throwing out edible shoots all year round. It's true that pandas do sex differently from us, but there is no reason to think that their way of reproducing is any less efficient than ours. None of this sounds like a weak species to me.

But I have learned through experience that no amount of carefully reasoned argument can dislodge this perception of the giant panda as a figure of fun. It's like trying to take on Po, the unlikely hero of the 2008 blockbuster animation, *Kung Fu Panda*. The measured appreciation of the giant panda that I have is always going to lose out to a 'big, fat panda' that can bounce his opponents to oblivion with his generous girth. So rather than railing against the innocent and sometimes not-so-innocent misrepresentations of the giant panda, I will try instead to understand them. In particular, I would like to know when, where and why the giant panda became fair game for satire. On this, I have some ideas.

I have structured *The Way of the Panda* in three parts. The first covers eighty years from 1869 to 1949 and is dominated by an almost exclusively Western obsession with pandas: we will learn of the giant panda's formal scientific discovery by a French Catholic missionary in the 1860s, of the (mainly) European interest in what to call this strange animal, of the competition to shoot specimens for (mostly) North American museums and then the race to collect live animals to show off in Western zoos. Throughout this period, China adopts a passive role in the panda story, busy as it was trying to free itself from the grip of Western colonialism, to replace its downtrodden imperial establishment with a new republic and to fight off unbelievable Japanese aggression.

The book pivots around the second, central part, which takes us from 1949 to 1972. Here, we will hear about one particular panda – Chi-Chi – whose extraordinary story captures much about this confused period. We will learn of the Cold War tensions that surrounded her journey from China to the West, of her role in the foundation of the World Wildlife Fund in 1961, of attempts to pair her with a 'Soviet' panda, An-An, and of her peculiar but very real life after death. During this period, the People's Republic of China begins to assert its ownership of the giant panda, using the species and its image to strengthen its sense of national identity both at home and, appreciating the West's enthusiasm for everything panda, abroad.

In the third part, which takes us from 1972 to the present, science begins to direct the path of the giant panda. We will see how a pair of animals gifted from the PRC to the United States became the subject of a serious research programme, how China and the West (in the guise of WWF) began to work on pandas in the wild, how zoos and other institutions began to succeed in breeding pandas in captivity and we will contemplate the species' future. As this final part progresses, we see China taking control of the future of the giant panda and, perhaps, the future of the world.

So without further ado, let us set out along the way of the panda, to experience the stir this species has caused wherever it has set its hairy feet: for decades pandas defied classification; they outwitted hunters and escaped trappers; they have induced public elbowing and had zoo turnstiles spinning; they have been on diplomatic journeys; they have been branded on products and turned into logos for companies and charities; they have become the face of global conservation; and they have attracted great scientific minds and plenty of money to study them. I give you the curious history of China's political animal ...

Part I
EXTRACTION

I

A most excellent black-and-white bear

The huge, foreboding oak doors of the Dengchi Valley Cathedral are mostly locked. But once a week, on a Sunday, they are opened for the local inhabitants to attend a service in one of the oldest Catholic churches still standing in China's Sichuan Province. Occasionally, too, perhaps a few times a month, a peculiar kind of tourist will step off the beaten trail and head up the dusty valley to this Christian outpost. More than likely it is not God calling them but the giant panda.

For it's in this remote spot, in 1869, that a French priest and keen naturalist by the name of Armand David became the first Westerner to clap eyes on this extraordinary beast. His 'discovery' resulted in the formal scientific description of this animal and with it the panda bandwagon began to roll. Although the inhabitants of the Dengchi Valley and other rural communities had clearly encountered this species before David, they did so only infrequently. And beyond such communities, it would appear that the panda was simply not known at all.

This is a truly remarkable fact. How could it be that a species so instantly recognisable today could have been virtually unknown as recently as 1869? This is particularly surprising given that anatomically modern humans have been in China for tens of thousands of years, and we have ancient Chinese texts inscribed from almost

3,000 years ago, which tell of events still further back in time. Given the long history of humans in China, it's hard to imagine that no one ever bumped into a giant panda, particularly as (one assumes) there were once many more of them, so the chances of seeing one would have been that much greater. And if you were out in the forest and encountered this striking creature, you'd tell someone about it, right? Surely word about this animal would have found its way into one or other of the many historical texts. Surely someone would have dipped a pen into ink to scratch out a sketch of this alluring black-and-white beast. You'd have thought so.

Plenty of people have looked, setting out on literary or artistic expeditions in the hope of glimpsing a creature that resembles a giant panda. And there have been plenty of sightings, though big, brooding question marks hang over all of them. Part of the problem is that we inevitably come to these ancient texts burdened by what we now know about pandas. This makes it easy to rule out descriptions that don't match with the fluffy template panda that inhabits our minds, and impossible to be certain that any of these faunal fables do, in fact, refer to the panda. With that caveat firmly in place, let's take a look at the line-up of candidate pandas, ranking them in order of increasing plausibility.

In third and last place comes the *pixiu*. In the *Er Ya*, the oldest known Chinese dictionary thought to date from the third century BC, this animal is described as 'resembling either a tiger or a bear'. That might be a panda. Then again, it might not. According to Sima Qian's *Book of History*, written the following century, the *pixiu* was a ferocious animal that made it the perfect mascot to fire up warriors before a battle. Though it's hard to see the giant panda in such an overtly aggressive beast, it is just possible that a fanciful description of a panda by some over-imaginative hunter could have fed into the identity of this now mythical creature.

In second place, just ahead of the *pixiu*, is the *mo*. This crops up in the work of sixteenth-century natural history giant Li Shizhen, who described it as living off bamboo in Sichuan. It certainly sounds a lot like a panda, but Li and others frequently describe the *mo* as an aggressive animal, which does not. One explanation for this confusing blend of characteristics – some resembling pandas, others not – is that the descriptions of *mo* reflect not one but two different species – the giant panda and the Asian tapir. Though you'll not find these animals in the same forests today, with pandas confined to their elevated pockets of Chinese bamboo and tapirs tramping through rainforests from Myanmar down to Sumatra, their ranges once overlapped, with the tapir found as far north as the Yellow River until about 1,000 years ago. In her forthcoming book *Panda Nation*, historian Elena E. Songster suggests that it is possible that the tapir and the giant panda were mistaken for one another. 'Their coloring is strikingly similar and their size comparable,' she notes. The snag with this idea is that tapirs are no more aggressive than pandas. 'The tapir is famous for its docility,' says Gathorne Gathorne-Hardy, the United Kingdom's 5th Earl of Cranbrook and an expert on the Asian tapir. 'A bit of ferocity might have ensured them more space in a crowded world.'

The front-runner is the *zhouyu*. In the *Book of Odes*, a book of poems written some 1,000 years ago, the *zhouyu* was depicted as 'a giant animal that could be as large as a tiger, that had white fur but was black in certain areas. It was not carnivorous, and displayed a gentleness as well as a sense of trustworthiness.' That sounds like a panda, doesn't it?

If you buy into the idea that the *pixiu*, the *mo*, the *zhouyu* or any of the other vaguely panda-like creatures that inhabit ancient texts really are pandas, then they begin to pop up elsewhere with rewarding frequency: there might have been pandas amongst the rare animals kept at the Emperor's garden in Xi'an around 2,000 years ago; in the seventh century, an emperor of the Tang Dynasty may have rewarded a bunch of deserving subjects with a panda skin each; and his grandson sent a couple of live animals that could have been pandas to Japan as a goodwill gesture. And so on.

The problem with all these wonderful stories is that it's impossible to be certain that these ancient authors were really talking about pandas. If there is any truth in them and the Chinese have known about the giant panda for thousands of years, then why did nobody think of sketching or painting it, or glazing it onto any of the millions of fabulous Imperial vases? Because here's another strange fact: there is no known artistic rendition of the giant panda until the nineteenth century. What this suggests quite strongly is that the existence of these animals was not common knowledge until really very recently, even within China. As we will see in Chapter 3, explorers who subsequently marched into the mountains with the sole intent of seeing (and shooting) a panda found the mission far harder than they'd imagined. For historian Songster, this is pretty good evidence that this animal – so well known today – really was just the stuff of rumour until Armand David sent it global.

Even if you think you've never heard of this French priest, there's a very good chance that your garden owes a debt to him. Horticultural favourites like *Buddleia davidii*, *Clematis armandii* and *Clematis davidiana* were all collected by and named after him. The list goes on – *Prunus davidiana*, *Lilium davidii* and *Viburnum davidii*. Over the course of almost ten years in China, dozens of forays into the countryside around Beijing and three major expeditions, David fell upon 1,500 plant species previously unknown to science. Before him, these species were all confined to Asia, many endemic to remote areas of China. Today, if you don't have one of David's plant species in your garden, you wouldn't have to stray far from your front door to find one.

Though David had been something of an amateur naturalist for as long as he could remember, he had left his native town in the French Pyrenees in his mid-thirties on a mission of an altogether different kind. 'It was my ambition', he wrote, 'to share in accordance with my abilities the hard and meritorious day-by-day work of the missionaries who for the past three centuries have tried to convert the vast population of the Far East to Christian civilisation.' After years of badgering his superiors in the Catholic Church in Paris, David had finally been posted to China to spread the Christian word to a people considered ripe for conversion. From his arrival in 1862 until 1866, he'd been based at a mission in Beijing, although he'd been given the space to pursue his interest in natural history. As David put it, 'All science is dedicated to the study of God's works and glorifies the Author.' He read whatever texts he could get hold of, pootled out of the city on short collecting trips and sent his specimens back to the Muséum National d'Histoire Naturelle in Paris.

On one of these expeditions in 1866, David's natural curiosity got the better of him. He had heard rumours of a weird creature to be found at the Imperial Hunting Park a few miles south of the capital. It was supposed to have the antlers of a stag, the neck of a camel, hooves of a cow and tail of a donkey. In spite of the high wall surrounding the park, an armed presence to keep out intruders and a risk of the death penalty for anyone who killed this rare creature, David managed to get his hands on the skin and bones of a female and a young male. The desk-bound zoologists back in Paris sat up at the arrival of this hitherto unknown beast. They were so impressed that they named it after him – *Elaphurus davidianus* or, more commonly, Père David's Deer.

2. The Catholic missionary Armand David set the panda bandwagon rolling when he sent back giant panda specimens to the Muséum National d'Histoire Naturelle in Paris in 1869.

Growing in confidence and with financial support from the Paris museum, David then set off to explore the mountains to the west of Beijing, a region 'which had not yet been visited by a European'. By his own admission, the results of his eight-month trip were 'not brilliant'. His third and last expedition, from 1872 to 1874, took him into central China, but his efforts were curtailed by illness.

So it was his second expedition from 1868 to 1870 that provided the greatest natural history treasures. He sailed from Tianjin across the Yellow Sea to Shanghai before heading 1,000 miles up the great Yangtze River into Sichuan Province in the wild and expansive west of China. At the Dengchi Valley Cathedral and its associated mission, built some thirty years earlier to plant the word of a Christian God in the midst of this rural community, David settled down to preach but also to collect thousands of plant and animal specimens for his Parisian natural history masters. While out collecting on 21 March 1869, not long after his arrival at the mission, David was invited into the home of a local hunter called Li for 'tea and sweets.' It was here that he chanced upon the striking, wiry skin of a strange new creature, 'a most excellent black-and-white bear'.

Back at the mission, David had just enough time before dinner to summon some of the hunters he'd taken on. He described the black-and-white bearskin he'd seen that afternoon and told them to add it to his wishlist. 'I am delighted when I hear my hunters say that I shall certainly obtain the animal within a short time,' he wrote in his diary later that evening. 'They tell me they will go out tomorrow to kill this animal, which will provide an interesting novelty to science.' A few days later, David's hunters returned with a huge beast trussed up beneath two sturdy lengths of bamboo. It was not, however, the coveted black-and-white bear but a huge black boar. At a glance, David could tell from its short ears, long legs and coarse hair that it was different to the European wild boar of his childhood and after a bit of haggling, the naturalist had the specimen and the hunters had cash-in-hand. While they went off to make a fresh assault on the

9

black-and-white bear, David and his servant set out on their own in the direction of a massive mountain above the mission. It was an expedition from which they very nearly did not return. The entry in David's diary for 17 March 1869 leaves just one unanswered question: what on earth had he been thinking?

The two men left the mission at dawn and made good progress until eleven o'clock. Then the path they had been following along the banks of a rugged stream petered out at the foot of 'a series of splashing, foaming cascades'. They munched on a 'crust of bread moistened with icy water', while David had a think. Should they turn back or attempt to find a way up the precipitous slopes on either side of the stream? You guessed it.

> For four whole hours we pull ourselves up from rock to rock as high as we can go by clinging to trees and roots. All that is not vertical is covered with frozen snow … Fortunately the trees and shrubs prevent us from seeing too clearly the depths over which we are suspended, sometimes holding only by our hands.

When they eventually decided to turn back, it had become impossible to descend without slipping and falling on the ice.

> Sometimes we are plunged into half-melted snow, or the trees which we clutch, break and we roll to another tree or nearby rock. Fortunately my robust young man is seeing it through better than I might hope from a Chinese; twice, however, I hold him back when he is already slipping to the edge of the abyss. He says that if we do not die that day we never will.

Thankfully for David and for the purposes of this story, they didn't. His survival must also have come as a relief to his band of hired hunters who returned a few days later bearing the body of a young black-and-white bear. With David still breathing, they had an eager – almost desperate – buyer for the specimen and were able to sell it to him 'very dearly'. David carried the cold, stiff body into the room that the resident priest, Father Dugrité, had put at his disposal. He laid it gently on his work table, picked up his scalpel and quickly set to work.

During the nineteenth century, it was pretty standard for missionaries to dabble in natural history. In China at least, it was the Catholic missionaries like David that made the most significant discoveries. 'No Protestant missionary accomplished half as much as they did,' notes Fa-ti Fan in *British Naturalists in Qing China: Science, Empire and Cultural Encounter*. The reason, she explains, is that Protestants being Protestants came to China with their wives and families, were most commonly based in coastal cities and tended to hang on to their Western lifestyles. The more mobile, celibate Catholics, by contrast, managed to set up a network of missions across China that would act as staging posts for journeys into the interior where the richest and weirdest flora and fauna were to be found. The Catholics also tended to embrace the local culture, dressing and living as did the locals and drawing heavily on their knowledge of the natural world.

Given this Catholic talent for natural history, it is perhaps no surprise to learn that the missionaries who contributed most to lifting the lid on China's natural history were European. Blazing the trail was Évariste Régis Huc, who came to China in 1839. In 1844, he joined forces with a former Tibetan Priest and Catholic convert, Joseph Gabet, and headed for Tibet. His *Souvenirs d'un voyage dans la Tartarie, le Thibet, et la Chine pendant les années 1844, 1845 et 1846*, published in 1850 and packed with derring-do, inspired a generation of missionaries – David included – to go out and do likewise. The Muséum National d'Histoire

Naturelle in Paris was more than happy to offer such educated and well-positioned missionary naturalists the funds to support their collecting work. On his way to Sichuan in 1868, David had popped his head in at a Catholic mission on the outskirts of Shanghai. This 'fine, large establishment' had a zoological collection established by fellow naturalist Pierre Heude, though when David came calling, the man himself had been out 'collecting the fish of the Yangtze'. 'I hope their researches will also augment our national collections at the Museum,' wrote David.

There was also Jean Marie Delavay, a botanist working out of Guangdong and Kunming and who David would meet in France in 1881. Delavay sent more than 200,000 herbarium specimens back to France. Yet another Catholic missionary, Father Paul Farges, was based in Sichuan from 1867 onwards. He described and gave his name to an entire genus of bamboo – *Fargesia* – one of the staple foods of the giant panda. Finally, there was the missionary Jean André Soulié, working a little later in the century, who sent the Parisian botanists thousands of specimens from Sichuan and Tibet.

But in case you have the idea that such men spent their spare time frolicking about with a flower press, nothing could have been further from the truth. 'In this country good results can be obtained only by surmounting great difficulty,' David wrote. What exactly did he mean?

China was a nation in disarray. It would be going too far to peg the collapse of China's 2,000-year-long Imperial era on opium addiction but it certainly played a crucial role. Through the early nineteenth century, Britain pressed opium from India upon the Chinese and with the local population hooked, demand was only going to go in only one direction. The consequences for the addicted were dire. Wherever David went, he was witness to the devastation caused by processed poppy. And he disapproved in no uncertain terms. On his way into one city on his first expedition to Mongolia, for example, what had initially appeared to be a prosperous place began to look 'increasingly wretched' as he approached. 'The misery is undoubtedly due to the abominable practice of opium smoking to which the population is addicted, and which is causing it slowly to perish,' he wrote. On the *Hirado* – the vessel that took him from Shanghai up the Yangtze as far as modern-day Wuhan – he complained that the Chinese 'quietly smoke their opium, the nauseous smell of which is brought to us in gusts by the wind'. Further upriver, he described the mother of the boat's captain as:

> an intrepid opium smoker and a bold widow, who often undertakes to give orders to the crew. This pale, almost cadaverous-looking woman … spends almost all of her time in her little room, inhaling the vapours of the drug which undermines her health and her purse. But the tyranny of opium smoking is such that never, or almost never, are those who fall under its spell able to overcome the habit, even though they see clearly how it hastens their ruin and their death.

When China's ruling Qing Dynasty deciding to clamp down on the drug in the late 1830s, the British were not best pleased and flexed their military muscles. During the Opium War of 1839–42, the British naval fleet put the pressure on China's exporting activities by blockading a string of strategic coastal ports. The upshot was the Treaty of Nanjing of 1842, which effectively stripped China's rulers of the power to control foreign interests in China.

Other nations independently negotiated agreements that were similarly skewed in their favour. The United States inserted an article that would help American Protestant missionaries become established in several of the trading ports. The French obtained similar concessions with respect to the Catholic presence, a step that would pave the way for the arrival of Catholic naturalists like Heude, Delavay, Farges, Soulié and, of course, David.

The Chinese did not take well to these developments. Resentment of an increasing foreign presence and dissatisfaction with the weakened Qing Dynasty led to a string of violent uprisings and rebellions. By far the bloodiest of these – the Taiping Rebellion – began in around 1851 and its bizarre origins offer an insight into the violent clashing of cultures taking place during David's Chinese travels.

In 1837, a young, ambitious man called Hong Xiuquan, who was working to become a scholar, had a dream. In it, he met two men. A bearded man with golden hair handed him a sword, and a younger man, whom Hong referred to as 'Elder Brother' explained how he should use it to slay evil spirits. It was a vision that lodged itself in his mind, for six years later and still struggling to qualify for the privileges of a scholarly lifestyle, he happened to dip into a collection of biblical tracts pressed into his hands by a Protestant missionary. 'In a sudden shock of realisation,' according to historian Jonathan D. Spence in *The Search for Modern China*, 'Hong saw that the two men in his vision must have been the God and Jesus of the tracts, and that therefore he, Hong, must also be the Son of God, younger brother to Jesus Christ.'

Hong combined this audacious claim with a burning hatred of China's ruling elite to create what we would recognise today as a fanatical cult following. By 1850, he had 20,000 recruits and eventually began to march north declaring himself the Heavenly King of the Taiping. The Taiping took control of several big cities on the way, massacring anyone who stood in their way, gathering food, wealth and might as they went. Finally, Hong set up his Heavenly Kingdom in Nanjing, just 300 miles shy of Shanghai and not too much further to Beijing itself. Although the Taiping got no further than Nanjing, contained in large part by fierce groups of resistance fighters intent on defending their homes and land from being overrun and their families from slaughter, they remained a force to be reckoned with for more than ten years.

Even after the downfall of Hong's hybrid Christian revolutionary sect in 1864, the devastation wrought by his troops en route to Nanjing was still very much evident. It was something that David himself noted as he ventured along the Yangtze River in 1868 on his way to panda country. Having jumped ship at Jiujiang 'with the eagerness and enthusiasm only a naturalist can understand', he ventured into the walled city. There, he found it 'almost deserted since the Taiping rebels pillaged and burned it.' Although these were violent and dangerous times, David was not one to be intimidated. When faced with the prospect of running into a full-scale Muslim rebellion on his trip to Mongolia in 1866, he had been philosophical: '[I]t would be necessary', he wrote, 'to renounce all travelling to distant parts if one had to wait for peace in the Empire, where brigandage and armed rebellion have occurred everywhere, again and again for so many years.' With which he had promptly packed his bags and headed straight for danger.

On top of such large-scale unrest, David also had to keep a constant lookout for bandits, thieves and the occasional pirate. But again, he was resolute:

[I]f I am to be held back by fears of this kind I can do no exploring, since the wild places, reputed to be the haunts of thieves and malefactors, are precisely the ones that offer the most in the way

15

of natural history in China. For safety only and to cool evil fancies I shall be careful to keep my gun much in evidence.

This precaution saved his life on more than one occasion. In 1864, while he was still majoring in missionary work and minoring in natural history, he had been accosted by eight mounted brigands, some of them brandishing European weapons. With just his Chinese servant and a couple of cowardly porters, David was severely outnumbered, but they could see his rifle and he drew his revolver. '[T]hese gallants soon saw that I was not inclined to let myself be despoiled gratuitously, and still less to let myself be killed by these prosaic cut-throats: they would first have to engage in a combat in which some of them might well be hurt.' The aggressors backed off and went in search of more submissive prey.

With dozens of hair-raising encounters like this, it's a wonder that David survived. He put it down, in part, to 'Divine Providence' but also to the reputation of Europeans. 'We are readily believed to be endowed with extraordinary talents and superhuman powers,' he wrote. 'I feel that Orientals accord to Occidentals, by instinct and from the bottom of their hearts, a universal and incontestable superiority.' But if, as David imagined in 1866, the Chinese were prepared to kowtow to their foreign 'superiors', this was not a situation that would last for long.

For as the nineteenth century progressed, missionaries in China found themselves facing increasing levels of hostility. Throughout his travels, David had frequently been refused accommodation, deliberately delayed, charged exorbitant prices and possibly poisoned. While at the Dengchi Valley Cathedral, he had heard news of a plan to 'exterminate all Christians' in the region. 'I think the emissaries of the Chinese government spread these rumours to cause us annoyance, or perhaps to make us flee from the neighbourhood by making it appear to be dangerous,' he wrote. But just over a year later, on his way back to Beijing, he received terrible news. On his way out to Sichuan, David had spent about a week amongst friends at Tianjin's French consulate, Catholic mission and an orphanage run by the Catholic Sisters of Mercy, all of which sat on the same site. Now, on his return, they were in ruins.

In June 1870, the French consul – a man named Henri Fontanier – had blustered into the local magistrate's office to protest at inflammatory rumours circulating amongst the Chinese. The French Christians, it was alleged, were taking Chinese children off the streets from impoverished parents to torture them or worse. David had heard such claims himself at a Catholic orphanage he'd visited in Jiujiang: '[E]vil-minded pagans say the missionaries only take in these poor abandoned children to send them to bawdy houses in Europe,' he wrote in 1868. Unfortunately for David's colleagues at the French mission and orphanage, Fontanier had pulled out a pistol and let fly at the magistrate. When it missed but killed a bystander, the consul did not have long to regret his actions. Within minutes he had been bludgeoned to death by an angry mob, which then killed several French traders and their wives on the way to the French quarter. The rabble set fire to the Catholic Church, murdered Father Louis Chévrier (who had accompanied David into Mongolia in 1866) and burst into the orphanage, where they had stripped and killed all ten of the terrified nuns.

Such violence was only a taste of things to come. With the Qing Dynasty continuing to give way to foreign powers, European faces became an increasingly common sight in China, though particularly in and around the trading ports on the Yellow Sea. And with floods and drought hitting the Chinese people hard, tolerance of the Europeans' different standards, culture and religion gradually gave way to a brooding resentment. This would give birth in 1898 to a violent anti-foreign, anti-Christian movement – The Boxers United in Righteousness. This bloody clash between cultures would set the tone for the next half century and more. As we will see, tensions between East and West, forged in the crucible of the Boxer Uprising, turned out to have a profound effect upon the way of the panda as it muddled its way through the twentieth century.

Today, thankfully, China has to put this troubled history behind it and is a very safe and friendly place in which to travel. In 2009, the tourism board in Sichuan's Ya'an City put on a bit of David re-enactment, organising an expedition for panda fans to retrace David's journey from Chengdu into the mountains 140 years earlier.

David had set out from Chengdu on 22 February 1869 and it took him just seven days to cover over 200 miles of not particularly hospitable terrain. That's averaging over 30 miles a day, one heck of a pace. There was a lot to take in as he went: he passed through 'admirably cultivated' rice fields; he wondered at a band of a dozen or so 'true dwarfs'; when he witnessed onlookers laughing at a naked beggar in a ditch, he saw it as proof that 'in general the Chinese are entirely without heart, compassion, or affection. They have only egotism and pride.' He found broad beans and mustards in flower; he scribbled down sightings of white heron, peewits and plovers; and marvelled at one of his hired men carrying a 170-pound load. 'The Chinese are the most adroit porters in the world. It is astonishing how they can resist fatigue in view of their poor and almost entirely vegetarian diet.'

As hills turned to mountains, David entered a long, high valley

3. The Dengchigou Valley Cathedral just north of Baoxing, where Armand David 'discovered' the giant panda.

'frequented by tigers and still more often thieves'. Over a mountain pass, he descended by a crumbling stone stairway, before tracking 'a beautiful river with clear, tumbling waters'. Finally, eager to reach the Dengchigou Valley Cathedral, he pressed on ahead of his luggage, rounding an 'impassable mountain' and crossing another through a snow-bound pass at an altitude of 3,200 metres. By two o'clock on 28 February 1869, he was 'safe and sound, thanks to God'. Father Dugrité was there to greet him and showed him to a guest suite on the ground floor across the courtyard from the chapel.

So it was that David rolled up the dried skin of the young panda and packed it into a box. He finished off a letter he would send separately to Alphonse Milne-Edwards, his zoological contact at the museum back in France. As his collection would not arrive in Paris for a while, he urged Milne-Edwards to publish a brief description of this creature. If it was as important as he thought it was, he wanted to establish priority for its discovery. He tentatively proposed the Latin name *Ursus melanoleucus* – literally black-and-white bear – and went on to describe its extraordinary markings. 'I have not seen this species in the museums of Europe and it is easily the most pretty I have come across; perhaps it will turn out to be new to science!'

How right he was. But what would Milne-Edwards and others in the West make of it?

2

Skin and bones

Beneath the Muséum National d'Histoire Naturelle in Paris lies the Zoothèque – layer upon descending layer of storage space filled with the remains of millions of dead animals. With thousands of type specimens – the individual animal that is used by the global scientific community as a reference point for a particular species – it's one of the most impressive zoological collections in the world. Buried somewhere down there beneath the Parisian metropolis is Armand David's young 'black-and-white bear'. There is also an adult he collected, which his hunters brought him just days later. 'Its colours are exactly like those of the young one I have, only the darker parts are less black and the white more soiled,' he wrote on 1 April 1869. It is these two specimens that Parisian zoologist Alphonse Milne-Edwards used to write up the formal scientific description of this species.

The privilege to name usually falls to a senior taxonomist based in a major natural history institution. Back in Victorian days, these head honchos could resent the presumptive and often ill-informed decisions made by their inferior field-based counterparts. This was certainly the case for the botanist Joseph Hooker, director of Kew Gardens from 1865 to 1885. As the man responsible for making sense of the botanical specimens shipped to him from across the British Empire, Hooker was incredibly

4. The red panda as it appears in Frédéric Cuvier's formal description of the species published in 1825. Alphonse Milne-Edwards saw similarities between this creature and Armand David's 'black-and-white bear'.

5. Armand David's 'black-and-white bear' as it appears in Alphonse Milne-Edwards' formal scientific description of the species, which appeared in the early 1870s.

frustrated by 'splitters' or 'species-mongers', botanical collectors who emphasised difference over similarity.

Historian of biology Jim Endersby has drawn attention to one such man, the New Zealand missionary-cum-naturalist William Colenso. As each new species had to be carefully preserved with a type specimen and its formal description lodged in Kew's herbarium, men like Colenso threatened to complicate what was already an extremely complex task. On one occasion, Hooker made a direct assault on Colenso's propensity for mongering species: 'From having no Herbarium you have described as new, some of the best known Ferns in the world.' In such put-downs, Endersby sees Hooker asserting his authority: it was those with access to the biggest collections who were best placed to make the final call on whether or not something was a new species, what it resembled and what it should be called. 'Hooker routinely offered his vast libraries of books and specimens as an argument for keeping the right to name in the metropolis,' Endersby notes in his biography of Hooker, *Imperial Nature*.

In the relatively minor taxonomic fracas between the remote David and metropolitan Milne-Edwards, there is just the faintest whiff of similar tensions. By the time David penned his first panda-related letter to Paris, he had decided this creature was a bear. But Milne-Edwards overruled. He had noticed some interesting similarities between David's 'black-and-white bear' and another creature first described at the Paris museum: the red panda.

Almost half a century earlier, in 1825, the remains of a beautiful russet creature had reached the museum and it had fallen to Frédéric Cuvier, the head keeper of the menagerie at the Jardin des Plantes and younger brother of the more famous Georges, to describe it for science. Cuvier had stressed its differences to bears, similarities to raccoons and created a new genus for it that sat somewhere in between. 'I propose for the generic name of this panda that of *Ailurus*, on account of its exterior resemblance to the cat and for its specific name that of Fulgens, because of its brilliant colours.' Cuvier gave the world a completely new family – the Ailuridae – containing a completely unique species – *Ailurus fulgens*.

Milne-Edwards was particularly interested in the skull structure, the arrangement of teeth and the unusual hairiness of the soles of David's black-and-white bear, characteristics that bore a striking resemblance to those of Cuvier's red panda. 'From its exterior form, it does indeed greatly resemble a bear, but the skeletal characteristics and dental arrangement clearly set it apart and associate it with the pandas and raccoons,' he wrote with barely concealed condescension. 'It must constitute a new genus, which I have called *Ailuropoda*', literally 'panda foot'. In time, Cuvier's red panda would acquire another name – the lesser panda – to distinguish it from David's 'black-and-white bear' or 'giant panda'.

In a letter back to the administrators of the museum the following year, David had not completely given up on his initial judgment. 'Another interesting new animal which I have seen in the mountains is the black-and-white bear,' he told them. He was, however, gracious enough to concede that 'some of the skeletal characters distance it from the true bears and relate it to the pandas' as his superior had argued.

However, the central question over which David and Milne-Edwards differed has refused to die away. Is this animal more like a bear and less like a lesser panda or less like a bear and more like a lesser panda?

Soon dozens of experts began to wade into the debate. Some based their conclusions on single characteristics like the shape of the brain or the structure of the inner ear; others drew together a combination of features like skull and dentition, the dentition and the skeleton, or the skeleton and the skull; and there were comparisons with fossilised panda material. But for every study concluding that David's creature was most like a bear, there was another suggesting it was not. Instead of forging a consensus, this tennis-like tussle over the course of more than fifty years only succeeded in adding to the interest in the panda. Here was a creature that apparently defied all efforts to make sense of it.

In the 1960s, a Chicago anatomist attempted to come at the question afresh. Dwight D. Davis began his thwacking great monograph on the anatomical make-up of the giant panda with an overview of the stalemate. He made a simple but important observation: 'Quite different conclusions have been reached by a succession of capable investigators on the basis of the same data,' he wrote. This meant only one thing – 'that the data employed are not sufficient to form a basis for an objective conclusion, and that opinion has been an important ingredient in arriving at conclusions.' In short, if scientists continued to pass judgment on the basis of just skulls, skeleton and teeth, there could be no end to the debate.

This was harsh criticism but probably fair. His next cool observation was more damning. 'Opinion as to the affinities of *Ailuropoda* is divided almost perfectly along geographic lines.' He highlighted two studies in particular to make his point. The first was a lengthy paper published in *Proceedings of the Zoological Society of London* in 1885. In it, a British zoologist had sided with Milne-Edwards in suggesting that *Ailuropoda* was most closely related to the lesser panda and raccoons. Putting the Frenchman Milne-Edwards and one other non-anglophone paper to one side, this view, Davis argued, had been 'echoed by every British and American author down to 1943'.

The second study to which Davis drew attention appeared in 1895. Its author, a Danish zoologist, placed *Ailuropoda* in the bear family and, observed Davis, 'every subsequent continental authority has followed in his footsteps'. He went on: 'Such a cleavage of opinion along geographical and linguistic lines cannot be due to chance.' Indeed, it is perhaps telling that the Germans often refer to *Ailuropoda* as the bambusbär, literally 'bamboo bear', and have consistently grouped it with bears, while English-speakers who call it a panda have preferred to align it with the lesser panda. From this, Davis concluded 'that authoritarianism rather than objective analysis has really been the determining factor in deciding the question'.

This was ballsy stuff. Davis was not too far off suggesting that the 'cleavage of opinion' had come about because English-speaking researchers were pulling down English-language publications and non-English-speakers were dipping into exclusively non-English publications and both camps were simply rehashing what they'd read. Thankfully, Davis had a solution. He had an entirely new set of data to bring to the taxonomic table – the preserved remains of Su-Lin, the first giant panda to make it out of China alive (and an animal we'll hear more of in Chapter 4). Though she had died several years earlier, the taxidermists had thought to pickle her insides. Since nobody had ever scrutinised these body parts before, there was nothing written about them that might skew Davis' judgment.

Where studies of skulls and bones had produced equivocal results, the anatomy left Davis in no doubt where to put David's animal. '*Ailuropoda* is a bear and therefore belongs in the family Ursidae,' he wrote in his introduction. This pronouncement freed him up to move on to 'more interesting questions'. What Davis wanted to know was exactly how *Ailuropoda* differed from other bears and how those differences had arisen.

But in spite of Davis' best efforts to put a stop to all this wrangling, the central question of whether *Ailuropoda* was most closely related to bears or pandas would not go away. The reason probably lies in the emergence of new, molecular methods for ordering the natural world.

All living organisms, from a microscopic bacterium to a blue whale, are made up of one or more cells and each of those cells contains a string of DNA that acts as a template for making proteins – the stuff of life. This fundamental protein-making machinery, common to every cell on the planet, is the most compelling evidence that all cells have something very fundamental in common: their origin.

If you took two cells from your own body – one from the skin on your big toe and one from inside a strand of your hair, for example – you would find that the DNA they contain is identical. If you now extracted DNA from one of your cells and compared it to the DNA in one of mine, you'd find the molecule's make-up very nearly identical. But not quite. The tiny differences help account for what makes you you and me me. DNA from you and from a chimpanzee would have a few more differences. If you compared your DNA with that of a daffodil, it would be more different still (though you would perhaps be surprised at how much you both had in common). And you'd find the least similarity with something like a bacterium.

There is really only one rational way to interpret these observations. Few people can disagree that DNA exists, that it is passed from a parent to its offspring and that its sequence can change as it does so. These simple rules, which we know are followed by every living thing we've looked at, offer a powerful explanation for why everything has a different DNA sequence. It is the relentless process of reproduction and the DNA changes that come with it that have given us the spectacular DNA diversity from the bacterium to the blue whale. DNA, then, has some rather exciting messages for the taxonomist. Most obviously, it provides strong evidence that Charles Darwin was right: life on earth has grown like a tree, starting from some common ancestor, with its descendents branching over and over, over billions of years to leave a very luxurious canopy. How else and why would a toadstool, a gnat and a great white shark all have vast stretches of DNA in common that help them make the exact same cellular machinery to manufacture the same sorts of proteins?

Given the basic tree-like structure, the similarities and differences between two DNA sequences can help a taxonomist to work out the most likely route the branches took as they grew. Imagine three species perched on the tips of twigs at the top of the tree of life. Ignoring what each of them looks like for a moment, it should be possible to put them into position based solely on their DNA sequences. If you now redraw the branches based on the external appearance of the three species – with the most obviously similar two nestled more closely together – you'll almost always find that you have sketched out the exact same tree.

So what, you might ask, is the point of going to all this trouble with DNA? Well, the most obvious reason is that DNA is something that everything has. This means that you can use it to come up with a meaningful comparison between a butterfly and an oak tree, which would simply not be possible if you had only their appearance to go on: you just wouldn't know where to start. It also means that for species like *Ailuropoda*, where evidence from skulls and bones leaves opinion divided, DNA can be called upon to pull the consensus in one direction or the other.

So although Davis' anatomical data set from Su-Lin had swung things in favour of those backing kinship with bears, the opportunity to carry out some molecular comparisons was rather tempting. In fact, by the time Davis published his monograph in 1964, molecular biologists had already got in on the panda act. They were not yet studying the animal's DNA, for it would be another couple of decades before someone devised the technology to describe this important molecule. But in principle, the idea is exactly the same for the downstream products of DNA: proteins. Differences in DNA will sometimes translate into differences in proteins and from the early twentieth century onwards, there have been ways to study these.

The creation of a dedicated Serological Museum at the University of Rutgers in New Jersey is testimony to the growth of this field. Its purpose, according to an announcement in *Nature* in 1948, was 'for the collection, preservation and study of the proteins of the blood ... in the belief that such proteins are as characteristic as other constituents and are as worthy of preservation and comparison as skins and skeletons'.

At first this collection was just so there was one, but it quickly became a resource that budding young biologists could approach for samples. So it was that in the 1950s, a couple of biologists from Kansas University requested a sample of giant panda serum (blood minus the red blood cells and clotting proteins) that had come to the Serological Museum courtesy of one of the pandas then in the Bronx Zoo. The researchers hoped, amongst other things, to find out whether the proteins in this sample were more like those of bears or raccoons.

How did they do this? They made the quite reasonable prediction that if the giant panda were more closely related to bears than to raccoons, antibodies raised from giant panda serum should bind more readily to bear proteins than to those from raccoons. This, it turned out, was exactly what they found, leading them to conclude that 'the serological affinities of the giant panda are with the bears rather than the raccoons'.

Just before the death of London Zoo's most famous panda Chi-Chi in 1972 (who we will hear much more about soon), the keepers collected some blood samples and sent them to Vincent Sarich at the University of Berkeley in California. He used much the same approach and reached much the same conclusion. 'The association of the giant panda and the other bears is clear and unequivocal,' he wrote.

There remained, however, some discomfort at such confident assertions. In 1966, just after Davis had brought out his monograph, researchers at King's College Hospital Medical School in London had discovered that the giant panda has just forty-two chromosomes where most true bears have seventy-four. That didn't sound much like a close relationship.

So when another molecular method for ordering species – DNA-DNA hybridisation – appeared in the 1980s, it was inevitable that someone would use it to revisit the panda question: 'I could not resist this one, a century-old debate, unsettled and looking for a new approach,' wrote Stephen O'Brien, a geneticist at the United States' National Cancer Institute in Maryland in his 2003 book, *Tears of the Cheetah and Other Tales from the Genetic Frontier.*

Even if DNA-DNA hybridisation offered only a rough and ready measure of genetic similarity, comparing the DNA from one species with that of another was still better – much better – than comparing proteins. In an effort to settle the question once and for all, O'Brien and his colleagues subjected the problem to as many other molecular tests as they could muster. They used gel electrophoresis to separate proteins according to size and charge, they reiterated Sarich's immunological analysis and they used the latest staining techniques to look at the structure of

6. Most bears have seventy-four chromosomes whilst the giant panda has just forty-two, which raised doubts about whether the panda is, in fact, a bear. But by lining up chromosomes from a brown bear (UAR) and a giant panda (AME), researchers were able to demonstrate the striking similarities between these species. The fact that the panda has fewer but larger chromosomes than other bears is most likely a result of a series of chromosomal fusions that took place at some stage along the panda lineage.

the giant panda's relatively few chromosomes in unprecedented detail. With good quality photographs of the chromosomes from giant pandas and brown bears, they began to look for sections of similar length, width and patterning. They found them. 'Once we had the photographs, it was remarkably easy to see similarities between the bits of chromosomes,' says O'Brien. This demonstrated that 'giant panda chromosomes seemed to be composed largely of bear chromosomes fused together'.

From these different strands of molecular evidence, O'Brien's team came down unequivocally on the side of the panda as a bear. The differences they'd described also allowed them to put a time frame on key events in these carnivores' evolutionary past. This is based on the assumption that DNA and its protein products accumulate change at a steady pace through time. The more molecular differences there are between two species, the further back down the tree you have to travel before you reach their common ancestor. The evidence produced by O'Brien in 1985 and later work points to a scenario that went something like this. Around 40 million years ago, at a time when the tree of life was not quite so tall, there was a weasely little carnivore wrapped around one of its twigs. Today, where that twig once grew, there is a chunky fork in the tree, with one branch leading off to give rise to the giant panda and the other species of bear and the other branch growing into the red or lesser panda and its raccoon-like relatives. Most subsequent research has confirmed this picture, making slight refinements to the date at which these branches split.

If O'Brien hoped his evidence would settle the matter once and for all, he was to be disappointed. Some saw the anatomical similarities between the forepaws of the lesser and giant panda as evidence of common ancestry: both have a modified wristbone that acts rather like an opposable thumb, allowing them to handle bamboo with great dexterity. Others were persuaded by

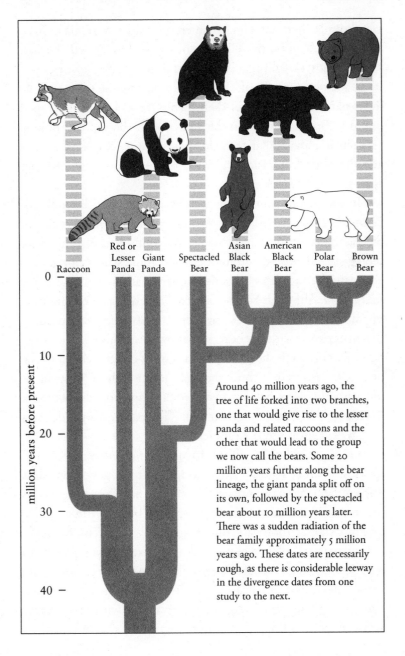

Raccoon | Red or Lesser Panda | Giant Panda | Spectacled Bear | Asian Black Bear | American Black Bear | Polar Bear | Brown Bear

0 –

10 –

million years before present

20 –

30 –

40 –

Around 40 million years ago, the tree of life forked into two branches, one that would give rise to the lesser panda and related raccoons and the other that would lead to the group we now call the bears. Some 20 million years further along the bear lineage, the giant panda split off on its own, followed by the spectacled bear about 10 million years later. There was a sudden radiation of the bear family approximately 5 million years ago. These dates are necessarily rough, as there is considerable leeway in the divergence dates from one study to the next.

faecal similarities. At a panda conference held in Virginia in 1991, Hu Jinchu, a respected Chinese biologist who co-led the first serious study of wild pandas in the 1980s (Chapter 10), stepped up to the podium to make his case for placing the giant and the lesser pandas in a group of their own. One of his slides jumped out at O'Brien, who sat in the audience. It showed two oblong and remarkably similar torpedo-shaped turds, one from a giant and the other from a lesser panda. 'I knew then what I was up against,' says O'Brien.

Hu was not alone in going with his gut feeling. The zoologist George Schaller, who had worked alongside him in the wilds of Sichuan, was sceptical of the strong assertions made by molecular biologists. 'Slick and ultramodern techniques may not always elucidate the incomprehensible,' he wrote in his 1993 book *The Last Panda*. Although Schaller asserted that he had 'no emotional investment in the outcome', he seems to have felt that grouping the giant panda with the bears somehow undermined its uniqueness. 'Even though the giant panda is most closely related to the bears,' he admitted, 'I think that it is not just a bear.' Instead, in line with Hu's view, Schaller favoured putting it together with the lesser panda in a group of their own. 'The panda is a panda', was his poetic solution to the problem.

In case you're finding all this to and froing between bears and the lesser panda a little exasperating, you're in good company. The eminent biologist Ernest Mayr made no effort to mask his frustration in a commentary that appeared in *Nature* in 1986. He took a swipe at those still unconvinced by Davis' monograph, writing that '[t]he few remaining doubts that the giant panda is a bear depend on the belief that it ought to be closely related to the lesser panda, and on controversial interpretations of molecular sequence differences'. Even though he agreed with them, Mayr also laid into O'Brien and his colleagues for the title of their paper – 'A molecular solution to the riddle of the giant panda's phylogeny'. Mayr felt this had 'unnecessarily overdramatised the issue' since 'it really was no longer much of a riddle'. If Mayr was correct, however, his own title – 'Uncertainty in science: is the giant panda a bear or a raccoon?' – hardly helped to bury the debate.

What all this shows is that taxonomy can be a tricky business. If teeth is your thing, then that – quite reasonably – is what you look at. It's relatively easy to demonstrate a similar dentition between two species – like the lesser and giant pandas, for example – and it's a very interesting observation. But it's another thing entirely to say that this similarity exists because the two are closely related. The equally plausible alternative is that the lesser and giant pandas have similar teeth because they have adapted to eat the same kind of food. This phenomenon of 'convergence' – where two rather unrelated organisms independently arrive at the same solution to one of life's little problems – appears to be quite a common feature of life on earth.

When things are uncertain like this, however, what you need to do – as the anatomist Davis was well aware – is throw more and different kinds of data at the problem. With geneticists able to produce DNA sequences from the 1990s onwards, such data has been coming in thick and fast. A detailed description of the giant panda's mitochondrial DNA pronounced that 'the giant panda is more closely related to bears than to the lesser panda.' Since then, there have been enormous advances in sequencing technology, making it possible to churn out ever-longer stretches of DNA sequence data in ever-shorter time frames at ever-reducing costs. There is now so much DNA data that it has become possible to use it to distinguish between different panda populations. This has even led some researchers to suggest that the

7. The cover of *Nature*, in which scientists described the complete genome sequence of the giant panda. This revealed that from a genetic point of view, the giant panda looks like a carnivore, boasting all the enzymes needed to digest meat and none of those needed to cope with an exclusively vegetarian diet. This suggests that the giant panda probably relies on some very important gut microorganisms to carry out the digestion of all that bamboo.

giant pandas in the Qinling Mountains at the eastern end of the species' range should be designated as a separate subspecies from those further to the west. As an indication of how far along the molecular road we have travelled, the giant panda received the ultimate treatment in 2010: a complete sequence of its entire genome. In this *Nature* paper, the researchers did not even revisit the panda question. By then, the conclusion was clear: the giant panda is a bear.

It's hard to argue against such a mass of molecular data, for it would require dismissing the overwhelming evidence that DNA changes as it is handed on from generation to generation. Outcompeted, behavioural or morphological evidence is now extremely unlikely to re-route the tree revealed by molecules. What it can do, however, is clothe the bare branches of the molecular tree with much-needed foliage.

So it would appear that David had it right all along. That said, Milne-Edwards' decision to highlight the similarities between David's 'black-and-white bear' and Cuvier's red panda is of immense importance for understanding the journey that pandas subsequently went on. It is because of this judgment call that this interesting species became known as the 'giant panda', so as to distinguish it from its red or lesser counterpart. From then onwards, this rare animal was able to boast the winning combination of good looks and a cracking name.

And as any marketer will tell you, an attractive, well-branded product is one that's going to turn heads. People will go to extraordinary lengths to get a glimpse of, or their hands on, something with this kind of appeal.

3

Game on

In the decades following Armand David's 'discovery' of the giant panda, the taxonomic debate surrounding this animal was fuelled by a few additional specimens that made their way out of China. But the tensions that came to a head in Tianjin in 1870 continued to rise, making travelling an increasingly treacherous pursuit for anyone wanting to follow up on David's work.

In 1900, the year that David passed away in Paris at the ripe old age of 74, these tensions between China and her unwanted imperialist guests came to a head. In the last years of the nineteenth century, the foreign powers had started to take ever greater liberties with the increasingly weak Qing Dynasty. Inevitably, this roused a strong sense of nationalism amongst the Chinese, most notably channelled into the Boxers United In Righteousness, a martial arts movement prepared to use violence to 'Revive the Qing, destroy the foreign'. When, in the summer of 1900, the Boxers began to attack anything that was remotely alien, the de facto Qing ruler, the Empress Dowager Cixi, sensing an opportunity, issued a declaration of war against the foreign powers. In Beijing the Boxers homed in on the foreign embassies. The diplomats from several different nationalities and their families barricaded themselves into a section of the city in the hope that help would reach them. It did in August, in the form of a 20,000-strong international force comprised of eight different nationalities. This Eight-Nation Alliance exacted revenge on the fragile

8. The British and other allied troops advance on the army of the Boxers United In Righteousness, which had taken control of Beijing in 1900.

Qing leadership in the humiliating Boxer Protocol in 1901.

As the West squeezed the Qing Dynasty to within an inch of total collapse, Western explorers continued to exploit China's natural wonders. For example, the British company James Veitch & Sons was one of the largest family-run plant nurseries in Europe and had collectors scouring every corner of the earth for botanical goodies. They took on a young botanist called Ernest H. Wilson to go to China to bring back seeds of the dove tree *Davidia involucrata*, a rare but striking species first described by Armand David in the 1860s. 'The object of the journey is to collect a quantity of seeds of a plant (Davidia),' the company director told him. 'This is the object – do not dissipate time, energy or money on anything else.' Wilson tracked down the exact same specimens that David had come across and sent back hundreds of seeds for his employer (along with those of several hundred other commercially viable plants and an even greater haul of herbarium specimens).

Over the next decade, Wilson made several collecting trips in Western China and in 1908 found himself in prime panda habitat accompanied by Walter Zappey, a zoologist from the Harvard Museum of Comparative Zoology. But neither he nor Zappey caught a glimpse of the panda's black-and-white form through the 'absolutely impenetrable thickets' of bamboo and when, in 1913, Wilson published *A Naturalist in Western China*, he gave a tantalising description of this shape-shifting beast. 'This animal is not common, and the savage nature of the country it frequents renders the possibility of capture remote.' Even then, however, there was commercial value in the panda. 'Skins are, on rare occasions, on sale in Chengtu, where they command high prices,' he wrote and he wrapped up his species description with the following pithy conclusion: 'It is the sportsman's prize above all others worth working hard for in Western China.' What's more, in noting that 'there is no record of a foreigner having killed a specimen' and 'no foreigner has so far seen a living example', Wilson laid down two explicit challenges: who would be the first Westerner to see a live giant panda and who would be the first to shoot one dead?

During the decade that Wilson had spent in the wilds of the West, Chinese dissatisfaction with the Qing leadership had steadily grown, most obviously in the shape of Sun Yat-sen's Revolutionary Alliance, which aimed to overthrow the Qing leadership, 'to avenge the national disgrace and to restore the Chinese.' Between 1906 and 1908, the Revolutionary Alliance coordinated at least seven uprisings against the Qing government. By 1911, the revolutionaries had succeed in infiltrating army units across the country and these began to mutiny, one after another. Powerless, the Qing court could do little but comply with the Alliance. On 12 February 1912, Puyi – the last emperor – abdicated and the Republic of China was born.

But this transition was never going to be smooth. Although a new Republican government attempted to occupy the vacuum left by the collapse of the Qing Dynasty, it was not able to hold China together and a series of military cliques began to gain in strength. The heads of these cliques, so-called warlords, dominated the Chinese political scene for the next fifteen years and, in the midst of this chaos, several Western expeditions came in search of pandas.

Just before Europe descended into war in 1914, a team of German collectors ventured into Western China and Tibet. They used hunting dogs to sniff out the trail of an individual, hoping to close in on it and squeeze the trigger, but the closest they came was to the sound of rattling bamboo stems in the near distance. As the panda seemed adept at threading its way to safety in its inhospitable natural habitat, the Germans tried a different approach. The expedition leader Walter Stötzner (or possibly expedition zoologist Hugo Weigold) bought a living baby panda from locals. It did not survive long but was enough for them to lay claim to being the first foreigners to see a living giant panda.

A few years later, in 1916, James Huston Edgar, an Australian missionary with a poetic bent, reported spotting a panda-like animal during his travels. 'I saw an animal asleep in the forks of a high oak tree which has puzzled me ever since,' he wrote to the *China Journal*. 'It was very large, seemed quite white, and was curled up in a great ball very much after the manner of cats. It was unknown, and a source of wonder to my Tibetans.' He was not armed at the time, so could not bag it and sat at a distance of around 100 metres, waiting for it to come down. It never did, even when a severe storm closed in, forcing Edgar into retreat. The sighting clearly niggled him for he wrote a poem entitled 'Waiting for the Panda'.

Waiting for the Panda
Or the piebald bear,
Which I saw a-sleeping
In an oak tree lair.

Waiting for the Panda
In the soaking mist;
Question: if he lingers
Can our camp exist?

Waiting for the Panda
On the snow-clad heights
How the hunters shiver
Through the dreary nights:

Waiting for the Panda
In the mountain pines,
Nomads watch his movements
Know on what he dines;

Yet the wily Panda
Not in bamboo grunts
But from crags uncanny
Sees the foeman pass;

And declares the Panda:
'What if lamas curse?
Bring your dogs and weapons

I'll be none the worse.'

Waiting for the Panda:
Will his gall unfold
Plans to turn the boulders
Into yellow gold?

No; we wait for Pandas
Not my child for that
But because he's something –
None can tell us what.

And the same old Panda
Is no garden pet
But inhabits regions
In or near Tibet.

And when wily Jacob
Sinned with kith and kin
Men desired the Panda
For his precious skin.

Waiting for the Panda
In a wilderness
And like Stoics scorning
Nature's storm and stress;

'But for this same Panda,'
Sneer the ancient men,
'You may wait 'till doomesday,
Yes, and miss him then.'

So we leave the Panda
Hoping that his bones
May some day be fossils
In the Muping stones

And you'll see the Panda
In a charming zoo
That a dreamer's fancy
Has prepared for you.

In 1921, the British soldier, diplomat and explorer Brigadier-General George E. Pereira spent over three months in Sichuan hoping to be the first foreigner to shoot one. He failed in his mission, catching only a fleeting glimpse of a furry white animal perched in a tree. He did, however, spend seven weeks laid up with an infected foot and, after walking almost 50 miles in native sandals through deep snow, he came away with severe frostbite. In spite of these setbacks he still managed to complete an epic journey from Beijing to Lhasa on foot.

All this served to ramp up the interest in the giant panda. Yet still, winding forward another decade, it was widely believed that nobody had managed to tick the second of Wilson's two boxes; no foreigner had yet managed to shoot a panda. This is perhaps the moment to ponder why anyone would actually want to do such a thing. At an entirely practical level, it's understandable. In the West, zoological museums in the business of studying and showing off natural wonders were obviously interested in displaying something as striking and rare as a giant panda and a gun was by far the most efficient way to stop one in its tracks. But why should men like Zappey, Weigold, Edgar and Pereira have wanted – really wanted – to be the ones to do the actual shooting? Sitting here in the twenty-first century, when most of us would be satisfied with seeing a panda or maybe taking a photograph, this is much harder to explain.

To arrive at a better understanding of why anyone would have wanted to shoot a wild animal like a panda, you have to imagine yourself into a different world. It was one in which there were still really rather a lot of wild animals, many of them capable of destroying crops and hence livelihoods or, worse still, taking lives. In these circumstances, shooting a wild animal doesn't seem quite so extraordinary. This was the kind of culture in which nineteenth-century museums set about building up their collections of natural history. Although it might seem strange, the actions of museum collectors, which often meant killing animals in as efficient a manner as possible, is really rather important for the emergence of a conservation mindset. After all, if you don't know what is out there, conservation is kind of meaningless. It is only with the greater understanding of the natural world, with the hard evidence laid down in natural history collections, that a conservation ethic could emerge. So it is of no coincidence that it was those hunting on behalf of museums who were among the first to express what we would recognise today as a conservation stance.

Here's a nice example. In his position as chief taxidermist at the United States National Museum (part of the Smithsonian Institution in Washington DC) towards the end of the nineteenth century, William T. Hornaday was well placed to notice that several impressive species, such as the American bison or buffalo, were fast heading towards extinction. Hornaday responded in the only way he knew how, with a proposal to stuff some of the last specimens for the museum. 'He believed that these population depredations should be brought to the attention of the public, and that compelling museum exhibits could encourage a more responsible environmental ethic across American society,' says Mary Anne Andrei, a historian of natural history at the University of Virginia. With the backing of his superiors, Hornaday set out for Montana in 1886 as the head of the Smithsonian Institution Buffalo Outfit with the aim of tracking down and shooting some of the last wild bison for the museum. There he saw a carpet of 'bleaching skeletons', scattered thickly like 'ghastly monuments of slaughter'. Nevertheless, he and his company still went on to shoot twenty-five animals. 'We killed very nearly all we saw and I am confident there are not over thirty-head remaining in Montana, all told,' he wrote back to his boss just before Christmas in 1886.

But, says Andrei, the Montana expeditions served as an epiphany for Hornaday, who went on to propose the creation of one of the first zoos that would champion the conservation of bison and other endangered species. The Smithsonian's Department of Living Animals opened to the public just over a year later and within a few years had transmogrified into the US National Zoological Park with talk of breeding animals in captivity. As we will see in Chapter 9, this institution entered wholeheartedly into the panda's story in the 1970s and continues to do so today.

Hornaday, however, was considerably ahead of his time. As museums went out for their specimens, private collectors set out on a parallel project to bring home as many impressive specimens for themselves. At the top of the hunters' wishlist were the big five – buffalo, elephant, rhino, lion and leopard. There were – relative to today – so many of these dangerous animals that there was an element of public service in taking them out. But the primary motivation of such hunting was to show off some machismo. Men – and it was an almost exclusively male affair – found it empowering to pit their wits against such awesome quarry (even if guns did stack the odds considerably in their favour).

There are few better examples of the testosterone-driven desire to hunt than Theodore Roosevelt, twenty-sixth President of the United States. In 1888, just as Hornaday was fighting to establish a national zoo, Roosevelt had founded his own organisation – the Boone and Crocket Club. It aimed to champion the virtues of the big-game hunter, who 'must be sound of body and firm of mind, and must possess energy, resolution, manliness, self-reliance, and a capacity for self-help'. According to historian of science, Gregg Mitman, writing in his history of wildlife film-making *Reel Nature*, 'Roosevelt felt that men of his class were threatened by the physical and moral effeminacy of modern times. By combating wilderness, and living the strenuous life that such a struggle entailed, they could reinvigorate them-selves with the prowess and republican virtues of their pioneer ancestors, making them once again worthy leaders in public affairs.'

Alongside this invigorating role, Roosevelt hoped that the more sportsmanlike hunting promoted by the Boone and Crockett Club would help turn opinion against the sort of industrial-scale hunting that had propelled big species like the buffalo to the brink of extinction. So even men like Roosevelt, who never gave up their desire to hunt, could be conservation-ists. Indeed, during his presidency (1901–9) Roosevelt channelled his utilitarian motives into some of the most important reforms in the history of the American environmental movement. He established the United States Forest Service and put it in charge of an area of forest about the size of the state of Michigan. He followed this up with further conservation reforms, including the creation of five new National Parks, four big game reserves, several national monuments and more than fifty areas for the dedicated protection of birds.

Such wide-ranging reform would help bring about a real

change in attitudes towards hunting. But in 1925, an elderly Hornaday still felt the need to make his voice heard, arguing that 'any duffer with a good check-book, a professional guide, and a high-power repeating rifle can kill big game, but it takes woodcraft, skill and endurance of a high order, to enable man or woman to secure a really fine photograph of a fine wild animal in its unfenced haunts.'

So the transition from shooting animals with guns to shooting them with the lens was not yet complete. For men like Zappey, Weigold, Edgar and Pereira, for whom the gun still held sway over the camera, big-game hunting – no longer possible in their own lands which had lost most of its dangerous fauna – was just a colonial expedition away. The giant panda – which according to some rumours could be ferocious, which had eluded so many hotshots over the decades and which was still under-represented in Western natural history collections – was an obvious target and the gun was the obvious weapon.

With this aside, it's perhaps easier to understand where Roosevelt's sons Theodore Junior and Kermit were coming from when, in the 1920s, they persuaded the Field Museum in Chicago to foot the bill for an expedition to collect (among other things) a panda specimen that would grace its new Asian Hall. In their 1929 book *Trailing the Giant Panda*, they began by making it clear how difficult was the task they had set themselves:

> The Golden Fleece of our trip was the giant panda ... From time to time such men as General Pereira, Ernest Wilson, Zappey, and McNeill had hunted it without success. We had slight hope of getting it. So slight in fact that we did not let even our close friends know what our real objective was.

9. This sketch of the giant panda appears in the Boone and Crockett Club's 1895 handbook *Hunting in Many Lands*, of which Theodore Roosevelt was one of the editors. One imagines that his sons Theodore Jr and Kermit took this image with them when they set out to become the first Westerners to shoot a giant panda in 1929.

When the William V. Kelley-Roosevelts Field Museum Expedition to South China (as it was officially known) reached Sichuan, they began their search in Baoxing County where David had found his panda. But six days passed 'without seeing a wild animal of any sort,' and that was with assistance from over a dozen native hunters. So they moved to the south and sent their interpreter, a Chinese-American teenager called Jack Young, in search of local hunters with knowledge of the panda. They found one or two men who had shot a panda, but only because it had wandered into their village to munch on their crops. One of their interviewees suggested luring a panda down from the hillsides by cooking up some pork bones, though to the Roosevelts this was 'rankest folly' and not their idea of good sport.

It was on 13 April 1929 that the Roosevelts stumbled upon a fresh trail of a panda and followed it for the next two-and-a-half hours. 'Unexpectedly close I heard a clicking chirp,' wrote Kermit in *Trailing the Giant Panda*. One of the hunters darted ahead, then turned back to urge the hunters to hurry. There, from inside the hollow of a spruce tree, emerged the head and fore-quarters of a giant panda. 'He looked sleepily from side to side as he sauntered forth and walked slowly away into the bamboos. As soon as Ted came up we fired simultaneously at the outline of the disappearing panda.' It bolted, but following a trail of blood through the snow for a distance, the brothers came across their prize. 'Both shots took effect,' wrote Kermit.

In Hanoi in modern-day Vietnam with the skinned panda a month later, they cabled a telegram through to the Field Museum in Chicago. 'Have extraordinary luck. Jointly shot for you splendid old male Giant Pandar', they wrote. 'Believe authorities agree this is the first Giant Pandar shot by a white man.' Others may have got their first, but history doesn't remember them. The celebrity status of the Roosevelts, their popular account of the expedition published later that year and the appearance of their giant panda in the Field Museum in 1930 had an almost inevitable consequence.

In the United States there was – probably still is – serious competition to be the biggest, most spectacular natural history museum in the country. If there weren't so many good ones, it's a phenomenon that probably wouldn't occur, but there's the National in Washington DC, the American in New York, the Carnegie in Pittsburgh and the Field Museum of Natural History in Chicago (to name just a few of the biggest hitters). In the last few years of the nineteenth century, these museums found themselves caught up in a fierce, testosterone-fuelled competition to boast the biggest and best dinosaur remains. There are striking parallels between this dinosaur rush and what happened over pandas in the 1930s.

Following the Kelley-Roosevelt coup, other museums mounted their own panda-hunting expeditions, each intent on collecting more and better-preserved specimens than anyone that had gone before them. In 1931, the Philadelphia Academy of Natural Sciences sent out Brooke Dolan and he took with him Hugo Weigold (who had got his hands on a young panda some fifteen years earlier) and another German zoologist Ernst Schaefer. It was Schaefer who spotted a panda cub lounging in a tree, lifted his rifle and shot it from its perch. The expedition acquired several more pandas from local hunters and sent them, along with the skinned cub, back to Philadelphia.

In 1934, the American Museum of Natural History got in on the act by sponsoring the Sage West China Expedition. Zoologist Donald Carter noted how local hunters would run a cord across a panda's trail that, when tripped, would launch a sapling-loaded spear at the animal's heart. But this tried-and-tested technique did not sound like fair play to the hunt-hungry Westerners. They began by trying to track pandas by foot; but once inside bamboo forest proper, they found the going impossible. 'We could see but a few feet ahead, and dried leaves of the bamboo on the ground made it impossible to proceed without a great deal of noise, and the roots of bamboo constantly tripped us,' wrote Carter.

> On account of the denseness, it was impossible to surprise our quarry, as we would announce our presence long before we had knowledge that game might be near. We would follow the stream

beds where travelling was not quite so precarious, and gaze up over the tops of the bamboos with the hope that we might be able to tell by the movements of the branches that a panda was feeding beneath. We would also, with our glasses, scan the spruces above the zone of bamboo in the expectation that we might be able to find an animal sunning himself among the boughs. But all to no avail.

They changed their approach, hiring hunting dogs from the locals. On one day, Carter and fellow zoologist William Sheldon did catch a glimpse of a pair of pandas. One disappeared over a ridge and the dogs chased the other for a short while, yapping ineffectually at its heels. But beyond this fleeting sighting, the dog approach turned out to be 'quite useless'. On another day, Sheldon came upon a track and followed it through thick undergrowth to find flattened vegetation where a panda had been sleeping. 'He was sure that he had heard the animal as it left its bed, but on account of the thick covering he was unable to see it,' reported Carter. He followed its tracks for the rest of the day, 'but never obtained a sight of it'.

Finally, on the last possible day of hunting, expedition leader Dean Sage and Sheldon let loose the dogs in a desperate bid to locate a fresh trail to follow. Sage climbed up onto a ledge and Sheldon had assumed another vantage point when suddenly the sound of snapping bamboo floated up towards them. Writing for the journal *Natural History*, Sage recorded the drama that unfolded:

Up the ravine came the dogs, their barking growing steadily louder, and the bamboos crackling at a great rate. Suddenly, I heard the deep, angry growl of a large animal, and I began to get really excited. And then – as if in a dream – I saw a giant panda

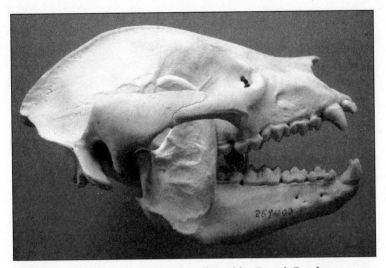

10. The skull of one of the pandas collected by David Crockett Graham for the Smithsonian Institution. This specimen, a female, was shot near Wenchuan in December 1934. Note the prominent crest on the top of the skull, which facilitates the attachment of the panda's powerful jaw muscles and also the chunky teeth, both adaptations for crunching into bamboo.

coming through the bamboos about sixty yards away from me. He was heading straight up the ravine with the dogs at his heels. I fired but missed. The panda made a right angle turn and came straight for the ledge I was standing on. I fired again.

Sage frantically worked the bolt of his rifle, but found himself out of bullets. The panda was just six metres away, now five and coming straight at him. 'Can I kill him with the butt of my rifle?' panicked Sage. The panda was four metres away when he felt a cartridge being thrust into his hand by his guide. Sage jammed it into the gun and, with the panda just three metres from him, he fired. Sheldon did the same from his vantage point 'and the

11. 'The Generalissimo' Chiang Kai-shek, the leader of the Guomindang, looking determined in 1928.

animal, struck simultaneously by both our bullets, rolled over and over down the slope and came to a stop against a tree fifty yards below. We had killed a giant panda.' The next day, they feasted on its flesh.

While all this very public, boastful hunting was going on, the Smithsonian National Museum of Natural History took a less conspicuous, more efficient approach to collecting pandas. In 1919, David Crockett Graham, a polymath missionary based in Sichuan, had popped his head in at the Washington DC museum on his way back to China to ask if they were interested in his collecting services. The museum agreed to provide supplies and expenses and over the next two decades Graham made dozens of collecting trips. Following the Roosevelts' high-profile shooting of a panda in 1929, Graham began to send back the remains of pandas to Washington DC. In just five years up to 1934, he supplied the National Museum with more than twenty panda specimens culled from Baoxing or Wenchuan counties. The skull of Graham's last panda specimen is still on display in the museum's Osteology Hall.

That so many Westerners were able to go about their colonial business as usual is an indication of the failure of the Republic of China to assert authority following the fall of the Qing Dynasty. But throughout this panda-hunting period, political forces – notably the Guomindang, or Chinese Nationalist Party, and the Chinese Communist Party (CCP) – had been at work in an effort to wrestle control back from the warlords and reunify China.

From 1919 onwards, the Guomindang offered an increasingly viable alternative to the chaotic status quo. By 1925, the party had set up a rival government in southerly Guangdong Province in direct opposition to the ineffective Beijing leadership and in 1926 its National Revolutionary Army began its so-called Northern Expedition. Over the next two years, this nationalist force, under the Guomindang's new military-minded leader Chiang Kai-shek, struggled north in one long, bloody battle against the warlords, the one-time ideologically sympathetic Chinese Communist Party and a 5,000-strong Japanese force. By 1928, however, Chiang and the Guomindang had taken control of China's east and moved the capital from Beijing to Nanjing in Jiangsu Province, where the revolutionary Sun Yat-sen had become 'provisional president' of the Republic of China in 1912.

During the Nanjing Decade from 1928 to 1937, the Guomindang established a one-party dictatorship and began to rebuild the still-fractured nation. The all-new Chinese leadership received support from several foreign countries, including the United States and Germany, which might help account for the preponderance of Americans and Germans on the panda-hunting expeditions during this period. With the financial, technical and missionary input of these Western countries, Chiang brought about reforms of the banking and education sectors, improvements of roads and railways and the expansion of industry. He also continued to use his military forces to rout out the Chinese Communist Party, forcing them to run for the hills, quite literally. When the Guomindang established an economic blockade around the communists' key stronghold in the border region between Fujian and Jiangxi provinces, they were left with no alternative but to attempt a surprise escape. Some 80,000 men and women broke through the blockade to freedom. Over the course of a year, from October 1934, this Red Army covered around 6,000 miles, hounded all the way by the Guomindang before regrouping in Yan'an in Shaanxi Province. It is thought that less than 10,000 of those that had left Jiangxi completed this 'Long March'. One of them was Mao Zedong, who emerged from the ordeal to become the chairman of the CCP.

Incredibly, when the Red Army passed through panda country in June 1935, crossing Sichuan's snowy Jianjin Mountain range on its way north to Shaanxi, Westerners were still taking pandas from the region. Just weeks earlier, for example, a British aristocrat and big-game hunter by the name of Captain Courtney Brocklehurst had been on his own self-financed panda hunt. He too noted the spring-loaded spear traps the locals set for pandas but did not like the approach any more than did the Americans before him. 'The only way was to find a fresh spoor and track it down,' Brocklehurst told the newspapers upon his return to Britain. After several weeks in pursuit of said fresh spoor, he heard a panda roar. 'It sounded like the cough of a leopard, but more prolonged,' he told the reporter. Quite clearly, here was a man who'd done some hunting before.

The next day, Brocklehurst found its tracks and followed them until, quite suddenly, he found himself staring into the blackened eyes of an 'unusually large panda' standing on a ridge just above him.

> Signalling frantically for the coolie who was carrying my rifle I scrambled as best I could after the animal. It was like night under the trees, and almost impossible to distinguish a vital spot for the only shot I was likely to get. To make matters worse, my dog ran after the panda barking wildly. Suddenly, however, the animal stopped and turned, and I took careful aim and killed him instantaneously with one bullet in the neck. I had come 28,000 miles to fire that one shot.

But by then, shooting pandas did not have quite the same allure. In 1935, Western hunters began to look for another challenge and so began the first serious talk of trying to get a giant panda out of China alive.

4

Live action

In the same year that the Field Museum of Natural History in Chicago put the Roosevelts' dead panda on show, it decided to invest in a ten-year survey of the fauna of Western China. Heading the operation was one Floyd Tangier Smith, a Japanese-born American who had given up banking for a life of adventure. The Field Museum issued Smith with strict instructions to ignore the panda and concentrate on obtaining specimens of other species, but the collector secretly had other ideas. Hoping to be the first to collect a living panda, he staffed a network of camps with local hunters who could go on collecting even if he himself were not present. 'I am highly expectant over what may have been accomplished while I have been away,' he wrote to his sister in the United States, 'and even dare to hope that a live panda or takin or two may be eating out of my hand when I reach the various present headquarters.'

Within two years, however, the Field Museum had wound up its formal agreement with Smith, possibly because they couldn't afford to keep him on in the wake of the Great Depression or possibly because they didn't want to. As journalist Vicki Croke explains in *The Lady and the Panda*, a gripping account of the search for a live panda, Smith turned out to be 'either the unluckiest or most incompetent collector going'. He blamed his poor results variously on bad weather, bandits, disloyal hunters, bureaucracy and political uncertainty. According to Croke, with

58

the Field Museum engaging with Smith on a freelance-only basis, the 'haggard and luckless adventurer would forever be chasing after the next check, straining to maintain a high profile while an army of Ivy League boys paraded through town'.

A youthful explorer by the name of William Harkness was one of the Ivy League boys who found Smith on his tail. In May 1934, Harkness and fellow Harvard graduate Lawrence Griswold had returned to the United States from Indonesia with a few live Komodo dragons, then something of an exotic rarity. In September, the duo set out on their next adventure – the Griswold-Harkness Asiatic Expedition – with the even spunkier goal of being the first to bring a live giant panda out of China. By the time they reached Shanghai in January 1935, Griswold had turned back. Harkness, on his own, fell into cahoots with Smith and a like-minded Brit, Gerald Russell, and the threesome set out for Sichuan. Without the necessary permissions to collect pandas, however, they were forced to return to Shanghai. It was there, in February 1936, that Harkness died, his body consumed by cancer at the age of just 34.

The Harkness involvement with pandas might have ended there had he not got married just weeks before leaving the States. Back in New York, feisty fashion designer Ruth Harkness resolved to use the $20,000 she inherited from her husband's estate to travel to China, disperse his ashes and complete his unfinished panda business. When she reached Shanghai in 1936, Harkness settled into the Palace Hotel, where her husband had shacked up, and began to take stock of the 'hot and sticky' surroundings of this 'flat sprawly city'. Vicki Croke captures the cosmopolitan thrill of 1930s Shanghai:

At the Chinese clubs, local gangsters danced the rumba to Russian orchestras. Chinese rich boys with jet-black hair, brilliantined to a lacquer finish, squired modern Chinese girls in stiletto heels and high-necked brocade silk sheaths slit up to the hips. Revelers could try a Polish mazurka or the Parisian Apache, the carioca, the tango. Crooners and torch singers bawled American jazz through the night.

As Harkness began to let her hair down, she found Smith – almost twenty years her senior – hovering over her money, which he wanted in order to keep his collecting operation alive. Within a week of her arrival, she'd seen and heard enough to know she could not pair up with him as her late husband had done and she let him know. 'He is anything but well and as much of a dear as he is, is totally impractical in many ways, and I cannot afford to take chances of any kind,' she wrote to her best friend back home.

Then, at a party in Shanghai, Harkness was introduced to Jack Young, the very same Chinese-American explorer who had accompanied the Roosevelts into panda land in the late 1920s. He was about to set out on a mountaineering expedition in the Himalayas, but his younger brother Quentin Young would make a first-rate partner, he suggested. The Youngs helped secure Harkness the necessary permits on the condition that Quentin Young also find another specimen for the Academia Sinica, then in the nationalist power base in Nanjing. With her new, more youthful partner in place, Harkness also cut her ties with Russell. 'The VRYENGLISH GENTLEMAN is no longer with the Harkness Asiatic Expedition,' she wrote home.

In September 1936, Harkness waved goodbye to Smith and Russell and stepped onto a steamer with the younger and handsome Young to head up the Yangzte just as Armand David had done almost seventy years earlier. They passed through Wuhan, then Chongqing and then travelled overland to Chengdu, before heading off to the mountains. Just about everyone Harkness met along the way could not understand why anyone – and particularly a woman – would contemplate such a dangerous journey and tried to warn her off. But the New Yorker remained steadfast in her commitment to the panda project. Given the degree of civil unrest in China at that moment – with Guomindang forces pitching battles against communists and bandits, it is surprising that Harkness did not witness more inhumane carnage on the journey. But she did get a feel for some of the realities of tensions not far out of Chengdu. Soldiers from the Guomindang army carrying machine guns continued to stream past Harkness, one posse with a couple of roped-up outlaws in tow. She saw one of them again a little later lying dead at the side of the road 'riddled with bullets, and by the look of him eight or ten had found their mark on his face'. With Young acting as translator, Harkness discovered that the dead man had been the leader of a pack of some 600 bandits, some of whom had tried to spring his release. The Guomindang soldiers, rather than let their man go, had filled him with bullets and scarpered. The other hostage appears to have got away.

In addition to Smith's network of hired hunters, who were supposed to be out scouring the countryside for pandas, Harkness also discovered that Russell had not behaved like the 'VRYENG-LISH GENTLEMAN' she thought he was; no sooner had she and Young boarded their steamer in Shanghai than he had jumped on a plane to Chengdu so as to beat them to the pandas. She could do little about this but press on to Wenchuan, where they hired the services of a wiry old Tibetan hunter who as good as promised them a panda. He led them west into the mountains.

In *The Lady and the Panda*, Vicki Croke makes a compelling case for a budding romance between Harkness and Young, first consummated in an abandoned Tibetan castle that boasted a room full of erotic statues and paintings. 'Hideous and disgustingly obscene' was how the botanist Ernest Wilson had described them when he passed through the region, but it's amazing what a difference three decades can make and the two travellers were clearly inspired.

In early November, Young established a base camp, another at a higher altitude and yet another higher still. They couldn't have quite known it, but it was the perfect time for a panda hunt. Catching an adult panda, as Smith seemed intent on doing, was always going to be hard. But female pandas, through a piece of reproductive cunning that we will visit in a later chapter, almost always give birth in late summer, and catching a six-week-old panda would be easy. One morning, they were out early to check a trap that Young had set when they heard a quiet, plaintive squeal coming from a rotting spruce tree; by some miracle, they had stumbled across a panda's den and the mother was away foraging as mother pandas are wont to do. Young reached into the hollow, carefully lifted out a tiny bundle of black and white and handed it to Harkness.

It was now time for the hard part – how to keep a baby panda alive – but while men like Smith entered into panda country armed with guns, Harkness had come armed with a baby bottle and milk formula. They slithered back to the base camp, located the unusual weapons and the panda began to suckle. Harkness called it Su-Lin, the nickname of Jack Young's wife. It was fitting, inasmuch as both Su-Lin the panda and Adelaide 'Su-Lin' Young were good-looking. It did not seem quite so appropriate when the panda Su-Lin, upon postmortem, turned out to be male. Less than ten days after the capture, Harkness and her panda were on a flight from Chengdu to Shanghai. News of the find had travelled fast and, fearing that publicity might create obstacles, Harkness promised interviews and photographs on the eve of

12. Ruth Harkness allows a local doctor to give Su-Lin a once-over before inviting the press into her room at the Palace Hotel, Shanghai, in November 1936.

her departure. Harkness stayed true to her word, and Shanghai's journalists convened in her hotel room on 27 November, the day before she planned to head off to the *Empress of Russia*, the vessel that she hoped would take her home.

But Harkness ran into difficulty over paperwork, perhaps because customs officials had got wind of her intention to take out insurance to the value of $10,000 against Su-Lin's death on the Pacific voyage, and the *Empress* sailed without her. Matters were made worse the following day when the *China Press* speculated that Harkness might get $25,000 for her panda back in the States. In a panic, Harkness brought powerful friends into the picture and money changed hands. Apparently satisfied, the Shanghai officials were prepared to issue an export permit for 'One Dog, $20.00'. Harkness and Su-Lin boarded the *President McKinley*, a steamer bound for Japan, then San Francisco.

As the panda sailed, Floyd Tangier Smith's barely contained bitterness erupted. It was bad enough to have been pipped to the live-panda post, but by a woman? For a man like Smith, in the 1930s, this was so unthinkable that he wove an alternative tale to the media. His men, he claimed, had been staking out the den and when Harkness got wind of its location, she snuck in and pilfered the panda, he whined to the *China Press*. But as he continued with his accusations in the days and weeks to come, the inconsistencies began to appear and, for a time at least, Smith found himself unable to steal any of the limelight from Harkness and her photogenic charge. The reporters swarmed all over them at the dockside in San Francisco, then in Chicago and finally in New York, where Harkness hoped to sell the giant panda to the Bronx Zoo. She was inundated with visitors, too, including Kermit, Theodore Jr and his son Quentin. According to Harkness, the experience of meeting her panda softened these hard men. When it was suggested that Su-Lin might one day join the Roosevelt's panda in the Field Museum's taxidermy display, Theodore Jr could not imagine it. 'I'd as soon think of mounting my own son as I would this baby,' he said. Dean Sage, the leader of the 1934 Sage West China Expedition on behalf of the American Museum of Natural History also visited Harkness and Su-Lin and was 'completely captivated'. 'You know, Mrs. Harkness, I'd never be able to shoot another Panda,' he told her.

At first, neither the Bronx nor any other American zoo would step forward to claim the panda. There were too many unknowns: such a fragile young animal might die at any moment, and would it be possible to source bamboo or would it take to some alternative diet? On top of all these uncertainties, there was also the rather large amount of cash they would have to fork out. But Harkness soon reached an agreement with the recently opened Brookfield Zoo in Chicago: it would take on the panda in exchange for funds to finance a return visit to China to obtain a mate for Su-Lin. It turned out to be a shrewd gamble on the part of the zoo. By the time Su-Lin went on show to the public in late April, the huge media attention over the course of several months had created an eager zoo-going public. More than 53,000 visitors came on the first day and, within a week, the zoo had recouped its financial outlay in gate receipts. In 1938, painter Frank W. Long produced a striking poster of Su-Lin as a part of the Federal Art Project, a government initiative to inject a bit of colour into the lives of Americans hit by the Great Depression (see cover).

While all this was going on, the Guomindang's grip on power had started to slip. Chiang Kai-shek's determination to stamp out the communists on their Long March had laid China's north open to occupation by the increasingly expansive Japanese. Then, just days after Harkness and Su-Lin had left China towards the end of 1936, anti-Japanese agitators managed to arrest Chiang in what has become known as the Xi'an Incident. It was time, they demanded, for the Guomindang and the CCP to put an end to their differences and show a united front against Japan. In order to secure his release, Chiang reluctantly agreed to their terms. The nationalists and communists were thrashing out details of how they might work together when events in the north overtook them. Japanese forces took control of Beijing and Tianjin.

Chiang responded by attempting to hit back at Japanese warships anchored in the Huangpu River in Shanghai. Unfortunately for the Chinese, their bombs missed the Japanese fleet, struck the city and killed hundreds of civilians. One of the

13. On 14 August 1937, a Chinese bomb – intended for the Japanese fleet anchored in the Huangpu River in Shanghai – landed in the city, causing damage to the Palace Hotel. Just a few days earlier, Ruth Harkness had checked in to the hotel but was not in the building when the bomb struck. This marked the start of the second Sino-Japanese War.

unintended targets was the Palace Hotel, which Ruth Harkness had used as her Shanghai base the previous year. Worryingly for her friends, Harkness had reached China just days before to begin her second panda expedition and she had checked back into her old home. Journalist Vicki Croke imagined the carnage in *The Lady and the Panda*:

> The explosions were deafening and deadly, shattering glass and smashing masonry. When the smoke lifted, 'a scene of dreadful death was uncovered.' The pavement ran slick with blood. Severed limbs and heads lay among the shards of glass and rubble. In burned-out cars, charred occupants remained upright in their seats. The smell of blood and burning flesh mingled with the

acrid bomb fumes. As the hundreds of dazed and dying came to, they writhed in pain on the debris-strewn street, filling the air with their sobs.

Thankfully, Harkness had not been in the building when it was ripped apart by the wayward bomb and the sight of the destruction had the kind of empowering effect that comes with a near-death experience: 'I know that this War will not be my finish,' she wrote to a friend in the United States. 'So with perfect confidence I can go to the Bund during the heaviest bombardment and know that it is not for me. A rather cozy feeling, although one does feel sorry for the other poor devils.'

Her panda calling strengthened, Harkness began to prepare her trip. This time, she would have to do so without Quentin Young, who had married his long-term girlfriend and was not in town. Because of the dangers of sailing up the Yangzte, Harkness opted for a circuitous journey to Sichuan via Hong Kong and Vietnam, re-entering China from the relatively safe south. With transport links collapsing as Japan and China descended into full-scale war, it is a testimony to Harkness' derring-do that she was back in panda country within a couple of months, arriving at the perfect moment to locate another young panda.

By that time, Japanese forces had taken Shanghai and started to march on the nationalist capital Nanjing. It was there, in what historian Jonathan Spence describes as 'a period of terror and destruction that must rank among the worst in the history of modern warfare', that the advancing Japanese army is estimated to have massacred 30,000 soldiers, murdered 12,000 civilians and raped 20,000 women. The Chinese, forced into retreat, moved their government further west up the Yangtze to Wuhan, which is why Harkness went there in January 1938 to clear the paperwork for exporting her latest fluffy charge to North America. Although she'd succeeded without Quentin Young, she clearly still thought of him. Believing the panda to be a female, she called it Diana after Young's new bride.

Back in America, though, Diana was renamed Mei-Mei; it would have been appropriate, as it translates roughly as 'little sister', except that Mei-Mei, as had been the case with Su-Lin, turned out to be male, too. There was great interest in the moment the two were brought together, but they only lived alongside each other for a matter of weeks because, on 1 April, Su-Lin unexpectedly died.

'Of her countless mourners none wept more bitterly than Mrs. Harkness,' read *Life Magazine* the following week. Su-Lin, it reported, had swallowed an oak twig, scratched her throat and developed quinsy, though the official verdict, when it came, was that she'd succumbed to pneumonia. On the previous page, *Life* carried a map illustrating the German National Socialist Party's designs on Europe. 'Wildly absurd is Germany's claim to two-thirds of Switzerland and most of Alsace-Lorraine,' read the accompanying caption. 'Much more immediate and ominous is the German tide lapping the Western boundaries of Czechoslovakia.' In spite of this looming threat of war in Europe and the bloody fact of the ongoing Sino-Japanese war, Harkness – determined to see a breeding pair at Chicago – set off for Sichuan once more. Her original partner, Quentin Young, had returned to the field and was holding two captive pandas in Chengdu.

But other zoos, seeing what Su-Lin and now Mei-Mei had done and were doing for Brookfield's gate receipts, were also getting in on the live-panda action. On 10 June 1938, the Bronx Zoo received a female – they called her Pandora – courtesy of a professor at the West China Union University in Chengdu, with plans to bring in a male, called Pan, the following year.

Panda hunter Floyd Tangier Smith had also been busy, his

14. The panda hunter Floyd Tangier Smith as imagined by author and artist Chiang Yee in *The Story of Ming*.

network of collecting stations having brought several pandas to Chengdu earlier in the year. But as the Japanese moved on from ravaged Nanjing to put pressure on the nationalist stronghold in Wuhan, the war came ever closer to panda country. Chiang Kai-shek ordered the destruction of dykes along the Yellow River to slow the Japanese advance, before abandoning Wuhan in favour of Chongqing in Sichuan. This seriously complicated Smith's task of exporting live pandas and he was holed up in Chengdu for months. Harkness, when she arrived, described the conditions of his captive pandas with horror. 'He keeps them in tiny dirty cages in hot sunshine; no shade, no freedom,' she wrote to a friend. 'He is simply collecting wholesale and letting them die.'

Finally, in October, Smith managed to get a haul of six live pandas away from the war in a gruelling three-week overland journey, to board a vessel that would take them through heavy seas to Hong Kong. One panda died en route, but the other five made it to Hong Kong. In a nod towards the blockbuster hit of the year, *Snow White and the Seven Dwarfs*, Smith named three of these animals Happy, Dopey and Grumpy. There was an old female he called Grandma and a youngster he called Baby. While he sought a safe passage to Britain (where London Zoo had started to express an interest in pandas), he allowed the animals to recuperate in the grounds of the Hong Kong Society for the Prevention of Cruelty to Animals' Dogs Home. Rosa Loseby, honorary secretary of the institution, was very much taken by her new charges, but the stressful journey they'd just endured was of concern. In a letter to *The Field*, she suggested that 'if the zoos of the world must encourage this trade in wild animals, they should, at least, supervise the trade and not leave it to private enterprise'.

Ruth Harkness had begun to feel the same way. When one of the two pandas that Young had captured turned suddenly savage during a thunderstorm, he had been forced to shoot it. The other panda was to have a different and rather surprising fate. The female explorer who had brought the first live panda to the West took this young captive all the way back into the mountains and set it free. She kept vigil for several days to be sure that the animal would not return. She saw it just once more. 'The little black-and-white furry youngster looked just once at civilization,' wrote Harkness, 'and ran as though all the demons of hell were at her heels.'

Arthur de Carle Sowerby, the editor of the *China Journal*, spoke out against the surge in panda extraction. 'A rare and not too plentiful animal at best, the giant panda cannot long survive such persecution,' he wrote. 'We, therefore, appeal to the Chinese government to intervene to save the giant panda from extermination before it is too late.' Quite incredibly for the period, and given the pressure the Chinese faced from the Japanese, within a matter of months the Provincial Government of Sichuan had brought in a ban on capturing pandas.

But Smith was already on his way, on board the *Antenor*, which reached London in a snow blizzard on Christmas Eve 1938. He was met at the docks by Geoffrey Vevers of London Zoo, who made arrangements to get the giant pandas across the city to the zoo. The eldest panda – Grandma – did not survive for more than a couple of weeks. On the eve of World War II, Happy was sold to a German dealer and went on a whirlwind tour of Nazi Germany before escaping Europe for the United States (where he and another panda, Pao-Pei, survived the war at Saint Louis Zoo in Missouri).

Grumpy, Dopey and Baby, meanwhile, were snapped up by London Zoo, who plucked three of China's imperial dynasties out of the bag to rechristen them Tang, Sung and Ming. Princess Margaret and her sister Elizabeth, the future Queen, were amongst the thousands who turned out to see the new arrivals – the first pandas on British soil. Also present was Chiang Yee, a Chinese poet, author and artist who had left China for Britain in the 1930s. With Vevers' permission, Chiang quietly observed the animals during the daytime and even when the zoo was closed at night. He also observed the public and their reaction to his panda compatriots. 'One old gentleman said that it was only an ordinary sort of animal after all, and he didn't know why people were making such a fuss about it.'

Chiang himself, however, was inspired to write and illustrate two engaging children's books. *Chin-Pao and the Giant Pandas*, a philosophical tale of a Chinese boy living wild amongst a family of five pandas, is dedicated to none other than Floyd Tangier Smith. The hunter appears late in the story to return the boy to his family and capture the pandas. *The Story of Ming*, directed at a younger audience a few years later, tells of Ming's journey to London. In it, Chiang noted the ambassadorial skills of the giant panda: 'Ming is a true representative of China,' he wrote. 'She is good-natured and friendly and so are the Chinese. She is patient, like all Chinese. She persists in her own way, and so do they.' He concluded: 'She is prepared to settle here for the rest of her life and to make permanent friends with the English.'

By the time that Chiang Yee wrote these words, political forces in China had also became alert to the possibility of using the giant panda to strengthen ties with the influential, panda-obsessed nations in the West. As the world plunged into war, China and the Western allies found themselves on the same side against the Germans and Japanese, and the US established the United China Relief to raise relief funds for the Chinese. As a token of its appreciation, the nationalist government sought a suitable and symbolic gift for the American people and quickly settled

15. During World War II, the United States established the United China Relief, Inc., raising funds to provide humanitarian aid to the Chinese people in the face of Japanese aggression.

on a pair of pandas. Once they'd reached the Bronx, they would become known as Pan-Dee and Pan-Dah, the first of their kind to find themselves tied explicitly to international political affairs. Presenting the babies to John Tee-Van of the New York Zoological Society in 1941, Chiang Kai-shek's wife made the following radio announcement broadcast back to the States:

> Through the United China Relief, you, our American friends, are alleviating the suffering of our people and are binding the wounds which have been wantonly inflicted upon them through no fault of their own. As a very small way of saying 'Thank you,' we would like to present to America, through you, Mr. Tee-Van, this pair of comical, black-and-white, furry pandas. We hope

that their cute antics will bring as much joy to the American children as American friendship has brought to our Chinese people.

The death of Tang and Sung soon after the outbreak of war prompted London Zoo to enquire after more. In return, the British Council was prepared to offer an all-expenses-paid opportunity for a Chinese biologist to spend one year studying at British institutions. It might not sound like much, but the arrival of Lien-Ho (meaning 'unity') plus a Chinese zoologist in London in 1946 marks the first time China received a tangible benefit from the export of one of its pandas. In another fifty years and under far more ethically satisfying circumstances, the loan of pandas to the West in exchange for a commitment to research, conservation funding and expertise would become standard practice.

Of course, by the time of Lien-Ho's arrival in London, World War II had come to an end. The atomic bombs falling on Hiroshima and Nagasaki in August 1945 had forced the Japanese surrender and, with US help, the Chinese nationalist forces had regained control of the east. But the war had eaten away at Chiang Kai-shek's hold on political power and the Chinese Communist Party under Mao Zedong had gathered in strength. With the Japanese as a common enemy, the Guomindang and CCP had managed to maintain a largely unified position. Now, as millions of Japanese troops and civilians began their withdrawal from China, the two parties turned upon each other in a brutal civil war. With the country going into financial meltdown and unemployment starting to soar, the communists continued to gain support. Its People's Liberation Army took control of the north of China, then pressed on to Nanjing which the Guomindang had reclaimed from the Japanese. Eventually, with nowhere else to go, Chiang Kai-shek withdrew to the island of Taiwan.

At a ceremony on 1 October 1949, the Chinese Communist Party's Chairman Mao Zedong announced the founding of the People's Republic of China. The West's exploitation of pandas was over. From now on, the CCP would insist that any foreign involvement with pandas would be strictly on their terms.

Part II
ABSTRACTION

5

Communist goods

During the 1950s, two pandas crossed China's borders that would re-route the way of the panda forever. Their names were Chi-Chi and An-An.

After all the upheaval during the first half of the twentieth century, China's first zoo, founded in the death throes of the Qing Dynasty in a western suburb of Beijing, was in a state of disrepair. But when the communists came to power in 1949, they began its transformation into a modern zoo, dispatching collectors into China's remotest regions to fill its empty cages and reopening it to the public. Soon, Beijing Zoo could boast a pair of snub-nosed monkeys – the first to be exhibited in any zoo anywhere in the world – golden cats, snow leopards, tigers, a golden takin and a handful of both lesser and giant pandas. But most of the rarities were to be found within China's borders and the collection hardly reflected planet earth's zoological diversity.

Which is why the zoo authorities were excited by the arrival, in May 1958, of a shipment of large African mammals – three giraffes, two rhinos, two hippos and two zebras, to be precise. The animals had travelled from Kenya to China in a matter of weeks, transported by a young entrepreneurial Austrian called Heini Demmer. What did he want in exchange? You guessed it. The Chicago Zoological Society had been on the lookout for a panda ever since the death of its last captive (a third panda called

Mei-Lan) in 1953. And they were prepared to pay good money for it, indicating to Demmer that they'd stump up $25,000 if he could get them one. Demmer and his wife had ventured with their large-mammal cargo from their operating base in Nairobi, via India, Thailand and Hong Kong, to China. Beijing Zoo's staff welcomed the foreigners: 'The Director was kind enough to give me complete freedom to choose one of their three pandas, which I thought was more than courteous,' remembered Demmer after the event.

He took his time in making his decision, more or less living in the panda house at the zoo for several days. 'My object in watching these rare animals for a whole week was not merely to choose one, but also to try and learn as much as possible about them in such a short time,' he wrote. At first, he found the pandas 'rather wild and absolutely not used to any human handling'.

> As it is my firm opinion that young animals in captivity should have some equivalent of their mother's love, I always try – in my compound in Africa – to ensure that all young animals freshly caught, immediately get a young African boy who can attend to the newcomers the whole day, feed them and play with them continuously.

Without a young African boy to hand, it fell to Demmer to act as a surrogate mother. When he first entered one of the panda's cages, the Chinese keepers were alarmed. And rightly so. 'I had to leave the cage as fast as possible,' he wrote. But it was not long before the youngest panda – a young female called Chi-Chi – had started to accept Demmer's presence in her cage. 'Her soul was sick and she was looking for someone to come into contact,' he later remembered. 'I think even she calls me quite a good friend.'

When Demmer attempted to arrange the freight of his new

friend to the US, he ran into trouble. In the words of *The Times'* Washington Correspondent, 'another would-be emigrant to the United States is being kept out of the country by the State Department'. Demmer and his panda had fallen foul of Cold War politics.

Since 1947, the United States had been clamping down on its military exports to the Soviet Union and its communist confidants. In 1949, several other nations, including Britain, France, Italy, the Netherlands, Belgium and Luxembourg, agreed to join the US on a Coordinating Committee for Multilateral Export Controls (COCOM) with a view to delivering a more painful economic squeeze on the Soviet bloc. With the CCP now in control of China, and the Soviet Union quick off the mark to pledge support for the new regime, the US National Security Council made it clear that China now fell under the same export controls:

> The United States should, as a security measure, seek to prevent the USSR, its European satellites, and North Korea from obtaining from abroad through China supplies of strategic material and equipment which are currently denied them by the United States and its European allies through direct channels.

Chairman Mao Zedong had anticipated this development and had used it to unleash the fighting spirit of the Chinese people and unite them against the American-led 'imperialist embargo'. 'Let them besiege us! Let them besiege us for eight or ten years!' he declared in August 1949. 'Why can't we live without the United States?'

Mao soon signalled where his interests lay, when he chose Moscow as the destination of his first state visit. He met with

16. The historic 1950 meeting between the Chairman of the Chinese Communist Party Mao Zedong and the General Secretary of the Communist Party of the Soviet Union Joseph Stalin was commemorated in this Chinese stamp.

Joseph Stalin for a couple of hours on 22 January 1950 and though the two men hadn't seen eye to eye, this and other talks held during the course of Mao's six-week stay in the Soviet Union resulted in a Treaty of Friendship, Alliance, and Mutual Assistance between the two great powers. In June, North Korean forces spilled over the 38th parallel and into South Korea. US President Truman, responding to the United Nation's condemnation of this invasion, offered American support for the South Koreans and troops from several other countries followed suit. This UN counteroffensive forced the North Koreans back towards the Yalu River, the border with China. But in October, hundreds of thousands of Chinese came to the North Koreans' assistance, pushing the UN troops back South and beyond Seoul.

Within the space of a few years, China's relationship with the United States had changed beyond recognition. In the years preceding 1949, the US had been China's strongest trading partner. Now the two countries were at war. With the Korean conflict in a state of stalemate in 1952, Western countries set up a China Coordinating Committee (CHINCOM) in an effort to control the export of sensitive goods from the West to China and North Korea and paralyse their war effort. They also began to turn down imports from the East.

Once a truce had been agreed the following year, support for the CHINCOM restrictions fell away rapidly. But not entirely. President Eisenhower's Secretary of State and diehard anti-communist, John Foster Dulles, remained a staunch advocate of taking a tough line with China. When he chanced upon Zhou Enlai at an international meeting in Geneva in 1954, the Chinese Premier offered his hand to shake. But Dulles refused the gesture and stormed from the room. In fact, it was not until President Richard Nixon's visit in 1972 that Sino-American relations began to thaw, of which more in Chapter 9.

In spite of the no-go stance taken by the US State Department, Demmer was not about to give up, hoping that 'some high person in Washington may close one eye and give Chi-Chi permission to enter and remain in the USA, despite her communist background.' In the meantime, he set off for Europe with a boxed-up panda, snow leopard, clouded leopard and several other zoological rarities in tow. The first leg of the trip was by aeroplane from Beijing to Moscow, though Chi-Chi was not the first panda to make this journey.

By the mid-1950s, the relationship between China and Russia had started to turn sour and Mao Zedong had tried to sweeten things by sending a panda to Moscow in 1957. Ping-Ping – assumed to be a female – arrived in Soviet Russia in May, just in time to be one of the many attractions on offer at the Sixth World

Festival of Youth and Students in July. So when Chi-Chi reached Moscow Zoo, where she rested up in 'a very large compound', she found herself in an enclosure alongside Ping-Ping. She would be back in altogether different circumstances almost eight years later, but on this occasion spent just ten days in the Soviet capital before Demmer and his animals continued their journey into Europe. At Moscow airport, they boarded a Lufthansa flight to East Berlin and at their destination were met on the tarmac by the Director of Tierpark Berlin and a truck that would take them there. 'Needless to say,' wrote Demmer, 'everyone was very glad to see the first Giant Panda to arrive in Europe since the war.'

The following day, Demmer began to make arrangements to transfer his animals from East to West Berlin. Although it would be several years before the first brick of the Berlin Wall was laid in 1961, Berlin was still a city divided along Cold War lines, with a Soviet sector in the East and the American, British and French sectors in the West. Even without a physical barrier, moving from East to West or vice versa was immensely tricky, particularly if you had to sign off a panda, a couple of leopards and bunch of other exotic beasts. Eventually, however, Demmer had the paperwork stamped and made his way to Tempelhof Airport in West Berlin's American sector.

The animals were transferred to a heated compartment of a Pan American Airways' flight to Frankfurt. At the destination airport, Demmer conducted a series of lengthy interviews with reporters and photographers. Finally, Chi-Chi made it to the city's zoo, 'where an absolutely magnificent large cage had been prepared for the young new little queen'. The turnstiles didn't stop moving and Chi-Chi began to move in higher circles, receiving on one day a visit from the Italian actors Marcello Mastroianni (of *La Dolce Vita* fame) and Marisa Merlini (*Pane, Amore e Fantasia*).

Like the 1940s panda Happy before her, Chi-Chi continued

the tour of European zoos, travelling from Frankfurt to Copenhagen and then from Copenhagen to London, arriving in the
British capital in early September 1958. Ever the showman,
Demmer was not one to miss a photo opportunity and on his
way to Regent's Park, staged a photograph of Chi-Chi's crate
balancing precariously on the roof of his car while he asked a
London bobby for directions.

At London Zoo, Demmer got up to further stunts, all aimed at
making a name for Chi-Chi. Once she'd had a few days to settle
in to her new temporary home in Regent's Park, Demmer led her
to the chimpanzee tea-party lawn to be filmed by a camera crew.
During the filming, Chi-Chi leaped over the low railings of the
enclosure and into the crowd. Knowing full well that the cameras
were rolling and stills were being snapped, Demmer hurdled the
fence in hot pursuit. A few days later Chi-Chi hopped out of her
pen and, playfully weaving her way around the legs of excited
onlookers, she pushed a woman aside and drew blood from her
leg. Such escapades, which made the news, only served to draw
in more visitors.

Initially, the Zoological Society of London had committed
to housing Chi-Chi for just three weeks. But as things turned
out, London Zoo was to become her home until her death in
1972. This would probably not have happened were it not for two
influential men and the emerging power of television.

In 1955, a distinguished zoologist called Solly Zuckerman had
taken up the all-important position of Honorary Secretary at the
Zoological Society of London. At that moment, the zoo was an
institution in decline, neglected during the war and now lacking
in funding and staff. Zuckerman – then aged 50 – set about
putting it on a more secure financial footing, efforts that saved
the zoo from almost certain extinction.

One of his innovative solutions to the financial crisis was to get in touch with an influential old chum, Sidney Bernstein, who just happened to be the founding Chairman of Granada Television, one of the first independent broadcasters to begin making programmes for British television. Zuckerman granted Bernstein and Granada Television permission to make natural history broadcasts using animals at the zoo. 'The hope that the programmes which the unit produced would add significantly to the Society's funds was fulfilled in the first few years,' wrote Zuckerman in his autobiography *Monkeys, Men and Missiles*.

One of Zuckerman's conditions was that the Granada TV and Film Unit should be fronted by a scientist. That scientist turned out to be Desmond Morris, a zoologist who had just completed his D.Phil at Oxford University. His thesis, on the reproductive behaviour of the ten-spined stickleback, hardly seems like a qualification for making television. And the new job came as something of a surprise to Morris. 'I was green and knew nothing about television, let alone been on it,' he recalled. But he took to the cameras like a ten-spined stickleback to a weedy river. The upshot was *Zoo Time*, a children's natural history series, which began in the spring of 1956.

In many ways, it was similar to a format that had been tried and tested across the Altantic, where the TV show *Zoo Parade* had transformed the fortunes of Lincoln Park Zoo in Chicago a few years earlier. In 1949, a producer had got in touch with the zoo's director to sound him out on the possibility of doing a series of half-hour live broadcasts from the zoo; the director, appreciating that the 'lifeblood of the zoo is publicity and promotion' jumped at the opportunity. Even though only around a third of American households had television, some 11 million people sat down to watch the show on a Sunday afternoon. 'Attendance at the Lincoln Park Zoo soared to over 4 million in 1952, as crowds flocked to see their favorite animal celebrities,' wrote historian of science Greg Mitman in *Reel Nature*. The programme, which made household names of Judy the elephant, Fuad the fennec, Sinbad the gorilla, Nero the lion, Sweet William the skunk, and the chimpanzee Heine II, was considerably ahead of its time, anticipating reality TV by decades.

The UK's *Zoo Time* followed on from *Zoo Parade*'s trailblazing example. 'So many animal programmes have a phoney "studio" atmosphere which is all too easy to detect,' wrote Morris several hundred episodes later in a 1966 book that looked back on the series. 'Most animals hate being moved into a strange, unfamiliar place and simply sit and sulk, or cringe in a corner.' So instead of transporting the animals from Regent's Park to a TV studio, Morris was adamant the cameras would have to come to the zoo as they had done in Chicago. More than that, Morris wanted a proper studio built inside the grounds where he could acclimatise the animals in the run-up to the broadcast. Not only would this avoid stressing the animals unnecessarily, it would also result in better television, he suggested. Bernstein agreed and a portable TV studio that had been destined for the Wimbledon Tennis Championships came instead to London Zoo. Though little more than a shed plonked at the back of the Bird House, 'The Den', as it came to be known, was where most of the live filming took place.

These live shows – in these days before videotape – could be volatile, which is of course what made them such compelling viewing. 'Things often go wrong when one is working with something as unpredictable as a mongoose or a monkey, and we have always felt it would be cheating to leave it out,' wrote Morris. The very first episode of *Zoo Time*, which went out live on 8 May 1956, contained just such an event. In the run-up to the broadcast, a baby bear called Nikki arrived at the zoo, a gift from Nikita Khrushchev, the First Secretary of the Communist Party of the Soviet Union, to Princess Anne. Nikki's connections guaranteed him a slot in the opening show, but he immediately grabbed hold of Morris' arm. 'Luckily of course we were in black and white because people couldn't see the blood,' he recalls. It was a baptism of fire that stood him in good stead for future mishaps. 'If you've actually got a bear that's clamped onto your forearm, and you're bleeding rather badly and it's your first television programme ever, and it's live,' then, suggests Morris, 'everything else seems easy.'

Nikki's star status set the tone of the show. From then onwards, Bernstein and his Granada producers were constantly scouting for animal talent to appear on the show. Chi-Chi, with the aura that had begun to follow her across Europe and her reputation for mischief, would fit in nicely. Granada began to haggle with the Austrian animal dealer. Eventually, after hours of negotiation, a price of £12,000 was settled on, roughly the figure that Brookfield Zoo and Demmer had bounced about in their informal communications. Granada would part with £10,000 and the Zoological Society of London would make up the difference.

On 23 September, the ZSL went public with the news of their new acquisition. In its statement to the press, it stressed that it was not in the business of encouraging the collection of creatures as rare as the giant panda but since Chi-Chi 'had already been exported from China under the authority of the Peking Government', it felt duty-bound to give her a good home.

China, meanwhile, was about to embark on the so-called Great Leap Forward. Early in 1958, Mao Zedong had unveiled his plan to subject China's heavy industry and agriculture to rapid Soviet-style reform. 'Man must conquer nature,' he declared. This, he argued, would result in steel production doubling before the year was out and overtaking that of Britain within fifteen years. In military fashion, Mao put his 600-million-strong Chinese army to work on impressive yet hastily concocted engineering projects; he got them clearing forests to make way for crops; and he pushed farmers to extraordinary limits.

For historian Judith Shapiro, author of *Mao's War Against Nature*, the Great Leap 'was one of China's most wide-ranging and convulsing campaigns'.

> Its defining characteristic was speed: urgency in recognizing society, urgency in catching up with Britain in industry, urgency in raising agricultural yields, urgency in building water conservancy projects, urgency in ridding China of pests, and so on. Mao sought to use the Leap to vault China toward a future utopia, realize his revolutionary vision, and capture his place in history.

In the west of China, in the pandas' stronghold, the forests suffered as the people cut down trees to fuel steel-smelting furnaces and to open up new land for crops. Ironically, the drive to press every possible hectare of agricultural land to its productive limits, and some extremely unhelpful ideas peddled by some very unscientific Soviet scientists, helped contribute to the worst famine in the history of the human species. One of the guilty was Soviet agricultural specialist Trofim Lysenko, who rejected the idea that genes were responsible for passing characteristics from one generation to the next. Instead, he claimed that the characteristics of an organism could be changed simply by giving it an appropriate set of environmental stimuli, like immersing seeds in cold water, for example. In the Soviet Union, he had pushed his views so persuasively that he convinced Stalin and, by publicly denouncing his many opponents as traitors to the Soviet Union, found them conveniently scrubbed out by the secret service.

One of Lysenko's more destructive assertions was that seeds of the same variety would not compete with each other for sunlight and soil nutrients but would survive – even thrive – when sown at unthinkable densities. It was an idea that appealed to Mao, who pressed the practice of 'close planting' upon Chinese peasants in an effort to increase yields by an order of magnitude. Another crazy idea that filtered through from the Soviet Union came from Lysenko's crony Terentsy Maltsev, who argued that 'deep plowing' would churn up more fertile soil. 'In some cases, furrows ten feet deep were dug by hand in exhausting and senseless marathon efforts to force the earth to become more fertile,' notes Shapiro. The consequences of such ideas were predictable and tragic: crops withered and died as did anywhere between 20 and 40 million Chinese peasants.

In contrast to such unimaginable suffering, Chi-Chi's London lifestyle could not have been more lavish. On hot days, visitors might see her reclining on blocks of ice or basking in a fine mist of water sprayed down from on high. A keeper with his own special uniform was assigned full-time to take care of Chi-Chi's every need and to play with her in front of the crowds. 'He was dressed in black leather gear, looking rather like Marlon Brando in one of his early movies,' recalls Morris. 'All this was to add glamour to what was indeed a very glamorous animal.' And within a few years, she'd moved into new accommodation, a custom-built enclosure complete with an air-conditioned indoor den.

When it came to her food, Chi-Chi appeared to be fussy, ignoring the bamboo specimens the ZSL offered up to her. In a cartoon published in the *Daily Express* shortly after her arrival, the famous cartoonist Ronald Carl Giles joked about the unfolding bamboo crisis at the zoo. He had Khrushchev's bear

17. As a young panda, Chi-Chi's playful antics thrilled the British public. Here, she plays football with her keeper Alan Kent, in his mucking-out clothes, at London Zoo in May 1959.

Nikki writing a letter to his new 'Comrade Chi-Chi'. 'I see you're complaining already,' wrote Nikki. 'No bamboo shoots to your liking … Believe me, Comrade, you'll have to get used to worse than that before you've been over here much longer.' This is one of the earliest examples of satire that Chi-Chi would inspire and endure, of which more – much, much more – later.

An elderly gentleman responded to the ZSL's call for new sources of bamboo. He lived in a cottage on the edge of Menabilly woods on the Menabilly Estate in Cornwall (which, incidentally, made him the next-door neighbour to the novelist Daphne Du Maurier who then rented Menabilly House). 'The Captain', as the man was respectfully known by the locals, cut down a sample of the bamboo from the dense thickets growing around his cottage and sent it up to London. Chi-Chi ate some of it and the ZSL engaged the Captain to provide a regular supply. The Captain enlisted the help of the local scout troop and a handful of scouts soon became the official bamboo suppliers to Chi-Chi. 'The boys would drop it at my house on Sunday when they normally cut it,' recalls Mike Kerris, who has been associated with the Polkerris Scout Troop since the 1950s. 'My first duty on a Monday morning would be to take the bamboo … on the roof-rack down to the station.'

In spite of this effort, bamboo made up only a third of Chi-Chi's diet. As a baby, the zoo staff topped her up with boiled rice or porridge, a couple of raw eggs, some chicken or steak, a cup of milk, fruit, a sweet potato, sugar and a sprinkle of wheatgerm. There were also treats. 'Chi-Chi ate much chocolate throughout her life and, after 1966, often drank tea, a taste apparently acquired in Moscow,' admitted ZSL's curator of mammals after her death.

This is a world away from the situation today, where panda nutrition has become a serious science. As we shall see in Chapter 11, the focus is now firmly on feeding pandas bamboo and keeping the extras to an absolute minimum. There are many benefits of giving captive pandas a diet that more closely resembles that seen in the wild, but one of them is that the animal has to remain active, shredding stems for much of the day. Indeed, it was perhaps partly because of Chi-Chi's instantly gratifying diet that she did not quite live up to Granada's expectations. 'Chi-Chi, we soon found, spent a great majority of life sleeping and this of course is not good on television,' recalled *Zoo Time*'s producer. 'The poor creature had to be poked out and woken up in order to at least appear to be animate. Sometimes on a good day – hungry perhaps – she would perform fairly well. But there were many, many days in which she was not accessible through sleep.' It was a hard but important lesson about giant pandas. They sleep a lot, especially if you feed them porridge.

Still, just as the *Zoo Parade* celebrities had drawn millions to the Lincoln Park Zoo in Chicago in the early 1950s, so the punters rolled in to London Zoo to see Chi-Chi and other *Zoo Time* favourites in the late 1950s and early 1960s. Chi-Chi was entertaining, for sure. But, as the next chapter will reveal, the mass media attention heaped upon her had rather more important and long-lived consequences for the way of the panda and also for the emerging conservation movement.

The face of conservation

It was during Easter 1961 – on April Fools' Day, to be precise – that a man called Max Nicholson sat down with pen in hand. He scrawled the heading 'HOW TO SAVE THE WORLD'S WILDLIFE'. In a grand old farmhouse in the charming folds of the Cotswold countryside, shut off from the relentless pace of life as director general of Britain's Nature Conservancy, Nicholson penned a rhetorical masterpiece that aimed to focus minds on the desperate situation facing mankind's natural heritage. It would result, within the space of just six months, in the World Wildlife Fund, now the world's largest non-governmental conservation charity, with more than 5 million members worldwide.

There were, Nicholson acknowledged, plenty of organisations committed to the emerging conservation cause. But, he wrote, '[t]he threat of defeat which faces us is primarily a question of resources and above all of money.' This money, he believed, was there for the taking, but to get it would require 'appropriate organisation and leadership', something he felt existing organisations lacked.

He was in a position to know. Throughout his long life, which spanned almost the entire twentieth century, Nicholson had a hand in organising or leading dozens of environmental initiatives and organisations, several of which are at the forefront of the modern conservation movement: he was instrumental in setting up the Oxford Bird Census in 1927 (which provided the foundation for the world-famous Edward Grey Institute of Field Ornithology); he established the British Trust for Ornithology in 1932; he drafted the constitution for the International Union for Conservation of Nature (IUCN) in 1948; he kick-started the Nature Conservancy in Britain the following year; he helped found the International Institute for Environment and Development in 1971; he was instrumental in the instigation of the Trust for Urban Ecology in 1976; he was president of the Royal Society for the Protection of Birds in the 1980s; and he was chairman of Earthwatch (Europe) at around the same time. And that's just skimming the surface of his achievements. When it came to organisation and leadership, Nicholson was quite simply second to none.

As he surveyed the conservation landscape from his Cotswold hideaway, he saw a gap that desperately needed filling:

> Existing organisations add up to something rather like a car with a half-pint fuel tank replenished by an occasional cupful. What is needed is not a new organisation to duplicate and compete with the work of existing bodies but a new co-operative international project to make their efforts effective by providing them with adequate resources – a new fuel tank with a petrol pump to fill and refill it.

Rousing stuff. On his return to London, Nicholson invited ten leading figures to a meeting at the Nature Conservancy's offices in Belgrave Square to mull over his handiwork. Three of the names – Julian Huxley, Victor Stolan and Guy Mountfort – should probably be circled with a fluorescent highlighter, for Nicholson credited each of them in turn with prompting him to put pen to paper that Easter.

As the grandson of 'Darwin's Bulldog', Thomas Henry Huxley,

and the younger brother of Aldous Huxley, author of *Brave New World*, Julian Huxley could have been forgiven for steering clear of the limelight. But he didn't. As a founder and the first director general of UNESCO, one of his first acts had been to set up the IUCN. Throughout the 1950s, a handful of IUCN ecologists began to report on the way that overgrazing by livestock and man-made fires were irreversibly changing the African landscape. So in 1960, just as African country after African country was preparing to break from its colonised past, IUCN began its African Special Project to make the case for wildlife conservation across the continent. Simultaneously, Huxley – reporting to UNESCO – went on a whirlwind tour of ten Central and East African countries to see the state of play for himself. A series of three articles published in *The Observer* in November that same year portrayed a continent at a crossroads. 'Politics we shall always have with us,' he wrote, 'but if wildlife is destroyed, it is gone forever, and if it is seriously reduced, its restoration will be a lengthy and expensive business.'

His uncensored account of the threats facing Africa's rich biodiversity struck a chord with many in his mainly British audience. One of them – a hotel-owner called Victor Stolan – was moved by *The Observer* articles. Aside from highlighting the problem, however, he felt that Huxley had not offered much in the way of a solution. '[A]las,' he wrote to him in early December 1960, 'however excellent your suggestions to remove the danger threatening the African wildlife, I feel that without vigorous and immediate action to raise the great funds needed, the irreparable detriment will not be prevented from becoming a fact.' Stolan had a point. 'I am proud to call this Country mine,' he went on, 'but I cannot help feeling that it has become a country of under-statements, of gentle talk with not enough push behind it.' What was needed, he suggested, was a 'single and uninhibited mind' to find a way to raise money – a lot of money – and soon. 'Would you care to put me in touch with somebody with whom ideas can be developed and speedilly [sic] directed towards accumulating some millions of pounds without mobilising commissions, committees, etc. as there is no time for Victorian procedure.'

Huxley did not have to think long. Nicholson was about as perfect a 'single and uninhibited mind' as one could hope for and he passed Stolan's letter on to his friend. Nicholson suggested that, if Stolan were 'seriously interested in this and willing to give some time to it', he should come by in the New Year to discuss matters. Stolan did just that, outlining his idea in 'a confidential memorandum' to Nicholson in early 1961. In it, he stressed two ideas in particular: the importance of weighty support from authority figures – the Archbishop of Canterbury and the Pope might be interested in 'the rescue of creation', Stolan suggested – and the value of tapping into the wealth of 'the new Tycoons'.

Nicholson proceeded cautiously, expressing to Huxley the need for 'the most thorough possible preparation anticipating all the questions which might be asked and all the practical problems which would arise'. He was wary of Stolan too, seeing him as 'too much the naive enthusiast and rather too little the practical man of affairs to be very much help'. What Nicholson was after was someone 'with ideas and drive and practical business experience for money raising'.

That person turned out to be Guy Mountfort, an advertising executive and – like Nicholson – an avid ornithologist. Standing on the stairs of the Royal Station Hotel in York following the Annual General Meeting of the British Ornithologists' Union towards the end of March, Nicholson asked Mountfort if he thought it might be possible to coax serious money from the very rich. 'Had the response been adverse the idea would probably have been dropped there and then,' wrote Nicholson. 'But it was encouraging.' And so Nicholson put his thoughts to paper that Easter on 'HOW TO SAVE THE WORLD'S WILDLIFE' and invited Huxley, Stolan and Mountfort along with a select handful of other influential folk – including naturalist and artist Peter Scott – to mull over it.

Annexed to Nicholson's draft document was a military-style series of timetables and targets necessary for success and one of them was to get the go-ahead from IUCN, an organisation in danger of collapsing for lack of funds and a major potential beneficiary of any money raised by the new charity. So Nicholson wrote what became known as the Morges Manifesto, a rousing document signed by sixteen of the world's leading conservationists at an IUCN board meeting at the organisation's Morges headquarters in Switzerland on 29 April. It concluded: 'Mankind's self-respect and mankind's inheritance on this earth will not be preserved by narrow or short-sighted means.'

With IUCN backing, Nicholson chaired nine meetings of his 'preparatory group' over the spring and summer of 1961. On Mountfort's recommendation, a public relations guru named Ian MacPhail turned up to the second and most of the subsequent meetings and began to focus minds on the importance of a name. To start with, everyone liked the idea of calling the new organisation 'Save the World's Wildlife', though they soon alighted on the more succinct 'World Wildlife Fund'. And it was MacPhail who got them thinking about a logo. Everyone agreed 'that a symbol which could speak for itself and overcome all language barriers, and which could be easily reduced in size, was of the utmost importance' and someone – most likely Peter Scott – proposed a panda. Motion seconded and carried. That was it.

Few committees in the history of committees can ever have reached such an important decision so effortlessly. Although the frequency of these preparatory meetings, the influential attendees and the care given to 'the most thorough possible preparation' is impressive, it's clear that consensus over the panda was reached pretty quickly. According to Nicholson it was 'one of the most valuable trademarks that has ever been devised, and it took about twenty minutes.' It seems unlikely, then, that the WWF founders took time to consider what this animal meant to the Chinese.

For by the 1960s, the panda had already emerged as a widely recognised image in cities across China, says historian Elena Songster. 'Renderings of the panda image in art and manufactured goods began during the 1950s and became even more popular during the course of the Cultural Revolution,' she says. Songster begins her analysis by pointing to an energetic electronics company originally based in Nanjing, which offers a nice example. In January 1956, a full five years before the WWF settled on its trademark, Mao Zedong paid a visit to the Nanjing Radio Factory, a Chinese state-owned electronics company. That same year, the company rebranded as Panda Electronics, with a fetching, bamboo-munching panda as its upbeat new logo. Songster cites a company representative quoted in the *People's Daily* in 1961: 'The "panda" is China's most famous precious animal', he announced in an article about a one-off radio manufactured for the company's fifth anniversary. 'Upon seeing "Panda" one would, therefore, immediately know that it is a Chinese product.'

Songster has brought together a list of other panda appearances in China from the 1960s onwards, each contributing to what she calls 'the emergence of the panda as a national icon': a dairy in Inner Mongolia adopted the panda to sell its condensed milk and butter; a Shanghai-based plastics company turned out a flexible plastic panda to showcase its innovative technology; and a set of panda stamps by famous Chinese artist Wu Zuoren appeared in 1963.

18. When traditional Chinese painter Wu Zuoren was commissioned to produce a series of stamps for the People's Republic of China, he settled on the giant panda. Ever since then, the panda has been a symbolic ambassador for the Chinese nation.

The Cultural Revolution, rather than stifling such artistic use of the panda, may even have propelled this emerging icon further into the mainstream, argues Songster. While the PRC clamped down with brutal efficiency upon any intellectual or artistic offerings that might be associated with China's imperial past, the panda seems to have escaped unscathed. Its relatively recent discovery and complete absence from any old-style art meant it was free from such associations. Its appearance as the front for enterprises like Panda Electronics, supported as they were by those at the very top of the Chinese Communist Party hierarchy, sent out the message loud and clear: pandas were fair, even desirable, cultural game. 'By the mid 1960s, the giant panda became synonymous with modern China,' says Songster. 'Studying it, painting it, and mass producing it were all means of glorifying one of China's prized possessions, and thus China itself.'

The WWF founders saw the panda rather differently. They needed a symbol that would communicate the idea of endangerment,

that looked good and that would be recognisable when reproduced in miniature in black and white. From where they sat, a
world away from the dripping forests of Sichuan, around a plush
boardroom table in a swanky town house on the edge of affluent
Kensington, the panda ticked all the boxes.

As the preparatory meetings came and went, the link between
WWF and IUCN became stronger; it made sense that a representative of IUCN should be coaxed along. That happened to be
its Secretary-General Gerald Watterson, who had worked for the
UN's Food and Agriculture Organisation before moving over to
IUCN in 1960. Watterson is credited with knocking up the first
sketches of a panda-based logo for the new organisation and,
according to WWF legend, they were based on London Zoo's
Chi-Chi. It's more than likely they were. In mid-July, Watterson
met up with Peter Scott at his home on the Bristol Channel,
and the two men shut themselves away in Scott's studio to draw
pandas. Watterson probably had his sketches of Chi-Chi with
him that weekend, Scott stylised them into WWF's first logo and
Watterson, more than likely, carried Scott's creation with him
back to London to show off at the seventh preparatory meeting
of WWF on Monday, 17 July 1961.

This was a meeting that Scott did not attend. Instead, he was
busy attracting figureheads for the organisation, targeting royalty
rather than the religious leaders that Stolan had suggested. He
was personally acquainted with many royals, including Prince
Bernhard of the Netherlands, the sort of nature-loving royal who
would give WWF an entrée to the leaders of countries around
the world and get conservation firmly on their agenda. Several
decades earlier, just before the war, Bernhard had visited Scott
at his lighthouse home in Norfolk, where the men had supped
tea and the prince had filmed some birds. Now, in 1961, Scott
arranged to meet Bernhard in Claridges Hotel in London to ask

him to become the WWF's first president and to head a board of international trustees. The prince agreed.

The idea was that as many countries as possible should establish their own National Appeal, with a similarly celebrated figure to act as chairman and with its own locally accountable board of trustees. For the British National Appeal, the obvious person to collar was the Duke of Edinburgh, Prince Philip. In 1947, Scott had been engaged by the BBC as a commentator for Philip's wedding to Princess Elizabeth; he was subsequently invited to Buckingham Palace to make portraits of Elizabeth and her younger sister Margaret, and was to be a frequent sailing companion for the Duke. Scott leaned persuasively on his influential friend. Once Philip had agreed to be Chairman of the British National Appeal of WWF, Scott even tried to effect a mention for wildlife conservation into a speech the Queen was due to give at the Commonwealth Parliamentary Association's biennial conference later that year. 'Is there a chance that Her Majesty could make reference to wildlife in her speech,' he asked of Michael Adeane, a chum from Cambridge University days and now Assistant Private Secretary to the Queen. Adeane, in reply, was polite but firm. 'I have drawn the Queen's attention to your suggestion,' he informed Scott, 'but I am more than a little doubtful whether it is the sort of thing which could be easily introduced into the speech.' It was worth a go.

By now, preparations were well under way for the organisation to launch on a global stage. The venue was to be Arusha, a city in northern Tanganyika (now part of Tanzania). The occasion would be the Symposium on Conservation of Nature and Natural Resources in Modern African States. The date, early September. One of the main purposes of this meeting was to encourage the newly independent African nations to embrace a conservation ethic. For if they didn't, Western conservationists feared that no amount of money raised by WWF would save Africa's wildlife.

Many Westerners were not overly optimistic this could be achieved. Writing in anticipation of Kenya's independence, Mervyn Cowie (the then director of the Royal National Parks of Kenya) feared for the worst. 'Up to date no Kenyan African leader has emerged who has the slightest interest in safeguarding either the national economy or the natural assets of Kenya,' he wrote in a confidential letter to Nicholson. 'I cannot escape a conclusion that the preservation of wildlife, and the continuance of the Royal National Parks in Kenya, have a relatively small prospect of success under an African government.'

But Arusha was a success. Watterson had laid the groundwork in late 1960 and early 1961 by visiting more than fifteen African countries to persuade their leaders to consider embracing a more conservative stance towards nature and to send delegates to Arusha in September. He had also written to Julius Nyerere, then prime minister of a Tanganyikan government en route to independence, inviting him to act as something of a conservation role model for his fellow Africans. Watterson enclosed the 'Arusha Manifesto', three pithy paragraphs drenched in powerful rhetoric and jointly drafted by Nicholson and MacPhail, and hoped that Nyerere and other African leaders would see their way to signing it. This is what it said:

The survival of our wildlife is a matter of grave concern to all of us in Africa. These wild creatures amid the wild places they inhabit are not only important as a source of wonder and inspiration but are an integral part of our natural resources and of our future livelihood and well-being.

In accepting the trusteeship of our wildlife we solemnly declare that we will do everything in our power to make sure that our children's grandchildren will be able to enjoy this rich and precious heritage.

The conservation of wildlife and wild places calls for special knowledge, trained manpower and money and we look to other nations to cooperate in this important task – the success or failure of which not only affects the Continent of Africa but the rest of the world as well.

Nyerere was not convinced of the need for all this fuss about nature. 'I, personally, am not very interested in animals. I do not want to spend my holiday watching crocodiles,' he confessed. 'Nevertheless, I am entirely in favour of their survival. I believe that after diamonds and sisal, wild animals will provide Tanganyika with its greatest source of income. Thousands of Americans and Europeans have the strange urge to see these animals.' But, as his permanent secretary responded to Watterson, the Tanganyikan leader was 'more than willing to lend his full support to the causes you are anxious to promote' and he and a couple of relevant ministers agreed to put their names to the so-called Arusha Manifesto. As this announcement was released to the world's media, the WWF became a legal entity under Swiss law and its panda logo – the new face of international conservation – made its first tentative appearance on a global stage.

The official launch of the British National Appeal followed quickly on 28 September at the Royal Society of Arts in London. With the press man MacPhail now orchestrating WWF's public image, nothing had been left to chance. The WWF panda was very much in evidence, with a large version of Scott's drawing draped behind the speakers on the platform. This, MacPhail anticipated, might pose the question 'why a Panda at a meeting about African Wildlife'? It would be an opportunity, he suggested, for the meeting's chairman 'to make the appropriate remark about the problem under discussion being a worldwide one'.

At the same time, for maximum impact, the WWF founders had engineered a massive PR coup. The *Daily Mirror* – then the most popular British newspaper with a daily circulation of 4.6 million and an estimated readership of 13 million – had started to run what became known as 'shock issues' dominated by a thorny, social evil. The then editor-in-chief, Hugh Cudlipp, had come up with the idea, describing them as 'an exercise in brutal mass education'. His first 'shock issue' in 1960 had highlighted the suffering of horses shipped from Britain to be butchered in France and Belgium, and Huxley had approached him over the summer of 1961 to persuade him to give the same prominence to the global wildlife crisis, timed to coincide with the Arusha Conference. For Cudlipp, an animal lover, the alarming evidence that WWF began to feed him would make perfect content.

'DOOMED – to disappear from the face of the earth due to Man's FOLLY, GREED, NEGLECT' ran the headline of 9 October. The main photograph was of a female rhino and her baby, animals that would 'soon be as dead as the dodo' without urgent action. The lead article went on to list the Galapagos giant tortoise, the Asian bactrian camel, the Indian elephant and the North American whooping crane to capture the global nature of the problem. Scott's spherical panda logo made a prominent appearance, stamped onto the bottom right corner of the front page. 'There is only one hope for them – symbolised by the lovable giant panda,' *Daily Mirror* readers learned, 'The WORLD WILDLIFE FUND.'

Other articles appeared throughout the paper, including the centre spread, which exposed how drought was killing wildlife across Africa and recommending 'building dams and drilling water-holes ... to alleviate the dreadful sufferings' of these animals. And, on the back page, normally reserved for sporting news, was a photograph of Chi-Chi munching on some bamboo. Beneath it was a cut-out form branded with Scott's panda logo, name-dropping the two princes and giving the address of where to send donations.

There was a massive response, with some 20,000 letters and donations flooding in over the next four days. In a follow-up article on 13 October, the *Daily Mirror* reported that two mailbags alone contained some £4,000 in stamps, postal orders and cheques. Again, Scott's panda was there, staring out from a poster on the wall in a photograph of two women frantically opening envelopes. In total, this single appeal is thought to have raised around £35,000 for the charity – more than £500,000 in today's money. This, according to Nicholson, provided 'good confirmation of our diagnosis of the publicity value of the World Wildlife emergency and the possibilities of converting it into effective money'.

But other countries were slow to follow Britain's lead, much to Nicholson's frustration. 'I find it increasingly difficult to explain why we are still without any firm news of any single other country joining in the campaign,' wrote a stern Nicholson to Jean Baer, president of IUCN and the temporary president of the WWF towards the end of 1961. The Swiss, the Dutch, the Americans and the Germans set up their own national appeals in the years to come, but in general the WWF movement was slow to spread throughout the world. For example, WWF offices only appeared in Canada in 1967, France in 1973, Kenya (on behalf of East and Southern Africa) in 1986 and Russia in 1995. The Hong Kong office appeared in 1981, with the Beijing office opening a decade later. As far as Nicholson was concerned, it was not until 1968 that the organisation really got going.

The slow take-up internationally prompted Scott and

MacPhail, in WWF's first report published in 1965, to set out a 'blueprint for setting up a National Appeal'. This earmarked four sources of money: small donations from the man in the street 'largely based on emotional aspects'; big donations from the wealthy 'in which social aspects may play an important part'; donations from commerce and industry; money raised from charity functions or through the sale of goods. 'If any two of these seem to promise success, it is worth starting an Appeal,' they suggested. They also provided an impressive list of ideas to drum up publicity. In an act that explicitly linked the panda to hard cash, many of these centred on the popular appeal of the animal, so those setting up a local branch of WWF might consider franking all mail with Scott's panda, turning out pottery pandas or ash trays, selling booklets of panda-branded matches, giving away rear-window stickers for cars or badges for children.

Other conservation organisations have done likewise and used a flagship species as their public face; but these are usually national charities that use some local species, like the US-based Defenders of Wildlife choosing a wolf, the UK's Royal Society for the Protection of Birds an avocet, or the Malaysian Nature Society an Asian tapir. Of the relatively few conservation organisations that have truly global appeal, Flora and Fauna International has its Arabian oryx and Conservation International a patch of rainforest. None – whether local or international – is capable of communicating the conservation concept so swiftly or shifting branded goods as fast as the giant panda.

In addition to exploiting the WWF brand, Scott and MacPhail also offered plenty of fund-raising ideas where the panda was not the focus – posters, calendars, Christmas cards, art exhibitions, concerts, film festivals, auctions, fancy-dress balls, luncheons, dinners, banquets. They were borrowing many of these ideas from more established charities, but this was the first time they'd been put to significant use in a conservation context. They proved remarkably successful. For example, WWF UK shifted almost 100,000 Christmas cards in its first year. Most of the very many conservation charities that exist today use some or all of these approaches to raise their funds.

In this first report, WWF also mapped out its three main lines of activity. In the short term, it would continue to support rescue operations 'to save the most endangered species at the 11th hour'. Looking beyond these species, it considered the safeguarding of habitats 'no less urgent' and voiced enthusiasm for National Parks. In the long term, however, the most important thing was to educate the public.

> Our task, impossible though it may seem, is to change the atti-
> tude of the great mass of human beings to the natural world, and
> we have at most one generation's span in which to do it. We are
> satisfied that it can be done.

It would take until 1979 for WWF to turn towards China and the panda.

At its 1961 launch, WWF had glossed over the threats to the giant panda. The choice of animal for its logo made sense, argued the organisation's literature, because the panda 'owes its survival to the sort of careful conservation which all wild creatures deserve'. This, of course, was far from the truth. With China vigorously taking control of nature under Mao Zedong and with the first dedicated panda reserve still a couple of years away, the idea of panda conservation had yet to be invented.

It fell to Nancy Nash, a journalist with a passion for animals and nature, to point out that the panda was not just a brand but also a species. Based in Germany in 1962, Nash had been an enthusiastic recruit to the new conservation charity and in mid-1979 found herself at WWF International's headquarters in Morges as a PR consultant. 'Since you have a panda as a symbol, why aren't you in touch with China about a panda study?' she asked one day. It sounds like an obvious question. It was rather strange that, after almost twenty years of operating, WWF had yet to make a contribution to the conservation of its emblematic species. Its excuses, if it had offered any, might have been as follows: WWF had spent the 1960s gathering strength as a global organisation and thrashing out the details of how it would allocate its money; it had been concentrating on Africa, where the wildlife had been relatively well studied, the threats facing it were reasonably well understood, and it was possible to see how money could be spent; and finally, the Cultural Revolution meant that nobody in WWF knew who in China to approach or how best to go about it.

Nobody, that is, except for Nash. In 1967, she had been a public relations manager at the Hilton Hotel in Hong Kong, where she met, organised events for, and became friends with a lot of influential people, including Wu Tai Chow, founder and then president of the left-leaning *Hong Kong Evening News* and a man with some serious Beijing connections. Nash also had a boundless passion for animals and for nature, something that proved to be crucial. 'I can get us into China,' she told the WWF leaders. But, says Nash, her bold claim was dismissed. WWF had already approached China and got nowhere. How could someone in Nash's position possibly make a difference?

However, Peter Scott and WWF's chief scientific advisor Lee Talbot encouraged her to go ahead and see what she could do on her own, figuring that a personal touch and abundant passion might succeed where more formal approaches had failed. She worked up a six-page proposal in her own name, which mapped her ideas for a China-WWF joint initiative. She took it to Wu, who was able to get it straight onto the desks of all the right people in Beijing.

The timing was perfect. At the Fourth National People's Congress in 1975, the ailing premier of the PRC, Zhou Enlai, had introduced the idea of the four modernisations, reforms in agriculture, industry, national defence, and science and technology, which promised to transform China into a world-leading economic force by the twenty-first century. With a tussle for power at the top of the Chinese Communist Party following Mao Zedong's death in 1976, it was several years before these ideas began to take coherent shape. But in 1978, Zhou's successor, Premier Deng Xiaoping was busy promoting science and technology as a 'productive force' and though restrictions on individual freedoms remained for several years to come, the rehabilitation of science and scientists in Chinese society had begun. In order to realise its modernising goals, China adopted a more inviting stance to the outside world.

Nash's proposal tapped into this new vibe. Following several days of talks, she had managed to get China to consider becoming a member of the World Conservation Union (IUCN) and the Convention on International Trade in Endangered Species (CITES). She also managed to get Qu Geping, director of China's Environment Protection Office of the State Council, to issue a formal invitation to WWF to attend talks. When Peter Scott and the other WWF officials flew into China in September 1979, it was the first time since the Cultural Revolution that the Chinese government had held talks with an international conservation organisation. After four days of meetings, with Nash acting as a go-between, the PRC and WWF formerly entered into a partnership that, in addition to getting China to sign up to IUCN and CITES, made a commitment to setting up a joint panda project. It was – is – a historic agreement.

19. In 1979, China's Environment Protection Office issued an invitation to the World Wildlife Fund to discuss collaborating in a project to study giant pandas in the wild. During a visit to Beijing Zoo, WWF delegates unfurled a flag bearing the WWF logo into the panda enclosure.

But the ink was hardly dry before WWF made the first of many diplomatic gaffes that threatened to scupper the relationship forever. The WWF press machine back in Morges released the news of the agreement to the world. 'China and wildlife group agree on help for endangered species' ran the headline in *The New York Times* on 24 September, but WWF's new Chinese partners and Xinhua, the Chinese news agency, had not been in on this publicity loop. 'Bad move,' says Nash. 'I got the blame until the Chinese realised I had nothing to do with it.' Then it fell to her to heal the wounds and set the project back on track.

There were more, many more, moments like this in the coming months. One source of tension was over the ownership of the panda. There were times, says Nash, when WWF officials spoke of pandas as their own property, apparently unaware that this species had now become a truly national treasure in China. On another occasion, in one of the most important meetings with EPO director Qu, WWF's director general Charles de Haes was showcasing some of the organisation's ideas for raising funds and passed round a sheet of panda postage stamps. It was a good idea, but one with poor execution, as the mock-ups were based on Taiwanese as opposed to Chinese stamps.

The CCP had recently stated that Taiwan had been 'the crucial issue obstructing the normalisation of relations between China and the USA' and that 'bringing Taiwan back to the embrace of the motherland' should be an entirely 'internal affair'. To the Chinese officials at the WWF meeting then, the Taiwanese stamps were particularly inappropriate, evidence of foreigners meddling yet once more in China's internal politics. Qu Geping grabbed the sheet of stamps, threw it onto the table and stormed out in disgust. His secretary remained in the room, but only long enough to say, in slow, clear English, 'That says Taiwan'. Nash, who had not seen the ill-advised offering until that moment, was horrified. 'It was so unbelievably stupid,' she says. 'If they'd shown it to me I could have said don't do it.'

To make matters worse, WWF representatives found themselves in negotiations with not one but three Chinese agencies – the Ministry of Forestry, the Chinese Academy of Sciences and the Environmental Protection Office of the State Council. It soon became clear that these three institutions rarely saw eye to eye, though not before WWF had invited four EPO officials (but none from the other two agencies) to a WWF gala in the Netherlands in June 1980. That upset a lot of people.

Another major sticking point was the establishment of a research centre. This was a commitment that appeared in the historic memorandum that Scott and others had signed in September 1979, but it soon became clear that what the Chinese had in mind was on an altogether grander scale to that envisaged by WWF: they wanted something concrete – quite literally – to show for inviting foreigners to study their national treasure.

On 30 April 1980, Nash was at the airport in Hong Kong to meet the renowned zoologist George Schaller, then director of conservation at the New York Zoological Society (what is now the Wildlife Conservation Society). Having carried out groundbreaking work on a range of animals, including gorillas, tigers, lions and wild sheep, Schaller was the perfect person for WWF to approach to study pandas. Indeed, several years earlier he himself had approached the Chinese with a view to setting up a panda study, but without success. 'It was the height of the Cultural Revolution,' says Schaller, 'and they obviously smiled and said it's not timely.' So when WWF approached him in early 1980, he began to look for someone to take over the reins of a jaguar project he was running in Brazil and, with the New York Zoological Society's blessing and financial backing, he headed out to China.

In the weeks that followed, Nash and Schaller had several meetings in Beijing, the first held in Nash's hotel room and attended by representatives of the three Chinese agencies. They then flew to Chengdu, where they met up with Peter Scott, his wife Philippa and a host of Chinese officials, including the deputy governor of Sichuan. In addition, standing quietly to one side, was leading Chinese panda expert Hu Jinchu (who we briefly met in Chapter 2), a small, reserved man who hid his uneasiness behind nervous laughter. 'His quiet project was being invaded by unknown outsiders whom he had been ordered to cooperate with,' says Schaller.

The Westerners were escorted to the Wolong Nature Reserve, which occupies some 2,000 square kilometres of the crumpled Qionglai Mountain range between the Tibetan plateau to the west and the Sichuan basin to the east, and had been established as a national park in 1975. 'Many foreigners have come to this part of China but none of them was invited,' their hosts told them. 'You have been invited.' The following day, they were taken on a three-hour hike up the mountainside where hemlock, pine and birch crowded over a canopy of bamboo. 'We traveled now in single file, our footsteps muffled on the soft earth, our voices subdued as if in a holy place,' wrote Schaller in his book *The Last Panda*.

Suddenly Hu signalled something on the trail ahead and Nash and Scott huddled round as Schaller scooped up two long panda droppings. 'The 21 Chinese in our entourage watch patiently, rather bemused at our delight in these artefacts of a panda's passing,' wrote Schaller of this moment, 'the first observation of a panda's presence in the wild by a joint WWF/Chinese team, the beginning of long-term cooperation to help assure this rare and precious species a future in its wilderness home.'

It was back at the reserve headquarters – formerly home to

several thousand loggers – that Wang Menghu from the Ministry of Forestry began to elaborate on China's vision for the panda research centre. This facility, he informed the WWF representatives, would be made up of around twenty research labs occupying some 800 square metres, an even greater area given over to living quarters to accommodate thirty scientists and technicians, an outdoor panda enclosure with 2,500 poles and 5 kilometres of fencing and a 250 kW hydroelectric station. The estimated construction cost? Two million US dollars. 'We were stunned,' says Schaller. The Chinese subsequently added an array of high-tech gadgetry to their wish list. For WWF, the most important thing was to begin a study of pandas in the wild. If, as was the case, the world still knew precious little about these animals, why was such a vast laboratory facility required with such urgency?

In spite of Scott, Schaller and Nash's best efforts to convince them otherwise, their Chinese counterparts refused to budge. As Schaller put it in *The Last Panda*, Wang's message was clear: no research centre, no panda project. WWF was being asked to stump up half of the $2 million or they could lump it. This threat was by no means idle. Other institutions were also keen to carry out field research on China's pandas. There was very real concern that the WWF would lose out on being the first Western organisation to study its own symbol. That just wouldn't do.

Given all the misunderstandings and mismatched expectations, it is truly remarkable that the China-WWF panda project came off at all. Important as Scott, Schaller and others undoubtedly were, it's unlikely that the negotiations of 1979 and 1980 would have borne any fruit were it not for Nash – or 'Miss Panda', as she's sometimes known. Not only did she set the ball rolling by effecting the initial invitation to Peter Scott and his fellow WWF leaders, she was also the one to whom it fell to iron out the very many difficulties. 'Without her the project never would have happened,' says Schaller. But with one foot in the East and one foot in the West, it was Nash that brought these two wildly different cultures together. And, as we'll learn in Chapter 10, come together they did, with Schaller and Hu co-leading the groundbreaking research that began in late 1980. For WWF, the $1 million it invested in the research centre at Wolong was a price worth paying for the privilege of entering the secret world of the animal inspiration for its logo.

By the time of its twentieth anniversary in 1981, WWF was able to boast the joint China-WWF panda project as a major new initiative that would help raise funds across the board. Nash established WWF's Hong Kong office that same anniversary year, though only remained with the organisation for a further five years. Her reason for leaving? In 1986, WWF had decided to rebrand. It changed its name from the World Wildlife Fund to the World Wildlife Fund for Nature (though not in the US and Canada). At the same time, Peter Scott's panda got a makeover. Different national chapters had started to tweak with the panda logo – notably WWF US – and it was hoped that a fresh panda logo could reunite the national organisations under one global emblem. Amongst other stylistic changes, WWF's new panda logo lost its bounce, its fluff and the sparkle from its eyes.

Scott, then in his seventies, was saddened by these seemingly superficial alterations. It had probably been his idea to go with a panda all those years ago. It had been in his studio at Slimbridge in July 1961 that he had created his Chi-Chi-inspired logo. It was his panda that had led the way for WWF and had become the face of global conservation. Nash, too, was upset: 'Sir Peter's panda looked like a panda and they turned it into this thing that looks like a dog.' For her – and probably for Scott too – the new logo was also symptomatic of other changes afoot in the organisation. Where WWF had once combined business with passion, it was gradually becoming strictly business, says Nash. 'That's not the way to do wildlife conservation.'

There's no doubt that WWF was no longer the small organisation that Nash had signed up to. In just twenty years of operating, it had raised and distributed some $55 million in support of 2,800 conservation and education projects worldwide. As we shall see, the path has not been entirely smooth, but today, half a century on, WWF remains the world's largest conservation charity with almost 5 million members worldwide. In the United States, home to WWF's largest national branch, it employs more than 400 people and the latest incarnation of Scott's giant panda logo helps raise some $180 million a year for conservation projects in the US and elsewhere. Though other national branches are on a smaller scale, the story is similar across the globe, with WWF now operating out of more than ninety offices across a network of forty countries.

In China, WWF's presence over the last thirty years has had a dramatic impact on the way of the panda. 'WWF has done a tremendous amount of good, because they've stuck in there and they're still in there,' says Schaller. Today, China and the Chinese have largely taken over control of the giant panda research with several generations of very talented researchers following in those first footsteps that Schaller and his colleagues took into the panda's world thirty years ago. 'WWF sort of pulled the whole thing together,' he says.

Whatever the future holds for WWF, it seems likely that giant pandas will be the face of the conservation movement for at least as long as there are still wild pandas and probably for a long time beyond. It was Chi-Chi that inspired this association. But that was not all she left us.

7

Sexual politics

In the autumn of 1960, Chi-Chi's mood suddenly changed and appeared to do so again the following spring. 'It was observed that at certain periods of the year she became faddy, less reliable, and showed symptoms of being "in season",' wrote London Zoo vet Oliver Graham-Jones in his 1970 book *First Catch Your Tiger*. 'She was noticeably attracted to her keeper, and at times appeared to be trying to make herself attractive to him!' It was time, everyone thought, to think about finding her a mate.

There were not many options. Beijing Zoo, by this time, had several pandas and was busy trying to get them to breed, and Moscow Zoo now had two. As recounted in Chapter 5, the PRC had sent the Soviet Union a presumed female, Ping-Ping, in 1957 and had followed it up with a male called An-An in August 1959. It would be safe to assume that the Moscow zookeepers, delighted by this pair of zoological rarities, did everything within their power to get the two pandas to mate. And one can only assume that Ping-Ping and An-An did not exactly hit it off, because when Ping-Ping died in 1961 it turned out that 'she' was actually a 'he'. In exiling Ping-Ping to the Soviet Union in 1957, Beijing Zoo had done itself out of what had then been its only male panda and in following him up with An-An had created an all-male enclave in Moscow. As the mistaken sexing of Su-Lin in the 1930s had suggested, assigning gender to a giant panda can be a tricky business.

Ignoring the political overtones of approaching either the PRC or the Soviet Union, honorary secretary of London Zoo, Solly Zuckerman, approached both, firing off letters to the directors of the Beijing and Moscow zoos in early 1962. The director of Beijing Zoo was quick to respond with a polite 'no'. Moscow was not much more forthcoming but Zuckerman was able to pursue the matter in person the following year when he found himself in Moscow attempting to get the Soviet Union and United States to agree to a ban on nuclear testing. For, in addition to his senior role at the Zoological Society of London, Zuckerman was also chief scientific advisor to the UK's Ministry of Defence (becoming the first Chief Scientific Advisor to the British government the following year). During a hectic three-week stay, which included several meetings with Soviet premier Nikita Khrushchev, Zuckerman managed to slip away to take up the panda matter with the director of Moscow Zoo, Ivor Sosnovsky. But still no firm agreement could be reached.

It's worth noting that the whole idea of captive breeding in zoos had yet to take off in any big way. As mentioned earlier, there had been inklings of a modern conservation ethic knocking around at the end of the nineteenth century. The National Zoological Park in Washington DC was founded in 1889 with its explicit goal 'the preservation and breeding in comfortable, and so far as space is concerned, luxurious captivity of a number of fine specimens of every species of American quadruped now threatened with extermination'. But the founders of the National Zoo made this sound rather easier than it is and, even in the 1960s, few zoos could claim to be making a serious contribution to conservation.

But things were changing. In 1960, the Zoological Society of London began to produce the International Zoo Yearbook, a publication that promised 'to provide an authoritative channel for the international exchange of information about zoos'. This made it a whole lot easier to find out what was going on at other institutions, who had what species and of which sex. It almost goes without saying, but this opened up a load of new opportunities for those who thought captive breeding was something they should be exploring.

The effort to save the Arabian oryx is one of the earliest examples of this new cooperative tendency in action. In 1960, Lee Talbot – who we've already met in his (much later) capacity as chief scientific advisor to the World Wildlife Fund – published a report for the Fauna Preservation Society (now Flora and Fauna International) that highlighted the plight of this handsome, straight-horned antelope. According to Talbot, it looked like the oryx would be extinct in the wild within years and its only future lay in captive breeding with the possibility of reintroducing it into the wild in years to come. In 1963, the Fauna Preservation Society launched Operation Oryx, which was, incidentally, one of the first big projects to receive funding from the newly formed WWF. The upshot was that a handful of animals – a few from the wild and a few from other collections – came together to form a 'world herd' at Phoenix Zoo in Arizona. Today, there are thought to be over 1,000 oryx in the wild with several times that number in captivity, many of them descended from this 1960s population.

Yet even with a precedent like Operation Oryx, the idea of effecting a relationship between two animals in different zoos (let alone between two animals in different zoos at opposite ends of a continent and across political and cultural divides) was still remarkably bold.

Then, in late 1963, Beijing Zoo announced that it had succeeded in producing the first ever captive-born panda. Early in the morning of 9 September 1963, a female called Li-Li with whom Chi-Chi had spent a few months in early 1958, gave birth to a cub weighing just 125 grams. It would later become clear that that is considerably above average for a newborn panda, which normally weighs around 100 grams or one-thousandth the weight of the mother. That is equivalent to a human female giving birth to a 23-week-old foetus, just over halfway through gestation. It's thought that this extraordinary reproductive strategy may be an adaptation to life on a tough bamboo diet, where mothers are unable to lay down sufficient fat to tolerate a longer pregnancy, but this peculiar feature of pandas remains something of a mystery even now. Here, the Chinese keepers describe the first few months of the baby panda Ming-Ming's life:

> His mother at first held him on her lap or in her arms day and night, not putting him down for a moment, neither when eating nor when sleeping. After the first month, Li-Li became less anxious and permitted the keeper to handle Ming-Ming. When the baby was two months old, Li-Li would play with him by tossing him from one arm to the other. When Ming-Ming grew impatient, she would soothe him with her paw just like a mother caressing a child. At three months Ming-Ming could manage to walk.

This compelling account can only have hardened the resolve of Zuckerman and his London Zoo colleagues to find Chi-Chi a mate. To begin with, however, and, given all the earlier mistakes made in assigning gender to giant pandas, it would be wise to confirm that Chi-Chi was indeed a female. The opportunity came in April 1964 when she scratched an eye on a stick of bamboo and developed an infection that required a minor operation. A large audience gathered in the zoo's operating theatre to witness zoo vet

Oliver Graham-Jones be the first to administer an anaesthetic to a giant panda. 'The pressures upon me were very great already,' he recalled some time later. 'But the pressures of being the first man to anaesthetise a giant panda and risk killing it were tremendous.'

Desmond Morris, by now curator of mammals at the zoo, watched as Chi-Chi squinted at Graham-Jones from her cage 'as if defying him to calculate the correct dosage'. With a deep breath, Graham-Jones injected her with a couple of trippy chemicals, one of which, phenylcyclohexylpiperidine, we more commonly know as 'angel dust', before he and colleagues lifted the limp but living body up on the operating table. With an oxygen mask placed over Chi-Chi's mouth and nose, it was time to introduce the general anaesthetic to her lungs.

Once Graham-Jones had cleared up the problem with her eye, he turned his attention to Chi-Chi's genital region in order to make his gender diagnosis. A photographer took some snapshots to convince London Zoo's Soviet counterparts, and the black-and-white prints were subsequently dispatched to Moscow. In mid-September, Zuckerman followed them up with a cable: 'The society would like it known that it would at any time be prepared to negotiate with the Moscow Zoo with a view to bringing the two giant pandas together,' he wrote. 'It is prepared to fly Chi-Chi out to Moscow or to have the Moscow panda as the guest of Regent's Park.'

The media pressed Sosnovsky and his staff for a response, which generated a flurry of conflicting stories. In some, Moscow was happy to go ahead. In others, the deal was off on account of An-An's virility and the harm he might inflict on Chi-Chi. 'These animals were not just animals, they were symbols of East and West coming together,' says Morris. 'If the animals had a fight it would be rather unfortunate in symbolic terms.' The deal seemed to be on the back burner once more.

Then suddenly, out of the blue in January 1966, the Soviet Ministry of Culture issued an invitation to the Zoological Society to discuss a plan of action in more detail. Given its political overtones, Zuckerman sought approval from on high. 'I am not sure that the proposal is consistent with our policy of détente, but we also have an interest in rapprochement. I recommend that this union be blessed,' wrote a senior advisor to the Ministry of Defence. A colleague at the Foreign and Commonwealth Office agreed, but with the British Prime Minister Harold Wilson due to visit the Soviet Union in July to discuss the Vietnam War, he had his concerns. 'Let us get this matter out of the headlines well before the PM goes to Moscow otherwise the two visits will become mixed in the public mind and worked to death by the TV comics and satirists.'

That, of course, is exactly what happened. No sooner had word gone out that Chi-Chi would, most likely, be flying to Moscow than the cartoonists sharpened their pencils. On 27 January, the *Daily Mirror* published a sketch of the Soviet premier Alexei Kosygin as An-An scaling a tree in hot pursuit of Wilson as Chi-Chi. 'I do hope nobody in the Prime Minister's office will be too upset about it,' wrote the zoo to the Foreign Office. The panda project was in danger of turning into a farcical spectacle before it had even begun. 'I have always suspected the F.O. of this sort of large-scale Dr Strangelove lunacy,' wrote one correspondent to a British newspaper, 'and this latest picture of diplomats and civil servants scurrying around the corridors of power debating the sexual habits of giant pandas is highly disturbing.'

The zoo people, too, were starting to feel the political pressure. Before Desmond Morris flew to Moscow on 4 February to talk things through with Sosnovsky and to meet the male panda An-An, he had to attend briefings at the Foreign Office and the Russian Embassy in London. Clearly, this was no longer a purely scientific endeavour motivated by animal welfare concerns.

For although most Western powers, including Britain, had started to foster new commercial and diplomatic ties with the USSR, Cold War suspicions remained strong. 'The Russians took it into their head that maybe this whole panda game was a cover for something more sinister,' says Morris. They did have their reasons. They were, of course, well aware that Morris' colleague Zuckerman had connections with the British Ministry of Defence. More alarming for the Soviet intelligence officials, though, was that Morris had worked with a man called Maxwell Knight. 'I knew Max as an avuncular, friendly old bloke, who loved animals and had written several books about how to keep pets,' recalls Morris. What he didn't know was that Knight's interest in nature, though real, was a cover for his role as a spymaster for MI5, responsible for coordinating the infiltration of the Communist Party of Great Britain and other groups that might be harbouring Soviet spies. Over the years there have been many names put forward as the inspiration for Ian Fleming's 'M' in his James Bond novels and Maxwell Knight's is one of them.

So when Morris got to Moscow he received the full treatment. 'They thought I was one of Max's boys,' he says. 'They bugged my room, they dismantled my electric razor … to see where my microphones were. I was followed everywhere.' Morris reports that in the state department store on the eastern side of Red Square, he was approached by a Russian agent provocateur who offered to show him plans for a secret factory. In spite of these obstacles, Morris and Sosnovsky managed to agree that Chi-Chi would come to Moscow that spring.

Back in London, preparations were made to ensure that the journey was as stress-free as possible. 'But when the animal is the cynosure of the world's communications industry, and its every move is faithfully reported to an audience totalling hundreds of millions in publications ranging from the *Cleveland Free Trader* to *Isvestia* and *The Times of India*, the path of the prodigy's escort is beset by a thousand pitfalls,' wrote Graham-Jones, who travelled with Chi-Chi should anything untoward happen. He was concerned that transported 'at varying altitudes, and exposed to varying pressures, Chi-Chi would be moved in a matter of hours from her snug accommodation in the temperate zone and delivered to a completely alien – and therefore suspect – environment held in the frozen grip of the Russian winter.' With a view to keeping her as calm as possible during the journey, Chi-Chi's favoured keeper Sam Morton was also along for the ride.

The zoo staff had designed and constructed a state-of-the-art box in which to transport their very important panda (or VIP). It was, wrote Graham-Jones, 'a cross between a crate and a mobile den that was far in advance of anything hitherto produced for the safety and comfort of a creature in transit'. But the size of the thing – 6 ft by 3 ft – meant that British European Airways had to remove thirty-two seats from one of their Vanguard aircraft to accommodate it. Before first light on the morning of 11 March, three vehicles drove in convoy from Regent's Park to Heathrow Airport, where Graham-Jones was surprised to find that well-wishers had gathered and 'a general air of carnival prevailed, to mock our dead seriousness'. He was less surprised to find journalists and photographers, eager to shoot the boxed-in panda.

It was this press attention – or the desire to avoid it – that resulted in a very strange welcome in Moscow. Chi-Chi was whisked unceremoniously away from the Western photographers that had accompanied her on the flight, as well as the flashbulbs waiting to fire from the tarmac. 'No sooner had the Vanguard cut engines and come to a stop, than the aircraft was enveloped by a horde of officials, most of them members of the brown-uniformed airport police,' Graham-Jones recalled. Several men unlashed Chi-Chi's crate, dragged it down the steps, heaved it onto a forklift truck and drove off. 'To say that we were surprised at these proceedings would be a masterpiece of understatement,' he wrote. Chi-Chi was transferred to a battered single-decker bus, which took her to the zoo. When an anxious Graham-Jones finally caught up with her, he watched as zoo workers manhandled the crate from the bus. 'It was dark by then, and as the crate hit the ground, its unfortunate prisoner gave vent to cries of anguish and rage!'

Chi-Chi did not calm down and it looked to Graham-Jones like the stress had affected her hormones and brought an early start and end to her oestrus. Recent research suggests he could well have been right. Injection of a hormone that stimulates the adrenal gland to produce and release the stress hormone cortisol seems to alter the normal levels of the two main female reproductive hormones: oestrogen takes a dive and progesterone surges, changes that probably reduce the duration of oestrus.

The 1960s was a watershed decade for the manipulation of female reproductive hormones. The United States Food and Drug Administration approved the first oral contraceptive pill in 1960 and the first drugs designed to boost fertility for those struggling to get pregnant soon entered clinical trials. One playful panda cartoon, published in March 1966 just before Chi-Chi and An-An's first encounter, gave a nod to the emerging field of fertility medicine. Two adult pandas – presumably the two celebrities then at Moscow Zoo – are walking upright across Red Square, chaperoning several baby pandas with dozens of others padding their way across the scene. The caption reads: 'More wives will test fertility drugs.'

The two animals were finally put together on 31 March. They stared. An-An inspected, licked and left his mark on a tree stump. Then all of a sudden he flung himself, snarling at Chi-Chi and

20. In March 1966, just before Chi-Chi and An-An's first encounter in Moscow, there was a spate of satirical panda cartoons in the British press. This one is typical. The Soviet premier Alexei Kosygin (right) and a couple of Soviet stereotypes look down from the balcony onto Red Square.

clamped his teeth into her hind leg. She fell onto her back, and An-An was on top of her, biting at her belly, when the zoo staff turned on the water hoses to drive off the assailant.

'Panda romance doubtful,' announced the *Montreal Gazette* and scores of other papers around the world. There would be no further mating attempts until the autumn when it was hoped that Chi-Chi would come back into heat. The London Zoo staff returned to the UK on 3 April.

Exactly six months later, Moscow cabled London to say that Chi-Chi was showing signs of coming into heat again. It was

21. Zoologist Desmond Morris watches on as An-An plods after Chi-Chi at Moscow Zoo in October 1966.

becoming increasingly clear that for panda mating, time was of the essence, so Desmond Morris dropped everything and was on a plane the following day. An-An seemed to sense that something was up and had started bleating like mad. Chi-Chi presented her rear to An-An through the bars that separated them. On 6 October 1966, Moscow Zoo closed early. Staff got into position, armed with water hoses, anaesthetic guns and wooden shields. A few carefully selected members of the press stood concealed behind a barrier of leaves and screens.

When An-An approached, Chi-Chi slapped him around the face. 'Though the pandas frolicked together and An-An made several romantic passes at Chi-Chi, it seemed the meeting was a failure and the animals were separated after 25 minutes,' reported the UK's *Birmingham Mail*. The following morning, the pandas were reunited, 'but the "bride" was even more nervous than at their rendezvous yesterday,' observed the *Leicester Mercury*. A photograph of Chi-Chi giving An-An a slap did the rounds in dozens of newspapers and the headline-writers went to town: 'Chi-Chi is playing hard to get'; 'Chi-Chi gives An-An a cuff'; 'Chi-Chi's right hook for the suitor'. They had even more fun the next day when it was decided that the pandas should bed down in the same enclosure: 'Two pandas spend night together'; 'Pandas' night of promise'; 'Strangers in the night'. But as panda relations turned from bad to worse, the headlines took on a gloomier tone: 'Time runs out for Chi-Chi'; 'Chi-Chi has only three nights left'; From Russia – without love'. And then it was announced that Chi-Chi would be heading back to London: 'Chi-Chi, An-An, say ta-ta'; 'Bride who never was flies home'; 'Return of the virgin panda'.

As the papers reported every conceivable development, the pandas became household names across the world. And as they did so, the whole adventure began to resemble the plot of a compelling but somewhat seedy soap opera; cheap jibes began to fly. Whilst zoologists tried their hardest to get their pandas to adopt more friendly relations, there was a rash of cartoons, many of them playing off the British Foreign Secretary's dismal efforts to forge a relationship with Moscow's politicians. As a typical example, on 18 November the *Evening News* ran with a cartoon of then Foreign Secretary, George Brown, dressed up in a panda suit with black rings around his eyes and bags packed for Moscow. Across the room, a tubby Prime Minister Harold Macmillan sits with his legs swinging off his desk. He is saying: 'Frankly, George, I reckon you'll cause a big enough sensation there without the gimmicks.' Others just poked fun at the pandas, like a *Daily Mirror* cartoon in which three American NASA officials chuckled as they chaperoned the two pandas into a space rocket. 'Happy to oblige, bud,' ran the caption, 'we only hope twelve months isn't rushing it.'

It was not just the public perception of pandas that took a bashing by the 1966 affair. So too did entrepreneurs, particularly in the UK, hoping to cash in on the birth of a baby panda. One company abandoned its plans to manufacture panda teddies. Another found itself staring at box-loads of Chi-Chi key rings. 'I'm afraid that we've been had,' the company's managing director told one journalist. In a drive to sell kidney pies, Walls, of ice-cream fame, offered cut-price toy pandas it could not otherwise shift. Late in the day, a pottery manufacturer scrapped his scheme for turning out mugs of Chi-Chi minor. A biscuit-maker, who had panda moulds tooled up and ready to cut pastry, decided instead to cut his losses. 'Never has such a gloom been spread throughout the industrial world by the mere lack of mateyness on the part of a couple of animals,' concluded a story in the *Daily Mail* shortly after Chi-Chi's return to London.

As if this weren't enough, there was more – much more – to come. Following a visit by Alexei Kosygin to London in February 1967, the Zoological Society of London issued a formal invitation to An-An to visit. The papers carried the news that there might be 'A return "match" for An-An', 'Another date for Chi-Chi?', 'Another marriage proposal for Chi-Chi?' Perhaps it would help Chi-Chi to be in familiar surroundings.

The timing seemed propitious. In 1967, thousands of people began to flock to the Haight-Ashbury neighbourhood of San Francisco, the epicentre of the hippy revolution, to have a piece of what would become known as 'the Summer of Love'. But the Russians did not jump at ZSL's offer. 'An-An is sick, so Chi-Chi's spring honeymoon is off,' reported one paper, and concerns over his health continued to emerge throughout the year. Finally, though, in early August 1968, the Russians gave a formal thumbs up to a reunion, in spite of all the tittering press attention they knew it would attract. The headline-writers relaxed into the panda groove once more: 'May be love at second sight for Chi-Chi'; 'A New Romance?'; 'Another date?'

Not long after this news broke, however, political events threatened to put the kibosh on the zoologists' plans. Czechoslovakia had been slowly pulling away from the Soviet Union, introducing reforms that would loosen restrictions on the press, introduce freedom of speech and make travel easier. It was a movement that became known as 'The Prague Spring' but in the early hours of 21 August 1968, the Soviet army (and troops from four other Warsaw Pact countries) moved in to shore up the solidarity of the Eastern bloc. There was widespread outrage in the West but the escalating tensions did not manage to thwart the panda plans. 'We have no reason to believe that the visit will be cancelled,' one London Zoo official said.

After the pandas' dismal showing in Moscow in 1966, there were several people doubtful that anything would come of the reunion. Ever since Chi-Chi had shown the first signs of coming into heat in the early 1960s, there had been suspicions that her lifetime spent amongst *Homo sapiens* rather than fellow *Ailuropoda melanoleuca* had resulted in her 'humanisation'. In preparation for her visit to Moscow, a mirror had been strung up in her den at London Zoo so that she could get used to what a panda looked like. But when in Moscow, she had adopted the full mating posture before one of the Russian zoo staff – 'to his intense embarrassment'. Following the 1966 meeting, the Russians reached the following conclusion: 'It appears that Chi-Chi's long isolation from other pandas has "imprinted" her sexually on human beings.'

The idea of imprinting had been popularised in the 1930s by the Austrian zoologist Kondrad Lorenz, who would later win a Nobel prize for his work on animal behaviour. He had wanted to know how it is that an animal comes to recognise its own species. Is this something that it just knows innately or is this something it has to learn? Lorenz's work suggested that in some species there was a critical period of learning during the first few hours of life. Newly hatched greylag geese, he found, would imprint themselves on the first plausible object they encountered. Under normal circumstances, this would be their mother. But when Lorenz incubated eggs artificially and was with the hatchlings in the hours after they'd broken free, he found they would imprint on him (and even an inanimate object) and eagerly waddle after him (or it) wherever he (or it) went. The purpose of this imprinting, Lorenz argued, was to establish a 'sort of consciousness of the species in the young bird', which would be crucial in later life when it tried to find a mate.

If a young bird imprints on the wrong species, this could have some strange consequences. Lorenz related how a male bittern, raised by a zookeeper, would drive away a female bittern it lived with whenever the zookeeper approached. When, eventually, the birds did mate and the female laid a clutch of eggs, the confused male would attempt to coax the keeper onto the nest to assist with incubation. Subsequent researchers followed up on this delightful anecdote in a more rigorous manner. In one study, German scientists took a clutch of eggs from a pair of zebra finches and had them reared by Bengalese finch foster-parents. After forty days of being fed and cared for by this different species, the young birds were kept alone for a further sixty days. Then, on day 100 of their rather extraordinary lives, the researchers began to explore the zebra finches' sexual preferences. The more their foster-parents had fed them, the stronger the preference for mating with Bengalese over zebra finch females, they found.

Such experiments have even been replicated in mammals. In the 1990s, researchers based in the UK and South Africa experimented with goats and sheep, taking eight newborn kids and switching them with eight newborn lambs. Once they'd grown up, the scientists tested their social and sexual preferences. The male goats raised by sheep wanted to hang out and mate with ewes and the male sheep raised by goats wanted to hang out and mate with goats. Females were not so easily fooled. 'This indirectly supports Freud's concept of the Oedipus complex and suggests that males may also be less able than females to adapt to altered social priorities,' concluded the researchers.

As an undergraduate student, the young Desmond Morris had been much impressed by Lorenz's work and had rushed to see him deliver a series of lectures at Bristol University in 1950. 'This man wasn't brilliant, he was a genius,' he pronounced afterwards. The idea of imprinting could help explain Chi-Chi's behaviour, Morris argued. 'Every indication was that, because she'd been raised by humans, without seeing another panda, Chi-Chi was humanised, not even recognising An-An as the same species,' he wrote.

The idea that Chi-Chi had become sexually imprinted on humans certainly had an intuitive appeal. But the emphasis on Chi-Chi's humanness only made it easier to crack wry jokes. 'Brought up by and in the constant company of humans she doubtless feels insulted by the offering of An-An as a mate,' read one letter to the editor of one paper. 'The problem, I suggest, can be solved best by dressing An-An in Morris' uniform ... and then stepping smartly aside.'

Though the zoologists plumped for humanisation as the most likely explanation for Chi-Chi's reproductive reticence, there were plenty of other explanations put forward in the popular press. For novelist Catherine Storr, writing in *The Guardian* in early September 1968, the wild and frivolous conjecture, most of it directed at Chi-Chi, exposed some of the stereotypes that women still faced in British society. 'Isn't it possible that without being cold, or homosexual or neurotic in any way, she can choose to remain single?' she suggested. 'Perhaps Chi-Chi could teach us something about integrity,' she went on. 'For instance that it could be "normal" to be not exactly like everyone else's idea of what "normal" is, but to be quietly and triumphantly ourselves?' So not only had Chi-Chi and An-An come to represent the political tensions between East and West and between Russia and Britain, now they were also being used to reflect on the gender stereotypes the flourishing feminist movement had yet to overturn.

By the time An-An arrived at London Zoo on 1 September 1968, Morris had moved on and Michael Brambell had become the new curator of mammals. He coordinated the reunion of the two pandas in stages: each animal spent some time alone in the other's paddock getting used to the smells; then they were given visual contact, allowed to interact through a mesh fence; and finally they were put together in the same den at night. As before, there were a few skirmishes and Chi-Chi was not at ease. The papers and the public tracked the pandas' every move: 'Reunion was hardly rapturous'; 'Chi-Chi plays it cool'; 'An-An snores as Chi-Chi love calls'.

After two months of this, there was no evidence that Chi-Chi had come into heat and it was looking increasingly likely that she wouldn't. London Zoo's agreement with the Soviet Ministry of Culture was that An-An should return at the end of October and the papers began to send up the whole affair once more. In one typical cartoon, published in *The Sunday Telegraph* that weekend, a bald man was depicted sitting against the bars of a cage. He is wearing a panda suit, has removed the head and, with a bead of sweat running down one cheek, he speaks into a walkie-talkie: 'Hello Moscow, this is An-An. They're sending me home. I have failed on my mission, but I've contacted two gorillas who could be useful to the organisation.'

With the deadline fast approaching, Brambell and his colleagues took a bold decision. In an effort to make the most of what they assumed would be the pandas' last few days together, they attempted to trigger Chi-Chi's oestrus by injecting her with a cocktail of hormones, something that no panda before had experienced. Indeed, at the time, the use of drugs to induce ovulation was decidedly experimental, even in laboratory animals like mice and rabbits. So, based on scant information from other species, Brambell and colleagues had to make an educated guess on the hormones to be injected into Chi-Chi's flesh, the dose they should give and exactly when they should give it. They ended up injecting an extract taken from the bloodstream of a pregnant horse which stimulates the secretion of 'follicle-stimulating hormone' from the brain stem, which in turn 'tells' the ovaries to start maturing eggs. Then, a few days later, on the assumption that this had done its trick, they prepared a syringe of the human equivalent of the horse extract – 'human chorionic gonadotrophin' – which is similar in structure to 'luteinising hormone', another brain hormone that triggers the ovaries to release any mature eggs they may contain.

From the sudden change in her behaviour following the treatment, something clearly happened. About six days after her first injection, she went off her food, just as they had come to expect when she was presumed to be in heat. She continued to fast for a further ten days before her appetite gradually returned. An-An also appeared to sense that something was up, showing more interest in the London panda's presence. But 'Chi-Chi did not present herself in a mating position nor did An-An persist in his advances,' Brambell and colleagues reported in *Nature* the following year.

As it turned out, they need not have bothered with this rather drastic experimental intervention, for the Russians eventually responded to London Zoo's request to relax the October deadline and agreed to let their panda sit it out in London until Chi-Chi's next heat. But with no feeling for when they should expect it, Brambell and colleagues decided to take control again and in February 1969 administered an increased dose of the mare's serum in the hope that it would push their panda to new reproductive heights. Her response, however, was very similar to that in the first effort: 'Chi-Chi went off her food and marked her den more frequently, An-An became more active and made several approaches but was not persistent and it is unlikely that they mated,' they noted.

From what we now know about panda biology – or, for that matter, the biology of any species you care to name – the 1968/1969 efforts to manipulate Chi-Chi's fertility were extremely unlikely to succeed. For it takes years, usually decades, of experimentation to work out the best way to stimulate the ovaries of a particular species and this is only one of many steps needed before a baby emerges.

So it was that on 21 May 1969, An-An finally returned to Moscow: 'An-An goes home, mission unfulfilled'; 'The panda love-in is over'; 'An-An gets back to the USSR'. The day after his departure, the *Evening Standard* published a wicked cartoon. In it, Chi-Chi sits in her pen alongside An-An's empty enclosure. The caption reads: 'Gosh, I feel so sexy today!' There were no surprises left in store. The affair had played out its natural course (as, by and large, had the pandas).

The zoologists might have failed in their mission but there is a real sense in which their pandas were not quite the reproductive failures everyone imagined. As the human sexual revolution unfolded around them, Chi-Chi and An-An found their image mass-produced in toys and trinkets, reproduced in hundreds of cartoons and thousands of photographs, illustrating news story

22. In 2009, the World Wildlife Fund decommissioned its Chi-Chi inspired collecting boxes and invited famous artists to turn them into works of art. Jason Bruges' 'Panda Eyes', an installation in which thermal sensors trigger 100 pandas to track the visitor, was shortlisted for the Brit Insurance Designs of the Year 2010.

upon news story released in dozens of different languages, in all continents on earth over the course of five long years. Su-Lin had caused a storm but that had been in the 1930s before either radio or television had really got going in any big commercial way. Chi-Chi and An-An, by contrast, were caught up on a global media merry-go-round. So much so that even in death, Chi-Chi was capable of causing a stir.

Life after death

As the 1960s became the 1970s, it was increasingly clear that Chi-Chi's days were numbered. She had begun to slow down, was suffering from regular bouts of anorexia, and the frequency with which she emerged to pad around her outside enclosure began to drop. Then, in March 1972, she fell ill and there was widespread concern for her health, with fan mail flooding into the zoo and the press office fielding phone calls from her alarmed admirers.

A presenter for BBC's news programme *Nationwide* telephoned the zoo for an update on her condition. The Zoological Society of London's Public Relations Officer Tony Dale was upbeat. 'When we last went to look at her she'd had her dish of tea, then retired into her bedroom for an afternoon nap,' he reported. 'She is asleep now, on her back, very happily waving her paws in the air.' But Dale was not confident that she would survive the summer. 'I don't think we can give any predictions on this because she's the oldest panda we know of in any zoo and fifteen in panda language is a very old lady.'

As she continued to decline, preparations were made for her death. You'll recall that almost a decade earlier, Chicago anatomist Dwight Davis had published the first really detailed look at panda anatomy based on dissection of Su-Lin, the first panda to be brought out of China alive. But Su-Lin was a young male and Davis had only had access to the 'embalmed and injected body'. Not only would a postmortem of Chi-Chi reveal the anatomical secrets of an adult female panda, the opportunity to dissect a recently departed panda opened up some avenues of enquiry that had not been open to Davis. So the zoo's curator of mammals, Michael Brambell, set about assembling a crack team of pathologists and anatomists prepared to drop all work and travel to Regent's Park in the event of Chi-Chi's death. The idea was to have her on the operating table within minutes, or, at most, hours of death.

By mid-July, Chi-Chi was very ill and when she declined her food, Brambell knew the end was nigh. Not long after the zoo closed to the public on Friday 21 July, Brambell administered a sedative to give her some much-needed rest. But it had no effect and, with the panda in considerable pain the only option left was to put her down. It was three o'clock on the Saturday morning, 'a very sort of stark and cold time of day to do it'.

That Sunday's newspapers mourned the passing of a panda that had 'won the hearts of millions around the world'. By this time, Chi-Chi's body had been carefully dissected by Brambell and the attendant pathologists. Brambell's first 'ghoulish' task after putting her to sleep forever was to remove her eyeballs from their sockets. 'One of the things we knew we could get from her postmortem would be information about the pigments of her eyes but we had to get them fixed in twenty minutes,' recalled Brambell. 'I still shudder to think about it,' he admitted. 'There I was looking after an animal ... and twenty minutes later I was acting as the pathologist with her on the slab.'

In reality, it took a little longer than the vision expert, Professor Herbert Dartnall, had instructed to get Chi-Chi's eyes into the freezer. What's more, because it was the weekend, Bramball could not send the body part to Dartnall's laboratory – the Medical Research Council Vision Unit at the University of Sussex in

Brighton – until Monday morning. It was there that Dartnall began his investigations into the pigments contained in Chi-Chi's retina, from which he hoped (amongst other things) to discover whether she had colour vision. Working under red light so as not to excite the pigments, he thawed out the right eyeball, slit it open and carefully removed the retina. Reporting his findings in *Nature* the following year, Dartnall concluded that the panda has two light-sensitive pigments, one most responsive to red and the other to white light. Here was an indication that the panda could see in colour, like most carnivores active during the day.

Other parts of Chi-Chi's body provided further insights into panda biology. In fact her postmortem takes up a whole issue of *Transactions of the Zoological Society of London*, with papers on her blood, gut and mammary glands to name just a few. These were gaps in our knowledge that Davis, working with less than fresh panda material, had been unable to fill.

With the postmortem complete, Brambell offered up Chi-Chi's remains to the Natural History Museum. It now seems the obvious place for her to go, but it's worth noting that this wasn't always the first-choice destination for the zoo's deceased inmates.

After it was formally founded in 1826, the Zoological Society of London set about landscaping Regent's Park to house a collection of live animals to interest and amuse the public. But almost as important was a parallel project to establish a museum in Bruton Street in Mayfair. So when the zoo eventually opened to the public, any of its exotic creatures that passed away went straight to the Society's museum rather than to the Natural History Museum, or the British Museum (Natural History) as it was then known.

In fact, at this period of the nineteenth century, most naturalists considered the ZSL's museum superior to the British

Museum, and the perfect place to lodge their specimens. As Charles Darwin wrote to a colleague on his return from the *Beagle* voyage in 1836, 'The Zoological Museum is nearly full & upward of a thousand specimens remain unmounted. I daresay the British Museum would receive them, but I cannot feel, from all I hear, any great respect even for the present state of that establishment.'

That changed in 1855 when the Zoological Society decided to close its museum and disperse its massive wealth of animal material. Their reasoning was twofold. First, the collection was so extensive that the accommodation – by now on the west side of Leicester Square – was wholly inadequate. More importantly, perhaps, the Keeper of Zoology, John Edward Gray, had done wonders at the British Museum, which was now considered Europe's preeminent zoological repository. So the ZSL sold its most important specimens to the British Museum for £500 and the Natural History Museum came to have first dibs on any ex-zoo animals.

It's a tradition that has continued ever since, with the zoo's most celebrated inmates wending their way in death across the capital. There's Winnipeg the black bear, for example, a mascot of the 2nd Canadian Infantry Brigade. In 1915, when they went off to Europe to fight in World War I, a lieutenant in the regiment dropped her off at London Zoo for safe keeping. It's there that Winnipeg won over a young boy called Christopher Robin Milne who decided he'd call his own teddy Winnie. By the time Winnipeg died in 1934 and made her way to the Natural History Museum, Christopher Robin was fourteen years old and his father, Alan Alexander (A. A.) Milne, had given the world the Winnie-the-Pooh stories.

Another example is Brumas, a baby polar bear born in Regent's Park in 1949, a first for any British zoo. She was so popular with the public that 1950 saw record attendance, with more than 3 million visitors, a figure that has not been surpassed since. Fortunately for the zoo, after Brumas died in 1958 and went to South Kensington for preservation, there was only a lull of a few months before Chi-Chi reached London and took over her crowd-pleasing duties.

Within a week of Chi-Chi's death, the museum had decided that they would put her on display. When mineralogist Frank Claringbull had assumed the director's chair in 1968, he took on the responsibility for giving the public face of the museum a much-needed makeover. The Chi-Chi exhibit was part of that and, on 27 July 1972, Claringbull issued a press release on the museum's plan for the panda:

> The skin will be mounted and put on display to the public as soon as possible but this process will take several months and the skin will not be available for inspection during this period. The skeleton will be added to the study collection and will be available only for research purposes.

At the bottom of the release, the museum offered up the curator of mammals, Gordon Corbet, as a source of 'further information'. In *Dry Store Room No. 1*, former palaeontologist at the museum Richard Fortey describes Corbet as 'a diminutive Scotsman with a hesitant manner and a nervous way of speaking' who reminded him of a vole 'the way these animals pause momentarily, whiskers twitching'. As Corbet's PhD was, in fact, on voles and most zoologists are rather fond of their study species, this description is perhaps not too offensive. Within days of the press release going out, Corbet found himself fielding calls from the media asking if 'special arrangements can be made to photograph her in various stages of preparation before going on display'. Had they had a query about panda biology, Corbet might have been able to help them, but these enquiries about Chi-Chi's display were wholly outside his remit and solely a matter for the Exhibition Department. The vole-like Corbet referred them to the Exhibition Officer, Michael Belcher.

The museum awoke to the media interest and began to hatch a grander plan for Chi-Chi's display. By mid-September, it was agreed that they should aim to have the exhibit ready to show off at the next trustees' meeting on 12 December and reveal it to the public the following day. At such meetings, the director asked the trustees to approve his policies and resolutions for the coming months and it was always nice to have a spectacular new exhibit with which to bring them onside. Unveiling Chi-Chi in mid-December would have the added advantage of enticing schoolchildren to the museum once they'd broken up for Christmas.

With this in mind, the museum made a couple of crucial changes in how they were to handle Chi-Chi's remains. Her skeleton, which had formerly been destined for the research collection in the museum's subterranean vaults, now found itself part of an expanded public display that would parade her bones as well as her mounted skin. In addition, the museum appears to have responded directly to the media's requests to witness the taxidermy. Contrary to Claringbull's first Chi-Chi-related press release, his second, sent out in early October, announced that there was to be a photocall at the Modelmaking and Taxidermy section based in Cricklewood the following week. Belcher kept his London Zoo counterparts informed of this development, and Tony Dale of London Zoo sent two members of the press team out to Cricklewood to meet the senior taxidermist, Roy Hale. '[W]e shall all be interested to learn what press coverage you obtain following the photocall,' he wrote to Belcher.

It was a good turnout and there was widespread interest in the process of taxidermy, in no small part due to Hale's pride in his work. 'A taxidermist is carpenter, metalworker, seamstress, sculptor and anatomist all in one,' he asserted. A journalist writing for the *Kensington News & Post* made the taxidermist rather than the panda the focus of her story. And the Australian Broadcasting Corporation, who interviewed Hale for a radio programme on Chi-Chi, considered him 'most helpful', and very good radio 'talent'.

Mammals are amongst the hardest animals on which to perform taxidermy. In the nineteenth century, it was still common practice to knock up a rudimentary wooden frame on which to hang the skin and then stuff it with straw or paper. But it would be very hard to capture the shape of an animal correctly and harder still to convey any impression of movement. What's more, as a skin dries it tightens and the stitching would inevitably begin to show. So poor were such preparations, in fact, that William Henry Flower, the director of the Natural History Museum at South Kensington in the last decades of the nineteenth century, penned the following scathing passage in 1889:

I cannot refrain from saying a word upon the sadly-neglected art of taxidermy, which continues to fill the cases of most of our museums with wretched and repulsive caricatures of mammals and birds, out of all natural proportions, shrunken here and bloated there, and in attitudes absolutely impossible for the creatures to have assumed while alive.

By the end of the century, however, the state of the taxidermic art had begun to improve. Based on precise measurements of the skinned carcass, the taxidermist would construct a skeleton-like

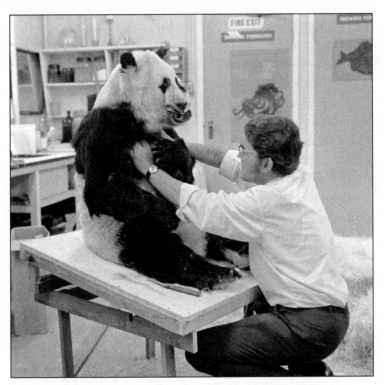

23. The Natural History Museum's chief taxidermist Roy Hale prepares Chi-Chi's skin at the Modelmaking and Taxidermy workshop in Cricklewood.

'manikin' from a combination of wood and wire and then build up the muscles with 'wood wool', the thin slivers of wood shavings you sometimes find in fancy packaging. The next step was to smear a thin layer of wet clay over the manikin. 'The skin should then fit over the model like a glove,' explained Hale, who had learned his trade working for Rowland Ward Ltd of Piccadilly, then the most highly respected taxidermy enterprise in the world. It could then be pressed onto the wet clay and sculpted into the desired shape. For Chi-Chi's head, Hale would mould her skin to a fibreglass cast of her skull, taking great care to get her expression just right. 'So many people have seen her in the zoo that they will soon say if they don't think she's lifelike when I've finished,' he told his audience.

Belcher was pleased about his orchestration of the media, purring to Tony Dale at the zoo that 'we got the press coverage we hoped for'. That is, with one notable exception. *Daily Express* columnist Jean Rook – also known as 'The First Lady of Fleet Street' – rarely missed an opportunity for satire. 'My readers,' she later wrote, 'love me to sink my teeth and typewriter keys into some public figure they're dying to have a go at themselves, more especially if it's some sacred cow – or bull – who's never criticised by journalists'. On this occasion, Rook championed Chi-Chi, who 'kept her virginity in an age when all around were losing theirs' and instead laid into her new custodians: 'Now that she's dead, dead and they'll never call her mother I think it's indecent of the Natural History Museum to exploit the remains when all that's left is a fibreglass model inside a giant fur coat,' she wrote. 'In life she may have chosen, in fact fought tooth and claw, to stay on the shelf. That's still no excuse for having her dusted.'

Dale responded to Belcher's letter with this wry consolation: 'I am sorry about Miss Rooke [sic] – if she appears again she could always end up in the polar bear pit!'

Back at the Museum, Belcher had set out some deadlines to museum staff. 'If the dates can be kept, we will endeavour to have the display open for the Trustees Meeting on 12 December,' he wrote.

Crucially, Belcher needed the scientists to come up with the contents of the second display case – the one that would house Chi-Chi's articulated skeleton. This, it had been decided, would address the problematic question of what, exactly, is a panda?

Belcher's team bought in some birch blockboard with which to construct the display and some cognac-coloured cloth to cover it. This was to provide the tasteful backdrop for the panda's skeleton and for some skulls and bones from red pandas, black bears and raccoons. Giving the public a chance to look at the similarities and differences between these species might help to explain how museum scientists went about their taxonomic business and might even communicate just how difficult it was to put the panda in its proper evolutionary place.

In addition, the exhibition team had a go at creating a 'habitat diorama' for Chi-Chi's mounted skin. A typical habitat diorama is composed of three elements: the stuffed animal, a three-dimensional foreground to convey the creature's immediate habitat and a concave background painting that draws the viewer into the scene.

Those that work best pull off the surprising trick of blending these three elements to create a single, lifelike image. In the age before natural history documentaries or affordable flights, these windows onto far-off worlds packed an incredible punch. Today, we are so familiar with such exotic places – either because we've been lucky enough to visit them or because we've followed Sir David Attenborough's career – that these displays are no longer out of the ordinary.

This is especially the case for Chi-Chi's diorama. Belcher did buy some artificial fronds of leafy bamboo to create a bush on the left-hand side, some lengths of genuine bamboo cane that would be propped up to the right, and three bags of granulated peat to cover the floor beneath Chi-Chi's bottom. He also commissioned an artist to paint a landscape, but his stark yellow palette is so at odds with the peaty foreground that rather than looking out from a mountain in Sichuan, Chi-Chi is quite clearly a stuffed and isolated element in a schoolboy diorama. Still, she was at least ready in time to for the trustees' meeting in December.

24. Chi-Chi on display in the North Hall of the Natural History Museum, where she has been – unmoved – since her death in 1972.

A few days before, Claringbull issued his final Chi-Chi-related press release inviting the press to a 'photocall' the day before the public opening. That might have been it for Chi-Chi, except that, before being sealed inside her glass case, she made one last journey.

Belcher was sitting at his desk towards the end of November when his telephone began to tinkle. He spoke quietly into the handset. 'Exhibitions?' It was the BBC. They had received the press release and wanted to know if they could feature the all-new Chi-Chi for their flagship children's show *Blue Peter*. Belcher could instantly see the value of the publicity. 'Blue Peter is a reputable programme and is watched by some 9 million children,' he wrote to Claringbull. But, he explained, 'all their programmes are produced live and they are not interested in coming here to film'. More than that, they wanted Chi-Chi to appear on the Monday show, the day before she was due to sweeten the trustees.

Claringbull agreed, 'providing it is at all times accompanied by a member of the museum staff at the expense of the BBC'.

So it was that first thing on Monday morning, Chi-Chi sat clutching a spray of bamboo in the back of a van as she was chauffeured from South Kensington to BBC Television Centre in Shepherd's Bush. A shaggy-haired Peter Purves was the *Blue Peter* presenter scheduled to introduce the stuffed panda: 'Lots of people were rather sad when Chi-Chi died, so it's good to know that she's been so beautifully preserved and that she'll be on display at the museum for ever and ever,' he comforted his youthful audience.

After the show, she was escorted back to the museum and placed inside her display case, ready to face the press and then the trustees the following day. On Wednesday morning, as the public got its first glimpse of Chi-Chi in her new home in the North Hall of the museum, the papers spread news of the exhibit far and wide.

What's a little surprising in all this toing and froing is that there was not more disquiet from the public or anxious nail-biting on the part of the museum's curators. Things could not have been more different a few years later when another famous zoo animal – Guy the Gorilla – died from a heart attack during an operation to remove a rotten tooth. Within days of his death, word had leaked out that the Natural History Museum was to give him a taxidermic overhaul and the headline-writers guffawed at the idea of 'stuffing the Guy'. The British public went beserk. Much to their irritation, zoo staff were inundated with a stream of vitriolic mail, all of which demanded a conciliatory and time-consuming personal response. There was everything from the sublime to the faintly ridiculous. Representing the sublime was a petition sent in by twelve-year-old Robin Tucker, signed by more than 100 of his friends, family and acquaintances 'in the hope that it will help prevent Guy the Gorilla being stuffed'. Staring out from the page was a haunting pencil sketch of Guy's pensive face resting on the caption 'Why can't they let him rest?'

Typing furiously for the ridiculous was Viscount Anthony Chaplin, a past Honorary Secretary of the Zoological Society, who wrote to his successor to express how 'utterly revolted' he was that Guy's remains were to be handed over to a taxidermist. Chaplin would rather Guy were 'buried or cremated and a memorial of some sort, however modest, placed in the Gardens of the Society'. He signed off with an eccentric rant: 'Are all future Hon. Secs, Presidents etc. of the Society to be stuffed and exhibited in a museum?'

The Director of Zoos, Colin Rawlins, wrote a stern letter to the Natural History Museum and forwarded some of this unsolicited mail. 'To many of the general public, "Guy" was almost human and the way in which news of the proposed use of his remains was put out offended them and led them to vent their annoyance on us!' he wrote. 'Although I do not suppose we shall have an equivalent situation for a long time to come, could I ask that, in future, if and when any of our well-known animal personalities are to be used for exhibition in the Museum, you could do what you can to see that the matter is not directly mentioned to the Press until it is absolutely necessary to do so.'

The situation was so delicate that Guy's half-cured skin was folded up and stored in the deep freezer for a couple of years. It was only in 1980 that the tricky subject bubbled to the surface once more. The then press officer Sue Runyard was worried about two pieces of information that had come her way. First, she'd heard that rumours were circulating at the zoo that something untoward must have happened to Guy's remains. Second, and more alarmingly, Arthur Hayward – one of Roy Hale's colleagues in the taxidermy department – had told her that 'a pelt is spoilt after two years in cold storage' – and two years was just about up.

'I am not a Guy fan by any means,' Runyard confessed to Ronald Hedley, who had replaced Claringbull as the museum's director in 1976. But she was more than aware of what would happen if she did nothing. 'My interest is that I should not have to explain to the press at some time why we allowed his remains to spoil,' she told her boss. 'The sort of passionate interest which surrounds this character seems rather silly to me – but it is very real. I regularly get calls from the press asking what is happening and to be informed of his re-appearance. The story will not die.'

Runyard's tone struck a chord and Hayward was instructed to take Guy's frozen skin out of storage to assess the damage. It did not look good. The connective tissue beneath the skin had tightened to such an extent that mounting it in its current state would be all but impossible. Hayward's recommendation was 'to use "drastic and shock" methods of relaxing the dried-up connective tissue' before attempting to mount the skin onto a model of Guy's body. This was a problem because Hayward couldn't be sure how Guy's skin would react to the chemicals he had in mind, raising the terrifying prospect of damaging it forever. So just as you should always test out a carpet cleaner on a spare scrap before going gung-ho at the real thing, Hayward ran some tests on some cured orang-utan skin to see what would happen.

It was a good job that he did, because one of his proposed softening treatments did the job 'but with almost complete hair loss'. In the end, there was only one thing for it. Hayward recommended mounting Guy's skin on a clay-covered model to grab hold of the hairs, rot away the skin and replace it with a fake latex version. This method, when it works, is 'absolutely brilliant,' says historian of taxidermy Pat Morris. 'But making it work is extremely difficult. It's very time-consuming, very smelly and no one likes doing it.' It's also expensive. Today, a job of this sort would cost tens of thousands of pounds, says Morris.

That the museum gave Hayward the go-ahead for such high-end taxidermy is testimony to the importance of getting this specimen right. And eventually, more than four years after his death, Guy went on show in the public gallery on 5 November 1982 – Guy Fawkes Day. While Hedley, the museum's director, praised Hayward for 'a lovely job', the public got lathered up all over again. 'Today is Guy the Gorilla's first day of purgatory', began an article in *The Times*.

So why was it that Chi-Chi's taxidermy was no big deal while Guy going under the knife just six years later triggered a national incident? In large part, of course, it's down to the fact that one is a panda and the other a gorilla; we humans are just that much more touchy about the treatment of our close living relatives. In addition, the 1970s experienced a surge of interest in the great apes. The work of primatologists Jane Goodall and Dian Fossey brought new knowledge of the intricacies of chimpanzee and gorilla societies, leading to the foundation of the Jane Goodall Institute and The Dian Fossey Gorilla Fund towards the end of the decade. It was also in 1979 that the BBC's Natural History Unit broadcast its most ambitious wildlife series to date, *Life on Earth*, which starred a young David Attenborough and featured his memorable encounter with Rwanda's mountain gorillas.

But this newfound wonder at the great apes was really just a reflection of bigger changes that were afoot as the environmental movement continued to gather momentum. The increasing frequency of natural history broadcasting during the 1970s – and in vibrant colour – resulted in far greater public awareness of, and sensitivity towards, the natural world. Apart from Guy's brief appearance in the galleries of the Natural History Museum in the 1980s, Chi-Chi was one of the last large mammals to be turned over to the museum's taxidermists for public display. By the end of the 1980s, stuffing animals for the public galleries had become so politically charged that the museum decided to shut down its Taxidermy Section for good, putting what little work they subsequently needed out to tender. Roy Hale, who had processed Chi-Chi more than fifteen years earlier, decided that the time had come to pack away his needle and thread.

Chi-Chi's passing left a panda-sized hole in British life and a strong desire to see it filled. Even before she passed away in the summer of 1972, the Conservative Prime Minister Ted Heath had been busy wooing China. In March, diplomatic relations began to look up when the two countries exchanged ambassadors. In May and June, the Parliamentary Under-Secretary for Foreign Affairs, Anthony Royle, went to Beijing to pave the way for a visit by Foreign Secretary Sir Alec Douglas-Home later that year, the first appearance of a member of the British cabinet on Chinese soil for almost a decade. 'I'm sure it is the start of much warmer relations and the ice having been broken we can now swim in the warmer waters together,' Douglas-Home announced to reporters. He was even asked whether he'd raised the subject of pandas with his Chinese counterparts. 'I'm not sure it's fair to ask the Chinese to produce a panda for us,' he replied with tact. But went on to make the following indirect request. 'If they would like to send us one, we should be very happy and as everybody's heard we'd like to have one.'

In late 1973, the Zoological Society of London sent China a pair of Père David's Deer, a species, discussed in the opening chapter, that had become extinct in China at the start of the twentieth century. Bolstered by additional animals sent over from

Europe several years later, this species has now made a comeback on its native soil.

On the back of all this groundwork, Heath had lined up a trip to Beijing in January 1974, but had to pull out on account of a major domestic inconvenience – the miners' strike. His visit might never have happened, because February's general election produced a hung parliament and Heath, with more popular votes but fewer parliamentary seats than Labour's Harold Wilson, had to pack his bags at No. 10. In walked Wilson and his minority cabinet.

But in spite of this change of leadership, the Chinese insisted that Heath stick with the proposed visit and in late May he met Chinese premier Zhou Enlai. 'At Peking airport,' reported *The Times* as its cover story, 'more than 2,000 young girls in colourful blouses and skirts danced, waved Union Jacks and shouted a warm welcome'. Heath had three days of talks, presented Mao Zedong with a copy of Charles Darwin's *The Descent of Man* and received a pair of eighteenth-century vases in return. But as far as his biographer John Campbell is concerned, Heath's Beijing triumph was 'crowned in the public mind with the gift by the Chinese Government of two giant pandas to London Zoo'.

When, in August, the pandas had not arrived, conspiracy theories began to circulate, with an article in the *Sunday Express* suggesting that Wilson was stalling on sending out an RAF plane to pick up the pandas 'for fears that they might prove electorally advantageous to the Conservatives'. As it was, the pandas – a male, Chia-Chia and a female, Ching-Ching – reached Britain in mid-September and, though received by Ted Heath at London Zoo amidst much media fanfare, Wilson still managed to sneak victory in the October election.

But just as Wilson found during his first term in office in the 1960s during negotiations to send Chi-Chi to Moscow,

Chia-Chia and Ching-Ching could pack a political punch. In November 1974, Solly Zuckerman of the Zoological Society of London approached Wilson to explain that 'being agent for friendship between the British and Chinese Governments was proving to be a pretty expensive business'. The government had a duty, Zuckerman politely suggested, to find some funds to support the latest acquisitions. It was something of a hot potato and Wilson flung it at Foreign Secretary James Callaghan, who passed it on to Parliamentary Under-Secretary Goronwy Owen Goronwy-Roberts. After a fact-finding mission to Regent's Park, Goronwy-Roberts reported that Zuckerman was after a contribution towards a £70,000 state-of-the-art panda house. 'I strongly think that we should make one,' Goronwy-Roberts recommended to Callaghan. Any refusal would be seen by the Chinese as 'a deliberate rebuff' and there was also the more immediate prospect of some 'especially damaging' headlines. 'The Press will make a meal of it ("Government leaves Pandas homeless" etc.),' anticipated Goronwy-Roberts.

But where, in the midst of a serious economic downturn, was Wilson's government to conjure up some spare cash? It was a tricky one. The Foreign Office shirked responsibility by pointing out that its budget had to be spent abroad. The Department of the Environment had already ring-fenced some £700,000 for new buildings at the zoo. Having failed to source even the most meagre government contribution, Goronwy-Roberts got back to Zuckerman to let him down gently. To Wilson's relief, his inability to support the pandas did not trigger the diplomatic incident Goronwy-Roberts had envisaged.

Unsurprisingly, the two-year-old Chia-Chia and Ching-Ching were a smash hit with the British public. But by the time they had settled into their new home, there had been an unmistakable shift in the balance of panda power. London Zoo could no longer claim to house the most celebrated pandas outside China. It was as if, upon Chi-Chi's death, her ghost had drifted across the Atlantic, taking fame and fortune with it.

For the next two decades, the National Zoo in Washington DC was *the* panda force to be reckoned with. And it's here that scientists began their effort to help conserve the giant panda.

Part III
PROTECTION

9

Presidential pandas

What do table tennis and pandas have in common? They are both symbols of a new friendship between China and the West that began to emerge in the 1970s.

In early 1971, with Japan about to host the 31st World Table Tennis Championships, it transpired that China would be sending a team. This was news because at the previous two tournaments – in 1967 and 1969 – the Cultural Revolution had kept the Chinese away. To mark their return to the table tennis table, the Chinese government issued an invitation to several of the then dominant nations in the game, including England, Canada and Colombia: did they fancy another game on the way home from Japan? When the invitation was extended to ping pong no-hopers the United States, the message was clear. There was more to this than a desire to bat a hollow lightweight ball back and forth. China was using table tennis to bounce itself onto a global stage.

The election of Richard Nixon as 37th President of the United States in 1969 was the first indication that Cold War tensions with China might be about to ease. By January 1970, ambassadors from both countries had begun to talk to each other again and, when the American table tennis team touched down in Beijing in April the following year, they became the first US sports team to alight in the Chinese capital for more than twenty years. This thawing of relations through table tennis became known as 'ping pong diplomacy' and just months later Chinese

25. Chinese Communist Party Chairman Mao Zedong shakes hands with US President Richard Nixon on 29 February 1972. Nixon's historic visit to China signalled an end to Cold War frostiness between China and the US and Mao gave the American people two pandas as a symbol of the new friendship.

premier Zhou Enlai asked Nixon to visit. In accepting the invitation, Nixon told the American people that 'there can be no stable and enduring peace without the People's Republic of China and its 750 million people'. Some six months later, in February 1972, he became the first US President ever to set foot on Chinese soil.

While Nixon was summoned to meetings with Mao Zedong and Zhou Enlai, his wife Pat got to see Beijing. The playful pandas at the city's zoo clearly thrilled her, a fact that was carefully noted by her Chinese hosts. For upon his return to Washington DC, President Nixon received the news that China was to give the American people a pair of pandas to commemorate their historic visit. This would help to convince everyone that it was OK to chum up with China. Nixon put a call through to the editor of the *Washington Star*, allowing them to break the news that a pair of pandas would be coming to the National Zoo. 'It's gonna be a hell of a story,' he told his wife later that day.

Even then, he did not appreciate quite how big. This was not just a story about a couple of animals, nor even about the first giant pandas to appear in the US for thirty years. This was a story about global politics. Since Chiang Kai-shek's gift of Pan-Dee and Pan-Dah to the American people in 1941, China has sent more than twenty pandas off down this diplomatic path. We've already heard about Ping-Ping and An-An heading north to Moscow, and Chia-Chia and Ching-Ching taking up Chi-Chi's place in London. Several went to the Democratic People's Republic of Korea, some to Japan, with others being flown to France, Germany, Mexico and Spain. But Hsing-Hsing and Ling-Ling are easily the most famous of these political animals.

History is heavily populated by animals used as gifts to cement relationships between individuals, families, tribes and even nations. And exotic creatures can have an extraordinary impact. In 1486, an Egyptian sultan, looking for military assistance from the wealthy Florence-based Medici family, is thought to have shipped them a giraffe. The animal caused such a stir on its arrival in Florence that several artists thought to capture the event in their paintings. In spite of attention lavished on the animal by its new owners, it did not survive long, getting its neck snagged in the rafters of its custom-built accommodation.

A similar case involved an Indian rhinoceros that arrived in Lisbon in May 1515. Later that year, King Manuel I sent the beast to Rome as a gift for Pope Leo X in a bid to gain his support for Portugal's colonial expansion in the Far East. It is from eye-witness descriptions of this armoured creature that Albrecht Dürer created his famous rhino woodcut. Sadly for this specimen, it too met an untimely death, in a shipwreck on the way to Rome.

Tu'i Malila, by contrast, had an extraordinarily long life. This Madagascan radiated tortoise, given to the Tongan royal family in 1777 by the British explorer James Cook, is widely considered the oldest known animal on record. It was one of the first to welcome Queen Elizabeth II to the islands during her royal visit of 1953 and only died a decade later at the ripe old age of 188.

Although this practice of panda diplomacy has slowed down in recent years, China continues to benefit from the careful deployment of captive pandas for explicitly political purposes. In 1999, a few years after the British handed Hong Kong back to the Chinese, the PRC gifted the region a couple of pandas and followed them up with another pair to mark the tenth anniversary of Hong Kong's return to Chinese sovereignty. In 2008, after several earlier offers, Taiwan finally accepted a panda gift from China. The names of the animals, Tuan-Tuan and Yuan-Yuan, meaning 'reunion', caused a stir in Taiwan. But let's return to the biggest of them all: Hsing-Hsing and Ling-Ling.

With the arrival of Nixon's pair of pandas in Washington DC in 1972, it was almost as if an election was imminent. The telephones at the National Zoo didn't stop ringing and its daily mailbag was full to bursting. Sibyl Hamlet, the institution's multitasking press officer, dealt with the increased workload with authority. As she tore open letter after letter, a theme quickly began to emerge. More than anything, the public wanted to know what the pandas would be called. As no official announcement had yet been made, several correspondents came up with their own suggestions. A Miss G. D. Shepherd of Marymount

College ventured to suggest Ping and Pong. It was a play on words that had occurred to others. 'I think this is just perfect for the two pandas as the ping pong stuff got us started going to China and the names sound Chinese,' wrote Mrs Emery Molnar. 'The names sound so cute and tickle one's humor – I can't imagine anyone not thinking they are cute and totally appropriate.'

Mr and Mrs Wen-Tsuen Lee, writing to the President, also thought Ping and Pong 'wonderful names' but ventured that they should, in fact, be Ping-Ping and Pong-Pong, as the double-barrelled feature is a sign of affection. 'For example, we have a little girl named Ling but we call her Ling-Ling at home.'

Hamlet drafted a template letter to post out to all of these enthusiasts. 'Although we do not, at the present time, know the names of the pandas we are receiving, we do know that they already have Chinese names as all pandas in captivity are given names,' she wrote. 'We do not plan to change their names but to continue calling them by the names they were given in China.' When the zoo finally announced their names – Hsing-Hsing for the male and Ling-Ling for the female – you can imagine the excitement of little Ling Lee.

Carl W. Larsen, then director of the Smithsonian Institution's Office of Public Affairs, sent Hamlet an encouraging memo. 'From our vantage point, we get the impression that you have provided the press with a fair but discreet, tantalising and appetising flow of information on a subject that some folks might have viewed as sensitive and subjective,' he wrote. Along with the note, Hamlet found a small sweet. 'As a junior "bonus" for your fine work, I am enclosing an authentic piece of Chinese candy,' Larsen explained.

Elsewhere in the zoo, staff were also busy preparing to welcome the new arrivals. Not long after the *Washington Star* broke the story that the pandas would be coming to the National

Zoo, its director Theodore H. Reed circulated a '9-point plan for the pandas'. This sent one member of staff off to the library to dig up everything about the species. Someone else set about sourcing bamboo. Yet another got on the phone to Western zoos with panda experience. There were plans to accommodate the animals in the short term and to take over and extend the existing white rhino enclosure in the longer term. Although there would be additional demands on staff, Reed was in no doubt about the benefits of hosting the pandas. 'This exhibit should prove exciting, fantastically popular, and profitable scientifically,' his memo concluded. 'The public and goodwill that can be engendered for the Smithsonian Institution is fantastic.'

With the entire nation bursting with anticipation, the two pandas eventually touched down in the US in April 1972. They had been flown from China via Paris in separate metal shipping crates, escorted by four high-ranking Chinese officials. Ironically, the pandas' entry point to the States was Dulles International Airport, the hub named after the former secretary of state John Foster Dulles who had prevented Chi-Chi's journey to Brookfield Zoo back in 1958. He turned in his grave.

Just days later, on 20 April, the National Zoo unveiled the animals to the public. 'Panda Day' as it became known, started with a press call attended by Pat Nixon, the four Chinese officials and a representative of the World Wildlife Fund. Mrs Nixon came away with a badge bearing the WWF's panda logo, a picture of the two pandas and an album of other panda photos. 'There were an awful lot of people there,' she told the President later that day. 'Boy it was well covered.' And it was. Over 20,000 people came to the zoo on Panda Day, more than double the number for the same day the previous year. But the media coverage that followed the press event on 20 April triggered even greater interest at the weekend. That first Sunday, some 75,000 people flocked to the zoo, jamming traffic right the way up Constitution Avenue.

There was no looking back. Although London Zoo's Chi-Chi was still alive at the time, the aura of fascination surrounding her had shifted, floating across the Atlantic from Europe to the States. Hsing-Hsing and Ling-Ling could now claim to be the West's preeminent pandas and a trip to Washington DC would no longer be complete without going to see them.

More than that, research on these pandas was to revolution-ise efforts to breed this curious creature in captivity, acting as a model for how to carry out research on an endangered captive and apply the findings to the wild.

Zoos, whatever the ethical arguments against them, do provide an unrivalled opportunity to get close to wild animals, something that zoologists have been alert to for several hundred years. French zoologist Frédéric Cuvier (the man who introduced the red or lesser panda to the world in 1825), was one of the first to take advantage of captive animals in order to advance our under-standing of the natural world. In 1804, when he became head keeper of the menagerie at the Jardin des Plantes in the heart of Paris, he had a vision for its future. 'The menageries that have existed up to the present have always been regarded as institu-tions of extravagance rather than institutions of utility,' he wrote. No more. Cuvier was going to study the animals' behaviour.

This menagerie was a surprise product of the French Revolu-tion, which had come to a head just over a decade earlier. In late 1793, a matter of months after the last French King, Louis XVI, had lost his to the guillotine, the Paris police department began a clampdown on street entertainers who paraded exotic animals to make a quick franc. With concern for public safety, the police were under orders to confiscate these crowd-pleasing beasts and march them to the Jardin des Plantes. Within a day they had rounded up a polar bear, a panther, a civet and a monkey, much to the surprise of the naturalists at the Paris museum who soon employed a couple of keepers, built some cages and put the animals out of sight in an empty carriage house. The next spring, the collection of live animals began to swell still further, with a lion, a quagga, a spiral-horned African antelope and dozens of other exotic creatures arriving from the now state-owned Royal menagerie at Versailles.

The menagerie quickly became a massive popular attraction, though when Cuvier took control in 1804 he focused instead on finding out all he could about living animals. 'Nothing has been written, nearly nothing has been seen, everything remains to be done,' he scrawled with a flourish of his quill. Over the next thirty years or so, Cuvier carried out some extraordinarily original research on the instincts of orang-utans, the intelligence of seals and the effects of isolation on beavers, to pick just a few highlights. He began to think seriously about the welfare of the animals in his care, working out their favoured diets and reducing their suffering as much as he could.

But Cuvier was way ahead of his time. Although there were others (like Charles Darwin, who made plenty of visits to London Zoo to observe its animals), it's only relatively recently that scientific research has become a serious concern for zoos.

There was very little coherent research on captive pandas until Hsing-Hsing and Ling-Ling reached Washington DC in the middle of April 1972. That same week, by some pleasing coincidence, the National Zoo acquired not just pandas but also Devra Kleiman, a young biologist fresh from London Zoo, where she had witnessed efforts to get Chi-Chi and An-An to breed in 1967. It was as if pandas were following her. 'At the time Hsing-Hsing and Ling-Ling actually arrived I stayed away,' says Kleiman. 'Number one, it was so highly political and number two it wasn't in my main sphere of interest to work on pandas.'

In the coming months, however, Kleiman began to observe them from afar and within a year she had begun to study them in earnest. She began by putting in place a system for monitoring and recording the activity and basic behaviour of the pandas. This is of fundamental importance. If you know nothing about what an animal is likely to do, when and in what particular setting, you've got no way of recognising the significance of unusual behaviour. For example, by carrying out a series of carefully planned observations on a daily basis, zoo staff had clear evidence of Ling-Ling's heat in 1974. This came as a total surprise, says Kleiman, as the female panda was thought to be just three-and-a-half years old. We now know that this is a full year before a female panda will typically become sexually active.

Over the course of the pandas' first year at the zoo, letters had been streaming in asking when they would be put together, when they would breed and when were they going to have babies. Frustratingly, given this expectation of the public, pandas usually come into heat just once in spring. What's more, the oestrus lasts a matter of days and no more. The National Zoo now took the signal from Ling-Ling and brought the pandas together for the first time towards the end of April 1974. When Hsing-Hsing failed to apply himself, the reporters saw the satirical side. *The Palm Beach Post*, for example, ran with the headline 'Pandas in zoo make lazy lovers, keepers find'. The zoo's director, Theodore H. Reed, was dismayed by the coverage. 'The low taste and vulgar observations of the American press continue to amaze me.'

With the playful publicity, yet more letters began to arrive from the public. Some were straightforward. Others tried to tempt the zoo with a cryptic approach, like this from Joshua

H. Batchelder of Batchelder & Associates Inc. 'Our organization believes that we have the solution to your problem,' he wrote to the zoo in May 1974. Though he didn't go into details of what that solution might be, Batchelder & Associates Inc. would not expect anything from the zoo unless successful. 'In this instance,' wrote Batchelder, 'we would consider adequate compensation as an all-expenses paid trip for four to see the zoo, for one week. Please advise of your interest.'

The zoo staff also had to field telephone calls from those keen to help. Following another unproductive oestrus in the spring of 1975, for example, Reed received a call from Tom O'Bradervitch, a representative of a waterbed company. 'They offered to give us a canvas covered waterbed for Ling-Ling and Hsing-Hsing,' Reed told his employees in a mirthful memorandum. He gently declined the offer. 'I agreed with him that it was a good idea but the animals were too destructive and the bed would not last long,' he wrote. 'This is another wonderful episode in the crazy memorabile of the pandas.' But the pressure on Reed was beginning to tell and he made it known that he wanted a baby panda at the next opportunity – 1976 – to coincide with the 200th anniversary of the United States Declaration of Independence.

This was too much to hope for. As it turned out, the pandas were not brought together until Ling-Ling's heat was almost over. Reed was furious. Kleiman offered an explanation. Ling-Ling's oestrus had come several weeks earlier than the previous year. 'This caught me (and I think, others) off guard,' she wrote to her boss in a conciliatory memo. With plenty of volunteers carrying out round-the-clock observations according to the now well-practised protocol, she had been confident – too confident – that any changes in Ling-Ling's behaviour would be detected. 'I was insufficiently flexible in my attitude and much too conservative,' she told Reed. 'Needless to say, I apologize.'

In spite of this setback, Kleiman pushed on with more basic research that would, within a few years, start to inform the captive management of these animals. In 1979, she added an unsavoury task to the long list of jobs required of the keepers. Each morning, they had to enter the enclosures of both pandas armed with a plastic pipette and use it to suck up urine from the floor. Once frozen, the urine samples were set aside for analysis. The idea was to describe the day-by-day changes in levels of key hormones circulating in the pandas' blood with a view to predicting the onset of Ling-Ling's oestrus more effectively.

Though the sample was small, based on just two animals over two years, the results looked promising. In the run-up to Ling-Ling's oestrus, there was a sudden and dramatic spike in the levels of breakdown products of oestrogen in her urine. Hsing-Hsing could clearly detect it as the amount of androgen derivates in his urine shot up a day later. Mating followed. '[D]etection of the receptive period of the female giant panda might be successfully accomplished by monitoring the excretion of oestrogens,' concluded Kleiman and her colleagues in the *Journal of Reproduction and Fertility*.

In addition, it was clear that as her oestrus approached, Ling-Ling became more vocal. This observation was straightforward because pandas are, for most of the year, silent animals, preferring to communicate with scent rather than sound (of which more later). But Kleiman reckoned that there would be subtle changes to the vocalisations that might give another indication of impending fertility. So she got in touch with Gustav Peters, then an up-and-coming German scientist with experience of working on the vocalisations of bears.

Peters, armed with a portable reel-to-reel recorder, began to lay down the pandas' calls as they became sexually active. This was not entirely unchartered scientific territory, for Desmond

Morris at London Zoo had succeeded in recording Chi-Chi's barks when she came into heat in 1963. 'She was so vocal at the time that it was only necessary to open the den door when she was inside her sleeping quarters and hold a microphone towards her to produce repeated loud calling,' recalled Morris in *Men and Pandas*. But the rationale for making these recordings was that they might help resolve the issue of the pandas' position within the tree of life. '[W]hen similar recordings become available for the red panda, the bears and the members of the raccoon family, it will be possible to carry out a detailed scrutiny of the different patterns and perhaps obtain some valuable relationship clues.'

Peters was also interested in how panda calls would compare to those of other carnivores he'd studied. But first and foremost, his goal was to obtain a thorough description of the panda's vocal repertoire. 'It was an exciting opportunity to study a species that was so little known,' says Peters. The fame of the pandas helped rather than hindered his work, with zoo staff providing all the assistance he needed to get the data he was after. He came away with the first insight into the acoustic range of the giant panda – a surprising mix of sounds produced by chomping its teeth and smacking its lips when nervous, honking when distressed, and moaning in the presence of danger. Crucially, there was also a set of very distinct calls – mainly short, sharp bleats and chirps – that Ling-Ling began to give out as her oestrus approached. Hsing-Hsing produced his own distinct vocalisations in response. In tandem with regular hormone assays, here at last was a reliable way to spot a randy panda.

It was at about this time that the decision was taken to try bringing the animals together outside oestrus. This ran counter to the recommendations of the Chinese. 'When we would put them together they spent most of their time kind of trying to figure out how to interact,' says Kleiman. By letting them get

26. Zoologist Devra Kleiman at the Smithsonian's National Zoo with Ling-Ling in 1982.

acquainted on a couple of other occasions, when the time came for mating their relationship seemed to go more smoothly.

In time, behaviour and vocalisations would also give an indirect measure of how comfortable the animals felt in their enclosure. Up until the early 1980s, the custom-built panda pavilion had been sparsely furnished, with few places to climb and nowhere to hide, or, as Kleiman describes it, 'the golf course type of facility where there was lots of grass and not much shelter'. With an interest in ways to enrich the lives of captive animals, this was of particular concern to Kleiman. So when Ling-Ling and Hsing-Hsing's enclosures received a radical makeover that gave them far more opportunity to climb, perch and hide, conditions more akin to those found in their natural habitat, Kleiman compared the pandas' calls and activities before and after the redesign. There was a dramatic change, says Kleiman. 'I was able to document a decrease in the frequency of aggressive and threatening vocalisations and the pandas began to play together much more frequently,' she says.

But even with the animals communicating better with each other, being brought together at the right moment and living in a more natural setting, the National Zoo had also been working on ways to give Hsing-Hsing and Ling-Ling a helping hand.

Several years earlier, the scientists at the National Zoo had raised the possibility of trying to get sperm from Hsing-Hsing. Although he looked in good health, they wanted to be sure his testicles were ticking over. Then, of course, if they succeeded in collecting sperm and freezing it, there was always the possibility of inserting it, at the appropriate moment, into Ling-Ling.

Artificial insemination is remarkably routine today, but in the late 1970s it was virtually unheard of. In the thirty years between then and now, the scientists at the National Zoo have attended to an impressive range of endangered species – black-footed ferrets, elephants, the Sumatran tiger – working out the best way in which to get sperm from them. This is not always easy. 'We are often talking about species that are dangerous, if not homicidal,' says David Wildt, who worked on the Nixon pandas alongside Kleiman and is now head of the Center for Species Survival at the zoo. For such creatures, a standard manual manipulation is out of the question. There are other methods, such as the artificial vagina offered to a male or vaginal condoms inserted into the female before copulation. But if none of these methods is a turn-on to the male, there may be no option but to electroejaculate.

Warning. Electroejaculation involves putting your target male under general anaesthetic, inserting an electrode into his rectum and slowly cranking up the voltage. All of these steps can injure the animal and may even be fatal, particularly if your male is the first of his species to be subjected to the procedure. In China, scientists had already started to experiment with electroejaculation and artificial insemination of their pandas. But Beijing Zoo's early success with natural mating, resulting in Ming-Ming in 1963, proved hard to repeat. In the wake of the Cultural Revolution, the Chinese began to pick up the pace of their research and turned increasingly to artificial insemination in an effort to increase the birth rate. In 1978, their work paid off when Beijing Zoo saw the birth of the first ever baby panda born as a result of artificial insemination. But, in spite of the new friendship between China and the US cemented by the Nixon pandas in 1972, details of China's artificial insemination programme were not available, and the Americans had to work out what to do for themselves.

To help things go as smoothly as possible, David Wildt called on the assistance of expert electroejaculator Carroll Platz Jr, then based at Texas A&M University. They had worked together several times before, including carrying out a successful procedure on a male lowland gorilla a few years earlier. Working with Hsing-Hsing, they delivered the correct dose of anaesthetic for a 109 kg panda, rolled him over and gave his genitals a gentle swab with a saline wash. Before bringing out the rectal probe, they used a micrometer to size up his testicles; their volume would give a quick and dirty indication of whether something was drastically wrong with his ability to produce sperm. All seemed to be well; his testicles were in good shape and each of four electroejaculations performed over a two-year period released plenty of viable sperm. Even the efforts to freeze and thaw out Hsing-Hsing's semen proved successful. Writing in the *Journal of Reproduction and Fertility*, Wildt's team concluded that 'standard electroejaculation procedures can be consistently effective in the giant panda without endangering the health of this rare animal.'

With hormone analysis and attention to vocalisations acting as reliable indicators of approaching fertility, and with sperm banked in liquid nitrogen, the stage was set to inseminate Ling-Ling artificially. When breaking new scientific ground, however, a few setbacks are inevitable.

The first artificial insemination, carried out in 1980, was performed a little late and there was no joy. The following year, another male panda – Chia-Chia – came to visit, on loan from London Zoo. As far as anyone could tell, Ling-Ling and Hsing-Hsing had never actually mated and the hope was that Chia-Chia would prove a more suitable mate for Ling-Ling. He did not. At their first encounter the two animals fought bitterly. They were 'totally incompatible,' pronounced Kleiman in an article for the zoo's newsletter *Tigertalk*, 'with Ling-Ling sustaining such serious injuries that we could not consider introducing her back to Hsing-Hsing or attempting artificial insemination.' They would have to wait for yet another year to pass.

Chia-Chia returned to London, but not before the folks in DC had put him through electroejaculation and frozen his semen. Some of this was used to inseminate Ling-Ling when she came into heat in 1982, resulting in signs that she might be pregnant; she began to build a den and could be seen cradling apples and carrots throughout the autumn as if nursing a baby. Unfortunately, this turned out to be a sham or 'pseudopregnancy', in which a female shows all the behavioural and physiological signs of pregnancy where there is none. Nevertheless, the scientists and keepers with an interest in the pandas entered 1983 with renewed energy. The mood strengthened as Ling-Ling came into heat in March. Kleiman and a volunteer observer watched as Hsing-Hsing and Ling-Ling mated for the first time in their decade together at the zoo. But the encounter had been brief, so Ling-Ling was also inseminated artificially with a batch of

Chia-Chia's defrosted semen. Then, in July, there was a sign that she was pregnant, and the sign came from her hormones.

In addition to oestrogen, Kleiman and her colleagues had started to study the variation in progesterone, sometimes nicknamed the 'pregnancy hormone'. In most mammals, progesterone levels increase shortly after ovulation, an indication that the uterus is being prepared for the possibility of receiving an embryo. If implantation does occur, progesterone will remain high throughout a pregnancy. If not, it won't. But pandas are not like most mammals. It turns out that progesterone levels do not rise until months after ovulation. This is because pandas are capable of 'delayed implantation', whereby an embryo is held in a state of dormancy for an unspecified period. In some rather extreme species, the delay between fertilisation and implantation can be a year or more. In the panda, it's usually between three and four months before there's a surge in progesterone, which probably signals the moment of implantation. A couple of weeks after that, it's possible to pick up the foetus on an ultrasound scan and a few weeks later still the cub pops out. This means that the foetus is actually only developing inside its mother for around four weeks.

So when, in July 1983, Ling-Ling's progesterone levels rose and remained elevated there was some excitement. Although a few captive pandas outside China had already given birth to babies that had survived – in Mexico City and in Madrid – the United States had yet to show off a captive-born baby panda to its public. There was, however, still a risk that the increase in progesterone was signalling nothing more than a pseudopregnancy as had occurred the previous year. From 11 July onwards, zoo staff and volunteers began a 24-hour watch, monitoring Ling-Ling's every move on CCTV.

In mid-afternoon on 20 July, Ling-Ling began to build a nest with bamboo in one corner of her enclosure. From about 7 p.m. onwards, she began to lick between her legs and remained restless until the birth at 3.18 a.m. the following morning. Zookeeper Barbara Bingham and collection manager Bess Frank watched anxiously for signs of movement in the baby. One minute passed, then two. Reluctantly, Frank picked up the telephone, dialled Kleiman's number and relayed the tragic news. But just seconds after she'd put the receiver down, Ling-Ling nudged her motionless cub and its tiny chest began to rise and fall. Overjoyed, she called Kleiman back. 'The early morning hours were wonderful,' wrote Frank in *Tigertalk*. Ling-Ling showed all signs of being a model mother, licking the cub and cradling it gently in her arms. But at around 6.30 a.m., suddenly, tragically and for no obvious reason, it stopped breathing.

By now, others had arrived and the growing crowd watched on in tears as Ling-Ling continued to lick and cradle the limp, pink body throughout the day. Even when they managed to retrieve it from her that evening, she scooped up an apple and rocked it for several days. The autopsy suggested that the cub had died as a result of bronchial pneumonia apparently contracted in the womb.

At an impromptu press conference, acting zoo director Christen Wemmer put on a brave face. 'Great expectations can lead to great disappointment,' he told the gathered rabble of journalists. 'Even though we lost the cub, we know Ling-Ling is capable of conceiving and giving a normal birth. We have come closer than ever before to successfully propagating this species.' Pencils scurried across notepads. In an effort to see the positive side of the setback, Wemmer turned attention towards the next breeding cycle. 'We are encouraged that we are on the right track and hopefully next year the young will survive to maturity.'

In 1984, this hope was dashed by a stillborn infant. Twins born in 1987 did not survive long. And like their first, Hsing-Hsing and Ling-Ling's last baby, born in 1989, died of pneumonia within a day of entering the outside world.

The media crawled all over these setbacks. Coming on the back of the very high-profile reproductive failure of Chi-Chi and An-An, Ling-Ling and Hsing-Hsing's non-achievement helped convince the West that the giant panda was a species uninterested in sex. Worse still, at least for the panda's reputation, the celebrated evolutionary biologist Stephen J. Gould settled on the panda's 'thumb' as an illustration of the non-optimal design he felt was a common feature in nature. In an incredibly influential essay published in *Natural History* in 1978, he described a visit to the National Zoo, where he had watched the Nixon pandas 'in appropriate awe' and became fascinated in the unusual anatomy of the panda's forepaw. 'The panda's true thumb is committed to another role, too specialized for a different function to become an opposable, manipulating digit. So the panda must use parts on hand and settle for an enlarged wrist bone and a somewhat clumsy, but quite workable, solution,' he wrote. 'The sesamoid thumb wins no prize in an engineer's derby.' China, too, was struggling to get pandas to mate naturally and the opening of the research centre in Wolong – the China Conservation and Research Center for the Giant Panda (CCRCGP) – in 1983 only served to increase the dependence on artificial insemination in order to turn out panda babies.

This is no longer quite the case. Building on the pioneering basic research carried out on pandas like Hsing-Hsing and Ling-Ling, scientists in China and beyond have been able to make some intriguing discoveries about panda biology that have, in turn, led to a dramatic improvement in the breeding stats. But before we find out more about these recent developments, it's time to catch up with research into pandas in the wild.

Born free

In the late 1960s, a small team of scientists made the first attempt to count wild pandas. They journeyed to the Wanglang Nature Reserve, the first of all China's reserves set up for the conservation of pandas, but the Cultural Revolution put a stop to the work. Then, in the mid-1970s, some 3,000 people took part in what would become known as the First National Survey, which produced an estimate of total panda numbers across the species' entire range (of which more later). But it was really only with the joint China-WWF project in the early 1980s that scientists began to study wild pandas in any meaningful way. They made the relationship between pandas and bamboo the focus of their work. 'Virtually all aspects of an animal's existence are influenced by the abundance, dispersion, and nutritional quality of the food it lives on,' wrote zoologist George Schaller and colleagues in their 1985 book *The Giant Pandas of Wolong*. 'How is the giant panda adapted to bamboo? That is the main scientific question our report attempts to answer.'

Some of the groundwork could be done without involving pandas at all and Hu Jinchu, co-leader of the joint project alongside Schaller, had already laid some of it. He had established a makeshift research base within the Wolong Nature Reserve and had started to collect preliminary data, like how the vegetation changed from 1,000 metres to 5,000 metres, how its make-up altered from season to season and how the pandas showed a preference for the sub-alpine coniferous forest at around 3,000 metres.

The China-WWF project built on this, monitoring the distribution and density of growth of different species of bamboo, discovering that this changed dramatically throughout the year, with some species at their most prolific sprouting up to 18 cm of new growth in a day. They carried out the first nutritional analysis of various parts of assorted bamboos, revealing that leaves have a higher protein content than do branches and stems and that species of the genus *Sinarundinaria* (of which there are several) have the greatest nutritional value.

They also gathered information about a panda's interactions with its surroundings. Tracks in the snow could be deciphered to give the researchers a rough idea of where pandas had been and maybe even the sorts of things they'd got up to, but they weren't helpful in distinguishing one panda from the next. Evidence of foraging for bamboo could give a good idea of which parts of which bamboo species were preferred at which times of year.

Panda faeces were pretty informative too, giving another indication of feeding preferences, how these changed through time, and the panda's ability to extract nutrients from this pithy food source. Dissection of bamboo fragments from a pile of faeces could also give a good indication of the animal's bite size, a measurement that made it possible to come up with a crude sense of panda numbers. Indeed, this was the method used in the First National Survey of giant pandas in the 1970s. There, the surveyors estimated a population size of just 145 animals in Wolong, an area of 500 square kilometres of suitable habitat.

Through long days and sometimes into the nights, the researchers were also able to get a feel for the secretive social lives of the pandas. Occasionally, they heard pandas communicating with each other with sound, made recordings and identified at least

27. Zoologist George Schaller ponders the challenge of getting to grips with a species that communicates largely through olfactory messages left on trees.

eleven distinct calls. These tallied well with the recordings that were made from Nixon's pandas at the National Zoo in Washington DC. Kleiman had also realised that smells seemed to be of immense importance to pandas. George Schaller and his Chinese colleagues soon found evidence in the field to support this idea. In March 1981, they had tracked an animal to a tree and could smell a 'faintly acidic odour' on the bark. Pandas, they realised, had 'scent posts', where animals came to claw, urinate and deposit their anal secretions. 'Once aware of how such posts looked, we discovered many, most of them above 2,700 m,' Schaller and friends wrote in *The Giant Pandas of Wolong*. As they began to record the location of these sites and what they looked like, some patterns began to emerge. The posts were typically found on conifers, with a lower area 'slightly darkened by secretions and smoothed by rubbing' and a higher region where the animal had clawed away at the bark. These posts seemed to be located where panda traffic was relatively high, 'around knolls on high ridges, in low passes, and along spurs projecting into valleys'. In tracking several known individuals and observing their propensity to make their mark, they concluded that it was probably males that were responsible for most of these odours, particularly since 'many trees were marked with a precise squirt'.

Though of immense interest, however, Schaller found himself thwarted by this secretive mode of communication. 'How would I ever understand pandas?' he wrote in *The Last Panda*. 'They moved from odor to odor, the air filled with important messages where I detected nothing.' It would take another decade and an abundance of captive pandas before scientists began to conduct some very cunning experiments to work out this interesting aspect of the panda's behaviour (see Chapter 11).

Beyond this useful background information, however, they would need to observe pandas being pandas in order to find out more. So in 1981, Hu and Schaller set about trying to trap some pandas so that they could radio-collar them. To help with the capture, sedation, collaring and tracking of pandas, Schaller called upon Howard Quigley, a young American biologist who had just completed a Masters thesis at the University of Tennessee.

In 1980, Quigley had chanced upon a news story about the forthcoming China-WWF panda project and had brazenly written to Schaller offering his services. Quigley's research on black bears in Yosemite National Park in California and the Great Smoky Mountains National Park in Tennessee had given him incredibly valuable experience. 'I had probably handled close to 200 black bears, involving their capture, immobilisation and release back into the wild.' When he did not hear back from Schaller he was not too surprised. 'I just thought that's probably the normal thing for someone of that stature getting a letter from a lowly Masters student', recalls Quigley. But then, towards the end of 1980, he got a call that saw him flying out to China early the following year.

They built two forms of trap – a log cage with a portcullis-style entrance that would drop shut when the animal wandered in, and a spring-loaded wire noose buried beneath leaves that would safely snare an animal by its foot. They set them in the places that pandas seemed to like, either along ridges or established trails or at the bottom of valleys, and baited them with meat to lure the pandas in.

Yes, you read that right. In spite of their predominantly bamboo-based diet, pandas still have a taste for meat. Armand David's local hunters had known this. They told him that the black-and-white bear seemed to live mainly off plants. 'Yet they say that it will not refuse meat if the opportunity arises,' reported David. During the Giant Panda Expedition in Wanglang in the 1960s, villagers reported to the researchers that they had found 'the remains of small rodents' in the stomachs of pandas. It was an interesting observation, though their ability to volunteer this kind of information – the poking around inside the insides of pandas – was a pretty good indication that habitat destruction was not the only threat to the panda. Over the course of the China-WWF project, Schaller and Hu would also note the occasional lapse into carnivory, finding the hair of a golden monkey in one panda dropping and the hair, bones and hooves of a musk deer in another.

So the scientists attempted to exploit this predilection, setting the traps with goat heads and pig bones. But for days – weeks – they remained empty. Then, in March 1981, one of the Chinese field workers came running excitedly from checking a snare trap. When they arrived on the scene, this is what Schaller saw:

The panda sits crouched at the base of a tree, one forepaw held by the snare. It has clawed the trunk in a brave and lonely effort to free itself, and now waits in the twilight of rhododendrons, a gentle creature with puzzled eyes looking into an uncertain future.

Quigley, at the age of just 20, was about to become the first person to dart a panda in the wild. He was certainly not complacent: he'd immersed himself in the relevant literature, talked to experts at the National Zoo about their experience of sedating Hsing-Hsing a few years earlier and, once in Wolong, had checked and rechecked his equipment. 'If I had time in camp, I would go over the process of making sure the dart gun was working, making sure that I could load and inject a drug into a dart,' he said. Yet no amount of experience and background research could prepare him for the sight of a real, live panda held fast by a snare. To Schaller, Quigley looked calm. But he wasn't. 'Inside I was chewing like a blender and my body felt like I was stiff as a robot.'

He sized up the animal and returned to his backpack to fill a dart with the appropriate dose of Telazol, a more benign relative of the anaesthetic administered to Chi-Chi in 1964. Though Schaller was not the one doing the actual injection, he too was anxious, just as London Zoo veterinarian Oliver Graham-Jones had been with Chi-Chi. The panda before them was not just any old animal, but 'a rare one, a national treasure, a symbol whose accidental death would forever haunt us'. Quigley set aside his nerves and focused on the task in hand. He mounted the dart on a stick, slowly approached the animal as if it were a black bear and jabbed the needle into its shoulder. Once the animal was under, the researchers measured, weighed and sexed it, and gave it a brief check-up before fitting it with a radio collar. Then, with

28. Howard Quigley and Hu Jinchu collect data from Long-Long, the first giant panda trapped and sedated under the China-WWF joint project in March 1981.

most of the job done and while waiting for the animal to come to, Quigley allowed himself a moment's reflection. This was no virtual panda – not a brand, not a photograph, not a cuddly toy. He ran his fingers through the wiry fur and felt the animal's warmth and the rise and fall of its gentle breathing. Until that moment, it was almost as if the panda existed only in a human world. But now, there before him, was a real, live, wild panda. 'It was truly a unique experience.'

The team went on to capture and collar a further six animals in Wolong. Though seven animals – two males, two females and three sub-adults – is a desperately small sample on which to base a serious scientific study, seven is an infinite improvement on zero and it provided the very first glimpse into the secretive world of the wild panda, mapping the behaviour of this elusive species onto the background information the researchers already had in place. Each panda appeared to occupy a pretty tight home range, an area of around five square kilometres. Males seemed to be slightly more relaxed about where they hung out than did females, who tended to spend most of their time in a dedicated patch within their range. From day to day, the animals they tracked did not move far – on average less than 500 metres.

On top of this rather sedentary picture, the researchers managed to obtain greater detail of what the pandas were up to. The radio transmitters they were using were fitted with motion sensors, pretty high-tech kit for the 1980s. The collars sent out different signals depending on whether the animals were asleep and motionless or awake and active. They found quite a bit of difference between each panda, which might have been down to their sex, age, reproductive condition, individual character, response to weather or any other number of factors. But in general, the activity pattern of the Wolong pandas made perfect sense for a creature that eats lots of low-nutritional food. They were active for a surprising fourteen hours a day, with peaks just before dawn and in the run-up to dusk. Over a year, they were most active in spring and least active in summer but never put on enough fat to hibernate.

By trekking in person to where the signals were coming from, the researchers were also able to get a feeling for what the pandas were doing during their bursts of rather relaxed activity. Sometimes they found the pandas on the move, at other times they were busy leaving their scent on a tree or engrossed in rubbing, scratching and licking various parts of their anatomy. Less frequently, they found a panda up a tree, and, on a couple of occasions, they stumbled across evidence of pandas having what appeared to be fun. Marks in the snow revealed that one panda tracked by Schaller had clearly flung itself onto its belly and tobogganed down the hill. 'I thought how much I would have liked to witness its lonely winter sport,' he wrote. But mostly, the pandas were busy grasping stems of bamboo, stripping off the tough outer wall with their teeth and then crunching into the soft, edible core.

Then, in 1983, some of the bamboo species began to flower in Wolong and elsewhere across the Qionglai Mountain range. This sounds very poetic but it's not good news for pandas and the China-WWF researchers knew it. Almost a decade earlier in the winter of 1975, villagers in the Min Mountains to the north began reporting sightings of dead or dying pandas. Local officials filed urgent reports, which soon reached the Ministry of Forestry in Beijing. They responded quickly and decisively, bringing together local officials and scientists based in the capital to organise an investigation into the mysterious deaths unfolding across the region. 'Such early and active national attention and the creation of a national task force to investigate the unusual and widespread panda deaths demonstrated the importance of the wellbeing and continued existence of the giant panda to the central government in Beijing,' according to historian Elena Songster. The 'Investigation Team' quickly reached their conclusion regarding the cause of the panda deaths: flowering of bamboo.

This is a problem for pandas because bamboo is what's known as monocarpic, a plant that flowers, sets seed and then dies. What's more, bamboo has a habit of flowering in synchrony, with almost every stem of a particular species on every slope across an entire range throwing out long wispy flowers, releasing pollen onto the wind and producing seeds. Since we can't step back millions of years to witness the evolution of monocarpism in bamboo, we can only guess at the advantages that this peculiar reproductive tactic affords these plants. There are two main schools of thought. One, proposed in the 1970s, is known as the 'satiation hypothesis', the idea that synchronous flowering is a strategy to overwhelm seed-eating species: if just a few bamboo plants go to seed each year, their tasty offerings will be hoovered up from the forest floor; if, however, all plants drop in the same year there will still be plenty of seeds even after the predators have had their fill. The other hypothesis for mass flowering is that the mature stands of bamboo make it difficult for seedlings to find the light and nutrients to establish; it's only if the old growth dies back that the youngsters can make their way in the world. There are other, more outlandish hypotheses but they are not so convincing, says Alan Taylor, a botanist currently at Penn State University who had joined the China-WWF project in 1984 to study bamboo. The 'fire-cycle hypothesis', for example, argues that a mass of dead and dying bamboo acts, quite literally, like a lightning rod, providing fuel for wildfires that enrich the soil and make way for the next generation. 'I don't buy it at all,' says Taylor.

During the Min Mountains episode, at least two – possibly more – different species of bamboo appear to have flowered at once. In the past, pandas could probably have coped with even this freak scenario, moving down the mountain into unaffected habitat. Indeed, it seems as if this is what they tried to do. But they found only agricultural land and no bamboo, which explains why villagers in the region began to notice a sudden spate of hungry pandas. These same people were there to help with the crisis facing their national treasure. They handed over any panda corpses they encountered to the authorities and subsequent autopsies confirmed that the animals had starved to death, their stomachs empty, their meagre fat reserves burnt out and their abdomens bloated with water. Earthquakes rattling the region were thought to have resulted in even more panda deaths and when the Ministry of Forestry's Investigation Team produced its definitive report on the devastation, they estimated the total death toll at 138.

Beijing introduced several protection measures that proved to have some very important consequences for the way of the panda in years to come. In some particularly sensitive regions, the Ministry of Forestry insisted on a stop to logging, and they tightened restrictions on hunting in panda habitat. It was also an offence to skin or otherwise tamper with the remains of a dead panda. There was a range of penalties – withheld wages, forfeit of holidays and fines – for any disobedience.

There was another, more controversial consequence of this tragedy. Local forestry bureaus encouraged an effort to rescue starving but not-yet-dead pandas by bringing them into captivity where they could be fed up to full fitness in relative warmth and safety. It might have seemed like a good idea at the time, driven by purely benevolent motives, yet returning a captive panda to the wild would prove to be harder – far, far harder – than it sounds. But nobody could have known it at the time or even when the arrow bamboo began to flower again a few years later, this time in the Qionglai Mountains, home to Wolong.

With the Min Mountains experience fresh in everyone's mind, there was a swift and decisive response. The plight of Qionglai's pandas became a national and, soon after, an international issue. Those on the China-WWF project were concerned that the situation their pandas were facing was rather different to that in the Min Mountains. 'I believed that Wolong's pandas would survive the bamboo die-off well,' George Schaller wrote in *The Last Panda*. 'It would harm rather than benefit the pandas if widespread rescue operations included areas where the animals were not in danger.'

The ongoing studies of bamboo also suggested that the pandas could probably cope; while there was, presumably, some genetic involvement in the synchronous flowering, there were patches that, for some reason, had failed to do so. The China-WWF researchers began to look at what these live patches had in common and found that the higher the altitude, the steeper the slope and the thinner the topsoil, the more likely it was that the bamboo would not flower. 'Broadly speaking,' says botanist Alan Taylor, 'local environmental stress created conditions where that genetic clock didn't go off.' Evidence from the radio-collared pandas indicated that they were able to locate these islands of living bamboo and move efficiently between them. The animals began to spend more time dealing with each stem, apparently appreciating that they had to get everything they could out of a resource that had suddenly become relatively scarce. And as the arrow bamboo began to run out, they just moved down the mountainside in winter to feed on a different species – umbrella bamboo.

But one of the China-WWF biologists felt so alarmed by the proposal to set up 'rescue centres' for wild pandas that he took decisive action. His name was Pan Wenshi, a character that would come to dominate the research on wild pandas for the rest of the twentieth century. He bypassed the Ministry of Forestry by sending a letter to the very top of the Chinese government, cautioning against a blanket rescue operation. 'I was not in favour of catching free-ranging animals and locking them up,' he later wrote. 'The last chance for the species' survival, in my opinion, was to offer a better, and larger, habitat.' But the tsunami of panda anxiety that swept across China and throughout the world meant his measured voice could not be heard.

One of the best-known responses took place in the United States, where First Lady Nancy Reagan launched a 'pennies for pandas' campaign in March 1984. 'I hope all children in our country will help this cause and give their pennies to help the pandas,' she told reporters at a press conference at the National Zoo. In April, when she and her husband travelled to Beijing, Mrs

Reagan handed over a cheque for $13,000 to the Deputy Forestry Minister Dong Zhiyong. The panda rescue effort continued for several years and, as had happened in the Min Mountains, dozens of pandas found themselves being taken from the wild and into captivity.

Stories of humans having to rescue pandas also did nothing for the panda's public image. The heroic but largely unproductive struggle to breed pandas in captivity during the 1960s and 1970s leant weight to the post-Chi-Chi assumption that pandas are not interested in sex. The high-profile episodes of bamboo die-off in the 1970s and 1980s took the panda to even more pitiful depths in the public imagination. Here was a species that needed human help to find enough food to survive. This could explain how, in the West at least, the panda came to be seen as an inept species at an evolutionary dead end for which extinction is the inevitable outcome. But few if any of the scientists who have worked with giant pandas in the wild would agree. 'I for one certainly did not think so,' wrote Pan Wenshi. The panda would be fine if only humans could find a way to let it get on with its life undisturbed.

In the 1960s, just as the conservation movement began to get going around the world, so China took its first small but significant step towards protecting the panda in the wild. The abortive Great Leap Forward had taken a devastating toll on wildlife. The people had been so hungry that they had even resorted to eating the reputedly unpalatable giant panda. Elena Songster has located and translated the PRC State Council directive sent to the Ministry of Forestry in 1962 that encouraged them to protect a handful of China's most endangered species. 'Wild animals are one of our nation's greatest riches,' the State Council announced. 'Not only can one obtain a great amount of wild animal meat, but also numerous pelts, deer antlers, and large quantities of musk.'

The Ministry of Forestry would now be responsible for managing this resource and was encouraged to protect nineteen species considered to be 'precious and rare'. In the State Council's directive, the giant panda sits at the top of this list. 'For these animals, hunting is strictly prohibited,' it went on. 'Moreover, nature protection reserves will be established in the primary habitat of these animals and in their breeding areas to better protect them.' This quickly led to the formation of dedicated panda reserves, so that today there are more than sixty such reserves that cover around three-quarters of all suitable habitat and over half of the population.

But in spite of the 1962 ban on hunting and the appearance of panda reserves, other forces continued to reduce the panda's chances of long-term survival. During the 1980s, there were dozens of cases of panda-poaching or pelt-smuggling that found their way into Chinese courts. The upshot was China's Wild Animal Protection Act, passed in 1989. Among other things, this ruled that anyone caught bumping off a panda, or even smuggling panda skins, would face at least ten years in prison, possibly a life behind bars and, in extreme cases, the death penalty.

According to standard economic theory, the law of diminishing returns would suggest that, as a species like the panda becomes increasingly hard to find, it would make economic sense for poachers to move on to a species that they can get their hands on more readily. But this, of course, ignores the immense value that humans place on rarity and several studies have demonstrated the tight relationship between rarity and value. Villagers in Papua New Guinea selling butterflies to wealthy collectors, for example, have a pricing system that reflects the rarity of their winged wares. Similarly, overfishing of the white abalone – a large, edible sea snail that lives off the Californian coast and is considered a local delicacy – has resulted in the population collapsing by more than 99.99 per cent, yet the soaring price of this commodity means that the fishery has pushed on in search of the remaining, lucrative, 0.01 per cent.

In 2006, researchers produced a mathematical model of exactly this kind of scenario and concluded that increasing rarity and therefore value can drive a species into an 'extinction vortex'. The very serious and well-publicised penalties imposed on anyone caught with panda blood on their hands had helped reduce poaching of this species, but the extraordinary prices some extraordinary people are willing to pay for a panda skin means that there will always be a minority willing to risk imprisonment or the death penalty. Between 1987 and 1998, Chinese authorities confiscated fifty-two panda skins, surely a tiny fraction of the total number poached. If not yet being sucked into an extinction vortex, the panda had been brought whirling perilously close to the brink by persistent poaching.

Along with the poaching, the transformation of forest into agricultural land continued apace even after the abortive Great Leap Forward. China's need for agricultural land can be understood when you consider that in the late 1970s it had only half the area of land that was then cultivated in the United States to feed almost five times as many people. Unfortunately, the agricultural reform pressed upon the Chinese people turned out to have disastrous short- and long-term consequences.

In August 1963, a bout of extraordinarily heavy rainfall all but destroyed Dazhai, a small farming community in the mountains of northerly Shanxi Province. But the villagers responded to the loss of life, homes and livelihoods with determination. It's hard to say just how successful they were at rebuilding their shattered world, but Mao Zedong leaped on this case as an example of self-reliance. Soon news stories and posters celebrating the Dazhai

29. When heavy rainfall destroyed livelihoods in Dazhai in Shanxi
Province in 1963, the villagers responded by terracing the hillsides
around them into agricultural land. Through posters like this
one, farmers across China were encouraged to do likewise, which
resulted in massive deforestation and contributed to the ongoing
fragmentation of panda habitat.

people's incredible tenacity began to appear and peasants across
China were urged to follow 'the Dazhai Road' to 'change the face
of rivers and mountains'.

Tragically, the idea that the Dazhai model would be a solution
to China's hunger proved misguided, and it laid to waste much
of China's wilderness without increasing the area of productive
land, argues historian Judith Shapiro. 'No matter how steep or
inhospitable the terrain, and regardless of how successful, appropriate, or time-tested other uses of the land, terraces were built
and grain was planted just as in the hillsides of Dazhai,' she wrote
in *Mao's War Against Nature* .

While researching her book, Shapiro interviewed a scientist

at the Chengdu Research Base of Giant Panda Breeding about the impact the Dazhai campaign had had on panda country. He wished to remain anonymous. He recalled seeing evidence of pandas in the hills around his childhood home in southern Sichuan but that the Dazhai approach had destroyed much of their remaining habitat. 'I remember vividly how we cut bamboo and trees to build Dazhai-style terraces and grow grain wherever possible,' he said. 'There was no awareness of the importance of what was lost.'

In the space of twenty years from the mid-1970s to the mid-1990s, it's estimated that half of the suitable habitat available to pandas was chopped down. More than that, it was becoming alarmingly fragmented. 'The realization that the panda has so suffered and declined in numbers while we chronicled its life burdens me painfully,' wrote Schaller in *The Last Panda*.

When fellow zoologist John MacKinnon arrived in Beijing in 1987 as WWF's senior advisor, he began to shift the charity's involvement with pandas away from basic research and towards management. As a joint China-WWF survey team scoured the countryside to produce a second and more reliable estimate of panda numbers, MacKinnon and a small team of Chinese colleagues bashed out the outline of a National Conservation Management Plan for the Giant Panda and its Habitat. 'It took about three months to write and then about three years to discuss it, argue it and get it approved,' he recalls. The Tiananmen Square protests of 1989 almost derailed that approval process when WWF HQ in Switzerland responded with orders to withdraw its operations in China. Fortunately for the management plan and therefore for the giant panda, MacKinnon studiously ignored this directive. 'I pretended I'd never got the message, I kept WWF in China and succeeded in getting the management plan signed off,' he says.

Meanwhile, in the West, an internal audit of WWF circulated in late 1989 made for some very uncomfortable reading. In his executive summary, the author of the report, Oxford University professor John Phillipson, accused WWF of neo-imperialism, charging around the world issuing its conservation orders without being sufficiently sensitive to local people and infrastructure. When it came to pandas, he did not hold back. 'The policy of widening WWF involvement to cover other interests has, in my opinion, been counterproductive and, in view of the virtual cessation of support for all forms of panda research, amounts to an abrogation of responsibility for the much-publicised "Panda Program".'

When word about the Phillipson Report leaked to the public in 1990, just a year after the Tiananmen Square protests, the organisation had some difficult questions to answer. In spite of WWF's continued presence in China, Prince Philip, then president of WWF, attempted to draw a line under the charity's involvement in the country. The panda experiment had been 'very disappointing,' he told a journalist for the UK's *Sunday Express*. 'One of those projects that was a good idea at the time.' He also dwelt on the charity's financial investment, musing that 'in spite of WWF spending a fortune on it, the chances of the panda surviving at the present rate of progress are not good.'

This mention of money is perhaps appropriate. For, in the decade since China had adopted a more open stance to the West, it had made swift economic strides. In 1980, just as the WWF won over its Chinese counterparts with a cash injection of $1 million to help build the China Conservation and Research Center for the Giant Panda (CCRCGP) at Wolong, China had met the requirements for membership of the International Monetary Fund and the World Bank. In 1983, direct foreign investment in China is estimated to have been in the region of $1 billion, with the PRC taking out around the same amount in international loans. In 1984, as if to underscore these changes, the British government agreed that its then colony Hong Kong – a jewel in the capitalist crown – would revert to Chinese rule in 1997. With such a radical reconfiguration of the PRC's fortunes, it is inevitable that this should rub off on China's approach to its pandas. Instead of gifting these valuable specimens to other countries (as had been PRC practice since the 1950s), it now seemed more appropriate to exploit their commercial value to the max.

This rather unsightly chapter in the history of the giant panda may even have started in the boardroom. In April 1984, the chairman of Occidental Petroleum Corporation signed a deal with the PRC to develop a massive open-pit coal mine in Shanxi Province. The Los Angeles-based company would put up $340 million to fund engineering equipment and bring in outside expertise and China would fork out an additional $240 million. It seems as though two giant pandas were also part of the deal, for the Occidental chairman personally paid $150,000 to bring two giant pandas – Yun-Yun and Ying-Xin – to Los Angeles Zoo for the Olympics later that year. Following their ninety-day stint in LA, the pandas went on a lucrative four-week trip to San Francisco Zoo. 'This commercial gesture precipitated much vigorous jostling by North American and European zoos to obtain pandas for exhibition, as well as by China to loan them,' wrote George Schaller in *The Last Panda*.

This jostling continued for almost a decade, with China sending out pandas on extremely rewarding, short-term loans. But there was a growing feeling that the money generated should be working harder and more transparently to benefit pandas. What's more, these purely commercial loans appeared to be in breach of the US Endangered Species Act and IUCN's Convention on

30. Pan Wenshi's team of researchers in the early 1990s photographed in what would become the Changqing Nature Reserve in the Qinling Mountains. Pan Wenshi and Lü Zhi are seated towards the back and Wang Dajun is at the bottom left.

the Trade of Endangered Species (CITES), which rule that the import of endangered plants and animals be for the advancement of science or to improve the prospects for the species. After legal action, the US Fish and Wildlife Service finally announced a moratorium on processing the permits necessary to import wild pandas into the United States.

Though these were difficult years, the China-WWF partnership had achieved some important milestones along the way of the panda: the first real observations of the behaviour and ecology of wild pandas, the second national survey and the first coherent management plan for the species, which was packed full of evidence-based recommendations. In addition, there was another, less obvious legacy of the China-WWF collaboration.

When Schaller left Wolong in 1985, so too did fellow zoologist Pan Wenshi who set up his own research programme in the Qinling Mountains in Shaanxi, the easternmost mountain range with pandas. And his team began to produce top quality research that built significantly upon the China-WWF's foundations. The emphasis in this study was on finding out as much as possible about panda reproduction in the wild and the factors that might affect it. Pan wanted to know whether the panda population was self-sustaining. Were there enough animals out there, breeding successfully, to keep the population topped up?

Pan's move to Qinling may have been motivated by the desire to get as far away from Sichuan as possible. During his years on the China-WWF project, his outspoken views had rubbed local forestry officials up the wrong way. Qinling, he hoped, would provide a fresh start. With its gentler slopes and less dense vegetation this mountain range would also prove to be a super place to watch pandas in the wild.

Pan had provisionally planned to work in Shaanxi's oldest and best-known protected area, the Foping Nature Reserve, but his troubles with the Ministry of Forestry followed him east and it soon became clear that he would have to find somewhere else, somewhere that did not fall under MoF control. Well aware of the irony, Pan settled on the Changqing Forestry Bureau, a state-owned timber enterprise established in the 1960s that employed several thousand local people. Here, in spite of the obvious conflict of interest with their hosts, the panda scientists were made welcome, given rudimentary accommodation in one of the logging camps and even loaned a handful of former hunters to help track pandas.

Just as it had been in Wolong, life in these remote, frequently snowbound mountains was not for the faint-hearted. 'The weather was humid and chilly, especially in the winter, and an open charcoal fire in my room was the only way to stay warm at night,' wrote Lü Zhi, Pan's first graduate student on the new project and now a director of both the Center for Nature and Society at Peking University and the non-governmental Beijing-based Shanshui Conservation Center. When she found herself poisoned by the fumes for a second time, Lü decided to do without heat.

And as in Wolong, it took a long time before data began to trickle in, in spite of what appeared to be a relatively dense panda population in the Qinling region. 'We were lucky to catch sight of a panda, never mind getting close enough to study one,' wrote Lü in *Giant Pandas in the Wild*. As the researchers on the China-WWF project had done, Pan's team constructed wooden cages and baited them with mutton. After a painful fifteen months, however, there were still no panda takers.

A tranquillizer gun would get round this problem. 'But,' wrote Lü, 'at a price of $2,000 – the equivalent of my five-year stipend and Pan's two-year salary put together – that was out of the question.' Then, a group of American zoo directors passing through Peking University agreed to donate a gun to the project and after that Pan and his followers were away. Between 1986 and 1999, they managed to trap, dart, collar and track a total of thirty-two individuals.

At this point, there was still almost nothing known about real, wild panda sex. Pandas appeared to be solitary animals, coming together over a few days to mate. The China-WWF project had added a few details about these fleeting encounters, as Schaller's first glimpse of panda action demonstrates. He was following a female Zhen-Zhen, who had hooked up with a large male and was being followed by another, smaller male. On several occasions, this hanger-on had a go at getting a look-in. 'The small male comes near, moaning, and is promptly attacked again, though I only hear growls, roars, and whines like a pack of dogs fighting and see the bamboo shake violently,' wrote Schaller. He continued to track the animals closely and in the twilight hour, he watched as Zhen-Zhen and the more dominant male mated more than forty times. This is clearly not a species averse to sex.

Still, the picture of wild panda pair-bonding and cub-raising remained pretty sketchy until Pan's study in Qinling. Over the course of ten years, from 1985 to 1996, he and his colleagues observed twenty-one mating events. It still doesn't sound like a lot, but it was enough to begin to generalise about what panda sex is like. Interestingly, of the mating events the researchers could get a really good look at, there was usually more than one male at the scene and in several instances the males got into a brawl and sustained injuries. Again, this strongly suggested that the rather strained affairs taking place in breeding centres and zoos were a world away from what pandas normally do in the wild.

With so many pandas sporting a radio-collar, Pan's team was also able to find the exact location of eleven births for five different females. This revealed that females typically give birth every other year in the wild, dropping down the mountainside to lower altitudes, identifying a snug cave or hollow tree, and giving birth in August. There was one panda – a female called Jiao-Jiao (meaning 'Double Charm') – for whom the researchers held a particular affection. In August 1992, Pan and Lü found Jiao-Jiao's signal less active than usual, an indication that she was giving birth to what would be the second of five cubs. Lü recalls the moment they located the den:

> Jiao Jiao lifted up her head, then snuggled down again. A pale, tiny creature, its voice as delicate as a puppy's whimper, then wriggled out from between Jiao Jiao's hairy chest and arms ... It was the size of a hamster, its pink body covered with sparse white hair ... Each time the infant squealed Jiao Jiao gave it a tender

pat with her hairy palm, cradling it the way a human mother does her newborn child.

The hours passed and as Jiao-Jiao gradually drifted off to sleep, Lü was taken by a bold wheeze. In the course of the three years that she had been tracking this panda, she had gradually earned its trust. How close would Jiao-Jiao let her get to her newborn cub? Imitating the panda's soft sigh, Lü moved forwards slowly until she was close enough to reach out towards the sleeping mother. 'The moment I touched her back, a peaceful feeling swept over me,' she says. 'What a reward! After three and a half years, Jiao-Jiao had finally accepted me.' She and Pan decided to call the newborn cub Xiwang. It means 'hope'.

Jiao-Jiao remained with her newborn cub for a surprising twenty-five days before heading out to grab a quick bamboo snack. She was gone for about an hour, in which time the researchers were able to find out that Xiwang was a female. At seven weeks, she opened her eyes, at four months she had started to walk, then climb, and soon began to follow her mother on her foraging expeditions. Tracking the two pandas on these trips, Pan, Lü and others in the team found that Xiwang would often climb up into a tree and sit there for hours, waiting for her mother to return. She always did. This was rather an important discovery because during the effort to save pandas from starvation in the late 1980s, more than thirty cubs – assumed to have been abandoned – had been taken into captivity where more than half of them had died within a matter of years.

So in 1994, when the researchers revealed what they'd learnt about mother-cub relationships, they made the following recommendation. 'The mother's absence during bouts of foraging should be considered when rescuing abandoned cubs in order to avoid adding to the decline of the wild population.' The Ministry

31. Jiao-Jiao's second cub Xiwang playing in a tree. It is normal for a young panda to be left alone for hours, sometimes days on end whilst their mother goes off to feed. Until Pan Wenshi and colleagues made this observation, most people assumed these babies had been abandoned and would take them into captivity. This can no longer be done without evidence that the mother has actually died.

of Forestry listened and in 1998 made it official panda policy that no cubs should be removed from the wild unless there was concrete evidence that the mother had actually died.

By the time Jiao-Jiao gave birth to her next cub two years later, she was so comfortable with the presence of the researchers that she let them wedge a metal box in a crevice near the entrance to her den. Inside it was a miniature video camera and microphone wired up to a video recorder hidden carefully at a distance of 30 metres. Incredibly, Pan and colleagues had this in place in time to make recordings of the newborn cub when he was just two days old. They continued to film his development for over half a year, building up a unique and important picture of the first few months in a wild panda's life. The cub appeared to stay with its mother for at least eighteen months.

Based on the observation that females give birth every other year and that well over half of all cubs will make it through the perilous first year of life, it looks like the population in Qinling is self-sustaining. 'On the basis of its reproductive potential, the giant panda therefore remains an evolutionary successful species,' wrote Pan and colleagues.

By the time that they arrived at this upbeat conclusion, those working on captive pandas had achieved a remarkable feat. By stepping back to take a fresh look at how they were keeping pandas, they were able to transform the breeding statistics and boast that their population – like that in wild – was self-sustaining too. It is to this achievement that we now turn.

Captive subjects

Even with the official opening of the Wolong China Conservation and Research Center for the Giant Panda (CCRCGP) in 1983, things were still slow to take off. It took until 1986 for the birth of the first panda in captivity there. Then, the following year, the Chengdu Research Base of Giant Panda Breeding opened in the north of the Sichuan capital, a high-tech, top-spec institution to rival that at Wolong. Though they too found that reproducing pandas in captivity was no mean feat, they achieved a significant breakthrough in 1990. When a female Qing-Qing gave birth to twins (as occurs in about half of all panda pregnancies), the staff managed to keep both newborns alive by moving one to an incubator, feeding it on bottled milk and then giving it a turn at its mother's teat by swapping it over with its twin. Up until that point, the abandoned twin had been left to die. Though it was a lot of work, it was worth it.

Yet the potential for panda breeding was still far from being realised. From the first captive birth in 1963 until the end of the 1980s, the number of mature pandas in captivity rose from twelve to eighty-eight, but this explosion was largely down to the removal of pandas from the wild during the bamboo die-off of the 1970s and 1980s. There were 115 cubs born during this period – which doesn't sound too bad – except that only sixteen survived long enough for them to begin breeding themselves.

By 1996, there were 134 pandas in captivity across China but of the animals that had reached reproductive age, only a third of females and one-sixth of all males had ever produced any offspring. 'The artificial insemination technology was not good enough,' says Zhang Zhihe, current director of the Chengdu Base. The voltage used for electroejaculation and the frequency with which the procedure was being administered was clearly not right, he says. 'Following electroejaculation, a male would typically lose his appetite for one or two weeks. Sometimes there would be blood coming from his rectum.'

At the Annual Technical Meeting for Giant Pandas in 1995 – a get-together for panda managers to report on the situation at their institutions – the then vice-director of the Ministry of Construction, Zheng Shuling, decided to shake things up and improve the way that zoos across the country pooled their panda expertise and experience. Her drive led the Chinese Association of Zoological Gardens (CAZG) to seek assistance from the IUCN's Conservation Breeding Specialist Group (CBSG), a US-based organisation with serious expertise in troubleshooting captive-breeding programmes of endangered species.

So, in December 1996, a five-person strong CBSG taskforce met with thirty Chinese colleagues in 'a cold and drafty conference room in a public building in downtown Chengdu'. The Americans put a question to the Chinese: 'What is your reason for having giant pandas in zoos in China?' Following a quarter of an hour of keen discussion, the most senior Chinese scientist at the workshop stood up. 'The goal is to develop a self-sustaining population of giant pandas that will assist supporting a long-term, viable population in the wild,' he announced. Over the next four days, the delegates broke out into several small working groups to tackle part of the panda jigsaw. There was a lot – it felt like too much – to take on board, says David Wildt, reproductive biologist at the National Zoo in Washington, DC and one of the CBSG team. But he had an idea.

Back in the early 1990s, Wildt had been part of a team that performed the first ever highly manipulative survey of an endangered species in captivity – cheetahs – with a view to improving the health and reproduction of the captive population. At that time, only 15 per cent of wild-caught cheetahs had ever reproduced in captivity and those born in zoos were even less active. It was easy to guess at possible explanations for these dismal stats, but without any coordinated, carefully planned research it was impossible to know for sure; any management decisions would be based on instinct rather than on evidence. The upshot was that more than 100 scientists, vets and keepers across the United States worked together on a 'Biomedical Survey' of more than 100 cheetahs housed across many different institutions. They found several reasons for the failure of cheetahs to reproduce but one finding stood out: it seemed as though the ovaries of many of the females were not working. This stimulated one research group to devise a method of monitoring female hormones through the analysis of faeces, and another team to discover how management changes could alter hormone secretion and hence kick-start the ovarian activity. Could a similar approach work for the giant panda?

The success of such a survey rests on being able to study a sufficient number of animals in order to make generalisations that can be rolled out to the whole captive population. With backing from the Ministry of Construction, the body with responsibility for China's zoo network, and given that the majority of China's captive pandas were held at only a few Chinese institutions, it certainly seemed feasible to think about a big study on a lot of animals.

Over the next year, the method for the survey began to take shape. Each panda would be anaesthetised to allow the researchers to

32. During the Panda Biomedical Survey, researchers brought together a wealth of basic data on the health of the captive population in China.

get to grips with any problems it had. Small teams would work on different parts of the animal simultaneously to minimise the time it was under: each individual would have an electronic tag injected beneath the skin on its back and a number tattooed under its lip as an identification back-up; someone would collect tiny samples of skin, hair and blood for genetic analysis; healthy males would be electroejaculated according to a tried-and-tested rectal-probe procedure; every conceivable property of the sperm would be evaluated, and each animal would get a full-blown internal and external examination, involving a dental check-up, genital inspection and ultrasound, amongst much else. On top of this, the researchers would collect data on feeding regimes at the different institutions and details of all past breeding attempts – whether successful or not. The survey got under way in the spring of 1998, with data feeding in from pandas at four of China's zoological institutions – Beijing Zoo, Chongqing Zoo, Chengdu Zoo and the Chengdu Base.

Since just five of the thirty-three males in captivity that were of breeding age had actually bred, there was a big drive to find out why this was. Most of the males they inspected had healthy sized testes. When it came to their ejaculates, things looked even more rosy. 'The semen of the giant panda contained prodigious numbers of sperm,' noted the scientists in the Biomedical Survey report. Since they were using an electric shock to eject these cells from their testicular hideaway, there's no guarantee that a male panda will deploy the same extraordinary numbers of sperm in a natural mating, but it would appear that an average male has around 3 billion sperm he can call upon if needed; that's many times more than are released in a typical human male ejaculate. Under the microscope, the panda sperm looked good too, with the vast majority wiggling away frantically with no obvious abnormalities. All this strongly suggested that most of the captive male pandas – whether they had a reproductive track record or not – seemed to have everything right in the sperm production department. Which was nice to know.

With all this sperm, the researchers also had the opportunity to improve upon the method for freezing the cells for later use, otherwise known as cryopreservation. For some, the idea of experimenting with sperm rather than using it to make babies did not seem a good one, but it did for Zhang Zhihe, then the vice director of the Chengdu Base. Still, as Zhang ordered dozens of sperm samples to be consigned to cryopreservation experiments, he had to face down a fair bit of criticism. 'Some people even accused me of using the sperm to make money,' he says.

Freezing a sperm cell, indeed any cell, frequently causes irreparable damage to its membranes and internal structures. To avoid this kind of ice damage, it's necessary to mix up the sperm with a cryoprotectant or antifreeze. But since the first efforts to freeze panda sperm in the late 1970s, subtle differences in the protocol had emerged between different institutions. The thorough investigation by the Biomedical Survey team made it clear how best to buffer freshly collected panda sperm and protect it from the stresses of the freeze-thaw cycle. Importantly, it looks as though sperm that's been properly frozen and then thawed according to this protocol should perform just as well as does fresh sperm.

So with electroejaculation pretty routine and a honed method for freeze-thawing panda sperm, it should be possible to hook up any captive male with any captive female. In captive breeding circles, this is considered rather important. Because if the same few males tend to breed with the same few females – as was the case with pandas up until the 1990s – then the genetic variation in your captive population starts to decline. This might not be a problem. After all, there are examples of species that seem to have pulled through a genetic bottleneck without any obvious health problems. But then again, it might be. If just a few individuals do all the breeding, the next generation tends to be rather flush with closely related individuals – brothers, sisters, half-brothers, half-sisters, cousins. When they come to reproduce, inbreeding is almost inevitable and this can cause all sorts of trouble.

The case of the Florida panther has become the textbook example. In the 1990s, the total population size is thought to have dropped to around twenty to thirty individuals. With inbreeding rife, reproduction began to become a serious challenge, with more than half the males struggling with undescended testes. Careful management of the population purged it of these troubling inbreeding symptoms and the population continues – just about – today. Although most of the males in the panda Biomedical Survey appeared to be healthy, there were a couple of individuals that appeared to be testicularly challenged. Inbreeding was certainly a plausible explanation.

The snag was that nobody knew for sure. Just as Christians have the Bible, Muslims the Koran and Jews the Torah, panda managers have their holy book – the International Studbook for the Giant Panda, a detailed record of the pedigree and reproductive output of every single captive panda that has ever lived. In 1991, the National Zoo's Devra Kleiman and a member of the Chinese Ministry of Construction travelled throughout China to draw up a full inventory of the country's captive pandas. But there were crucial gaps in this first attempt at an International Studbook for this species. Most notably, many of the captive-born pandas were of uncertain paternity. This was not because Chinese scientists had failed to record which male had mated with which female to produce which offspring. Rather, it had been standard practice to follow up one or more natural matings with a dose of artificial insemination using sperm from one or more of the less sexually competent males. The idea here was to improve the likelihood of fertilisation and to enhance the spread of the genes of under-represented males, but it meant that nobody could actually know which male's sperm had won out in the race to fertilise each egg.

The Biomedical Survey aimed to clear up this confusion, using the latest genetic techniques to work out which panda had fathered which offspring. Back in 1983, Stephen O'Brien of the National Cancer Institute (who we met in Chapter 2) had been called upon to carry out a similar forensic investigation on Ling-Ling's dead cub. If you remember, she was thought to have received sperm from both her long-term partner Hsing-Hsing (through a natural mating) and the brutish 'British' panda Chia-Chia (through AI). This was a full year before scientists elsewhere proposed what we now call DNA profiling or finger-printing, so O'Brien had to rely on the far less variable proteins to work out the cub's paternity. It made a paper in *Science*. 'Of the 300 proteins we examined, six showed genetic variation and these proved that Hsing-Hsing, and not Chia-Chia, was the baby's father,' he and colleagues wrote.

With O'Brien's track record in panda genetics, it made sense to bring him in on the investigation of paternity in China's captive population. Interestingly, in most of the forty-three cases where paternity was in question, the male that owned the first ejaculate (whether it was delivered by natural means or by AI) became the father. The important consequence of this exercise was that it suddenly made it possible to consider how best to manage the breeding effort in captivity.

One of the goals of those managing endangered species in captivity is to maintain 90 per cent of the population's genetic variation for a period of 100 years. It's a little arbitrary, but seems like a reasonable goal to shoot for. In spite of all the pressure the giant panda has faced, it would appear that there is still a lot of genetic diversity out there. By making projections of the number of panda births a year, an international team of researchers estimated that 'to maintain the genetic fitness of the giant panda into the future will require space and resources for the management of about 300 individuals'. But this calculation was based on everyone working together in one, big, happy cooperative family for the long-term good of the giant panda. You might be disappointed, if not altogether surprised, to learn this isn't quite what's happened.

The reasons are somewhat dispiriting. For most zoos it is necessary to make a profit, albeit not a large one, and a major source of operating costs comes from paying visitors. And with a strong and direct relationship between the number of pandas and gate receipts, it's almost inevitable that, historically, there has been intense panda rivalry between different institutions and almost no movement of pandas between them. On top of this basic urge to boast the greatest number of captive pandas, the free flow of animals has also been restricted by a degree of intellectual competition between different panda-holding institutions. Of course, panda researchers are no different from other academics in this respect – they seek to publish in the most prestigious journals, to secure ever greater research grants and expand the scale and influence of their research enterprise. But with pandas catching the eye of journal editors, funding committees and some very bright students, the normal academic rules of engagement are more exaggerated.

Finally, the movement of pandas between different institutions is further complicated by yet another layer of realpolitik. For China's network of captive pandas is not coordinated by a single government agency but by two. Some captive pandas – those housed in zoos such as the Chengdu Zoo and Beijing Zoo – come under the control of the PRC's Ministry of Construction.

Others – like those kept at the CCRCGP in the Wolong Nature Reserve – are the property of the Ministry of Forestry (or State Forestry Administration as it became known in 1998). Historically, these two federal agencies have ended up competing rather than cooperating for the benefit of the pandas. As the authors of one of the Biomedical Survey reports diplomatically put it 'there are bureaucratic obstacles to transferring animals between institutions'.

Hopefully, you can now see why being able to freeze and thaw panda sperm is so important. Not only is it much easier to courier a vial of sperm than to crate up a panda, but people are not nearly as touchy about the movement of a few billion cells as they are about the movement of a whole, crowd-pleasing animal. 'A vial of sperm just isn't as interesting to look at,' says David Wildt.

It's going to take time before these entrenched rivalries disappear completely but there are signs that it's starting to happen. The Biomedical Survey offers a case in point. When it began in 1996, this project was confined solely to the main Ministry of Construction facilities with captive pandas; it did not include the Ministry of Forestry's captive population at Wolong. That soon changed, when the Ministry of Forestry invited IUCN's Conservation Breeding Specialist Group to come in and add the Wolong pandas to the survey. This almost doubled the number of pandas under investigation, vastly strengthening the conclusions that could be drawn. By agreeing to work with the same ostensibly independent go-between – the CBSG – China's two biggest captive institutions – the Chengdu Base and the CCRCGP in Wolong – were working together.

Senior figures at both these institutions claim that such rivalries are a thing of the past. 'We are happy to work with any institutions,' confirms Zhang Zhihe of the Chengdu Base. Zhou Xiaoping, Assistant Chief Engineer at the CCRCGP gives the same assurance. 'We intend to cooperate with many institutions,' he says. 'We have cooperation with the Chengdu Base. That's no problem.' But it's also clear that there's room for more and greater cooperation.

In a report to the Giant Panda Breeding Technology Committee of China in November 2009, Zhang Zhihe called for greater effort to 'prevent the phenomenon in which institutions seek giant panda quantity while neglecting their quality'. He went on to stress the need 'to encourage the exchange and transport of individual giant pandas and sperm among different captive giant panda institutions, and to quicken the processing time of the related approval formalities'. Such changes take time.

In the meantime, there has been a complete rethinking of the way that China shares its pandas with the rest of the world. If you remember from the last chapter, the 1980s and early 1990s had been characterised by somewhat seedy 'rent-a-panda' schemes. The United States Fish and Wildlife Service (FWS) finally put a stop to this practice in 1993. Though the short-term, commercially driven loan of pandas continued elsewhere, the FWS began to forge a whole new approach to captive pandas, one that would have very important consequences for the way of the panda.

The Zoological Society of San Diego played a crucial role in this, working with the FWS on a panda loan policy that would be of real benefit to giant pandas, not just in captivity but also in the wild. San Diego Zoo had started to forge strong research links with the CCRCGP in Wolong (of which more in a moment) and Wolong began to discuss the possibility of sending pandas to San Diego on a long-term, rather than a short-term loan. Long-term loans would require trust between institutions – in this case Wolong and the Zoological Society of San Diego. Such collaboration and exchange of ideas could only be good for the scientists at both institutions and also, importantly, for the pandas. San Diego Zoo would also have the important opportunity to carry out its own programme of research on the giant pandas it received, something that would not have been possible during the era of short-term loans. Since San Diego would benefit financially, it seemed appropriate to pay the Ministry of Forestry for the privilege of having the precious animals. It turned out to be quite a bit of money – $1 million per pair per year – so it seemed appropriate too that there should be greater transparency of how these funds were spent in China. This was the kind of considered arrangement that the FWS could agree to and it granted a permit for the import of two giant pandas for a period of twelve years. In September 1996, Wolong sent a male, Shi-Shi, and a female, Bai-Yun, to San Diego on a twelve-year research loan (though the elderly, aggressive Shi-Shi was subsequently to be replaced by the keener, younger Gao-Gao).

When, in 1998, the FWS formally announced their new policy towards pandas modelled on the Wolong-San Diego loan, other US zoos were quick to follow suit. In 1999, the Chengdu Base and Zoo Atlanta in Georgia entered into an agreement that would see the loan of panda youngsters Yang-Yang and Lun-Lun for ten years. When Hsing-Hsing (who had outlived Ling-Ling) finally turned up his aged toes in Washington DC in 1999, the National Zoo paired up with Wolong to bring in female Mei-Xiang and male Tian-Tian in 2000, also for a decade-long stint. In 2003, Le-Le and Ya-Ya travelled from the Chengdu Base to Memphis Zoo under a similar agreement. Much to the delight of the North American zoo-going public, all of these couples have now reproduced.

This is of course a good thing. But the arm of the FWS loan policy has had a far greater reach. Importantly, it is a model that has now spread beyond the United States, with Chinese institutions entering into fruitful long-term research partnerships with zoos in Austria, Thailand, Japan and Australia, with others in the pipeline.

The Wolong-San Diego Zoo story is a perfect example of just how fruitful this collaboration can be. In the 1990s, while San Diego Zoo was working with the FWS on formulating the new loan policy, Donald Lindburg, then head of the behaviour division at the Zoological Society of San Diego, had started to send scientists over to China to work with their counterparts at Wolong. One of them was Mark Edwards, then a nutritionist at the San Diego Zoo. Up until that point, the animals' diet had altered very little since Chi-Chi's day in the 1960s; they were getting most of their food from a sloppy, gruel-like porridge topped up variously with eggs, bits of fruit and some vitamins. Almost as a token gesture, they were also being given some bamboo, but with all their energetic needs coming from one intense porridge hit, they showed little interest. Some interpreted this as meaning that pandas prefer porridge over bamboo, but in fact the porridge-based status quo was doing them damage, with frequent incidences of vomiting and diarrhoea, and the leading cause of death in captivity was gastrointestinal disease.

With all eyes on the pandas on long-term loan from Wolong to San Diego, it became especially important to have happy, healthy animals; and, with Edwards' input, the porridge fell off the menu and in came bundles and bundles of bamboo. The quite reasonable assumption behind this move is that it's best to feed a captive animal on the sort of food it would eat in the wild. The proportion of bamboo in a panda's diet certainly seems to have an effect on the consistency of its faeces. In fact, in panda husbandry circles there is now a 'standardised faecal grading system' that keepers use to monitor the health of their animals. At one extreme, there are faeces that are 'very loose, no form, diarrhoea, possibly blood' and these score zero. At the other extreme, there are those that are 'formed, very hard, dry, crumbly' as they are for wild pandas and these score 100. There are three categories in between. Healthy poo equals healthy panda.

As the experience with Chi-Chi had indicated, and the first serious fieldwork in the 1980s would confirm, pandas are rather picky about the bamboo species they like to eat. But captive institutions often struggle to meet these needs, so Edwards also worked on creating a special bread to deliver supplementary vitamins and minerals in a high-fibre form that matches the chemical make-up of their preferred bamboos.

All this emphasis on bamboo is quite a commitment. Pandas need to eat vast amounts of it – almost half their body weight in freshly cut stems a day – to continue to function; sourcing this quantity of fresh bamboo and the dedicated husbandry required to deliver it comes with a not inconsiderable price tag. At Schön-brunn Zoo in Vienna, to which Wolong loaned a pair of pandas in 2003, they provide their animals with a choice of two different bamboo species, cropped from a farm in France and driven in every week at an annual cost of around $200,000. On top of that, it's recommended that a panda's daily bamboo intake be delivered in at least three separate sittings; this is to prevent the stems and leaves from lying around and drying out, but such attention to detail creates a lot of extra work – and therefore expense – for the panda's human custodians. It has, however, made a vast difference to the welfare of these animals, putting an end to the vomiting, firming up the faeces and keeping the creatures more active.

In addition, the Wolong-San Diego collaboration also made significant changes to the way newborns are fed. In the early 1990s, it was still common to find hand-reared cubs receiving a cow- or yak-based formula. Not only were they struggling to digest it but they were also being weaned too early, turned away from

33. Captive-born giant panda cubs are now kept on milk (either panda and/or formula) for at least eighteen months before gradually being introduced to bamboo.

the bottle at around six months and encouraged to eat bamboo. Cubs between the ages of six and eighteen months were dying in terrible numbers, but once Wolong switched to a mixture of human formula and puppy formula, the baby pandas did much better. It was also important that the animals did not experience a sudden change of diet at six months. 'We encouraged and helped to keep the animals on formula to at least eighteen months of age,' says Edwards, now at California Polytechnic State University; cub mortality became, for the most part, a thing of the past.

In parallel with all this work on nutrition at San Diego Zoo, Lindburg went in search of a postdoctoral fellow who would work solely on panda behaviour. In the ad he circulated, there was mention only of 'working with solitary mammals in a third-world country for up to six-months a year' in order to avoid being deluged with applications from those in love with the giant panda rather than the research. Ron Swaisgood had just completed his PhD in animal behaviour at the University of California, Davis. He had studied the predator-prey dynamics between ground squirrels and rattlesnakes. It had all been very interesting but he was after something more applied when he came across Lindburg's advert. Swaisgood put himself forward and it was only during his interview that he learned of the study species. 'When I first heard it was pandas I was frankly a little bit doubtful whether I would be able to do research of the quality I had come to expect.' Where were there enough pandas to produce meaningful scientific results, he wondered. The answer, Lindburg told him, was the CCRCGP in Wolong.

So it was that Swaisgood first went to check out this mountainous refuge in 1995 and then to begin his work in 1996. 'At that time, there were about twenty-five pandas at Wolong and they were having about one or two cubs born and surviving each year,' recalls Swaisgood. 'I went over there with the goal of trying to work with them to conduct research and alter their management husbandry practices to promote natural mating.'

A stream of evidence was beginning to reveal just how important the surroundings of a captive animal could be, not only for its welfare but also for its reproduction. As usual, it was lab rats that paved the way, with experiments showing that animals with more to do end up with more developed brains and display a greater range of behaviours than rats kept in impoverished captive environments. In addition, the more dismal the captive conditions, the more likely the animal is to exhibit what's called 'stereotypy'. We've all seen it: the elephant shifting its weight from foot to foot and swinging its trunk like a metronome; the tiger pacing backwards and forwards, backwards and forwards, weathering away a deep track in the mud; the polar bear on its haunches slowly rocking its head.

Zoo people obviously took note and began to provide more 'environmental enrichment', an animal husbandry principle that 'seeks to enhance the quality of captive animal care by identifying and providing environmental stimuli necessary for optimal psychological and physiological well-being'. What was lacking, however, was real data on the consequences of enrichment for the animals and it was this that Swaisgood and his colleagues at Wolong sought to address.

The difficulty, of course, is that you can't just ask an animal how it feels about the ball you've tossed into its enclosure. Actually, you can ask but it's unlikely to answer. So you have to come up with indirect ways to measure the animal's well-being. Though it might not satisfy a philosopher, there is intuitive appeal to the idea that an animal that does not display stereotypy, exhibits lots of natural behaviour and occasionally breeds is going to be happier than one that rocks back and forth, has none of the behavioural range of its wild counterparts and cannot be coaxed to have babies. By measuring well-being in lots of different ways, Swaisgood is confident that it's possible to gauge how contented a captive animal is with its surroundings.

So the staff began to shake up the way that the pandas were kept at Wolong, much as the National Zoo had done with Hsing-Hsing and Ling-Ling in the 1980s. The pandas got larger enclosures, with different kinds of trees, shrubs and terrain. Swaisgood and friends tried introducing objects, such as a plastic ball, a bag of hay or an ice 'fruiticle', and then set about recording their reactions. As soon as the pandas noticed the enrichment item, they almost invariably approached, sometimes cautiously, to investigate. Once they'd gained confidence, they rolled onto their back and balanced the object on their paws before starting to play, biting, rolling, shaking, pursuing it. The pandas didn't seem to tire with these objects, even on seeing them for the fifteenth time. Importantly, they were more active and less inclined to stereotypy than a group of control pandas left to their unenriched lives.

In addition, the researchers took the opportunity to reflect on what had been learned about wild pandas from the China-WWF project in Sichuan, and Pan Wenshi's research in Shaanxi. How did mating in the wild differ from the set-up being offered to captive pandas? One thing stood out. The panda, living an intensely solitary life for most of the year, suddenly turned intensely social when it came to mating, with males drawn towards fertile females like moths to a lamp. How did they do it? Everything pointed at odour. So the Wolong-San Diego team set about devising a series of brilliant experiments that began to reveal just how rich is the giant panda's olfactory world.

One of the first things to do was to confirm that pandas were able to distinguish between odours from different individuals. To do this, the researchers collected odours on small blocks of fir tree (the variety that appears to be the preferred scent post of wild pandas). For a male, this meant rubbing it on known scent-marking sites within his compound and for females it meant dragging the fir block through a puddle of her urine. Then, over five consecutive days, the researchers used these blocks to expose one panda to the scent of another. So imagine one particular panda, let's call it A-A, encountering the smell of another, let's call it B-B. At first, Panda A-A shows interest in the whiff of Panda B-B but this falls away as the novelty wears off. Then, on the sixth day, Panda A-A finds itself confronted with two boards, one from the same old Panda B-B but the other bearing the novel, surprise smell of Panda C-C. The sudden and striking interest in the new smell is obvious. So pandas can distinguish between the smells of different individuals. But what else might they be able to work out from the aromatic scent posts so common in the panda's natural habitat?

In a follow-up study, the researchers divided up their pandas into three groups – males, non-fertile females and fertile females – and then performed the logistically challenging task of taking a resident panda from its pen, introducing a visitor for half an hour before returning the owner to its rightful home. By recording the visitor's response to the resident's smells and then the resident's reaction to the intruder's pongy deposits, the researchers made some important discoveries. Males encountering the smell of another male moved into territorial mode but they showed much greater interest in female odours and called out more readily if these were fertile. When fertile females came across male odours, they were similarly vocal, over and above the interest they showed in female smells. Clearly, these pandas were in their communication zone and the researchers reached the following punchy conclusion: 'This study strongly implies that chemical communication may be of critical importance for appropriate behavioural management for captive propagation of the species.'

By the time this study was published in 2000, the Wolong CCRCGP had already taken these findings and converted them into practice. The staff would watch out for signs that a particular female was approaching oestrus, supplementing their behavioural observations with regular analysis of the hormone levels in her urine. As soon as it became apparent that she was entering her fertile phase, they would move her into an enclosure adjacent to a target male. By using a carefully scented block as an olfactory

34. A panda cub tussles with a stem of bamboo at the Ya'an Bifengxia Base of China Conservation and Research Center for the Giant Panda, Wolong's sister base established in 2003.

go-between or through wholescale pen swaps, the Wolong keepers began to prepare the pair for their sexual encounter. Their meeting, when it happened, was no longer characterised by the kind of antagonistic behaviour that had stymied the relationship between Chi-Chi and An-An. 'Over time we went from less than a third of animals mating naturally to over 90 per cent mating naturally,' says Swaisgood. This development resulted in the explosion of Wolong's captive population, from just twenty-five individuals in 1995 to more than seventy a few years later. Zhou Xiaoping, Assistant Chief Engineer at Wolong's CCRCGP, is in no doubt that this tremendous success is mainly due to these management changes. 'If you do not allow olfactory communication, you cannot get the pandas to breed,' he says.

The Wolong-San Diego Zoo alliance carried out some more very cunning experiments on olfaction that are well worth a short digression. These revealed that pandas consistently show more interest in odours from adult pandas than in those from sub-adult pandas, suggesting that the animals could be using smells to work out age, reproductive condition and maybe even social dominance. Building on this idea, the same researchers tested an intriguing hypothesis: that the different postures the panda assumes to make its mark might add a whole layer of important information to the olfactory cues.

British zoologist Desmond Morris had observed Chi-Chi and An-An adopting different marking postures and Devra Kleiman, studying the behaviour of the Nixon pandas in Washington DC, had described them in detail. She gave them pretty self-explanatory names: squat, reverse, legcock and handstand. This last posture – the handstand – is particularly interesting. Only the Washington male Hsing-Hsing had performed this extraordinary feat and George Schaller and his colleagues working in the wild had noticed that pandas had sometimes left their mark at more than a metre off the ground.

Swaisgood and his colleagues wanted to explore the significance of the handstand and other postures. They began by making some interesting observations and found that all pandas will use the squat but it's most common in females and sub-adults. It's mainly adult pandas that go in for the reverse and legcock, though males seemed to be more keen on cocking legs than females. Finally, it's only males that do the handstand and they are not using it to smear their bottom on the scent post but to sprinkle it with urine. The researchers designed an experiment to find out how pandas of different ages and sex react to scent marks posted by adopting different postures. What was clear was that all pandas show more interest in high than low odours, investigating them for longer and performing the flehmen response more frequently, a curling of the upper lip that mammals use when investigating smells (picture a horse). This and other evidence led them to the conclusion that the height at which scents are posted may reveal key information about the social rank of the panda doing the posting. So in the case of handstands, for example, the higher up a tree a male can wee, the bigger and tougher he's likely to be.

With smells coming to the fore as the panda's communication modus operandi, chemists began to take a look at the molecular make-up of these secretions and excretions and identified almost 1,000 different compounds. There were striking differences between the composition of male and female odours, which lends reassuring weight to the idea that pandas can identify sex from smell. More than that, each individual had a pretty unique chemical signature such that given a sample at random, the researchers could, in the majority of cases, identify the individual it had come from. Though they needed a sophisticated analytical tool to do this – gas chromatography-mass spectrometry – pandas have been living with these smells for many millions of years so have, one imagines, evolved the ability to make sense of them.

In a lovely bit of lateral thinking, the same scientists then set about swabbing down a panda's body to see if the mix of volatile chemicals varied from place to place. The resulting olfactory map is quite remarkable. 'A panda's forearms, legs and back don't carry many smelly messages,' says Lee Hagey, an analytical chemist at the Zoological Society of San Diego. Their ears, however, are heavily scented with urine, as are the undersides of their forepaws, which presumably act to ferry the stuff from their genitals to their ears. Intriguingly, the black rings around a panda's eyes, which get rubbed a lot, have a completely unique smell and are completely free of urine. This is achieved by the panda being careful to use the back of a paw rather than the urine-scented underside to rub its eyes. 'The body of the giant panda is shown to be a kaleidoscope of scent patches and zones, each with a unique chemical make-up,' wrote Hagey and his fellow researcher. They went on to propose that the urine-scented ears act like miniature beacons, allowing these secretive smells to be caught by, and spread on, the wind.

The collaboration between the Chengdu Base and Zoo Atlanta is another great example of the value of the long-term research loan. While olfaction has been a big focus for the Wolong-San Diego pairing, the Chengdu Base-Zoo Atlanta partnership has paid particular interest in the relationship between a mother and her cub. This is a somewhat sensitive field of research because the standard captive practice in China has always been to separate a mother from her cub at six months in the drive to increase the production of baby pandas. Without the suckling stimulus, the mothers stop producing milk and their bodies prepare again for another reproductive cycle. But as discovered from the studies on wild animals, panda cubs usually remain with their mothers for at least eighteen and sometimes as long as thirty months, so female pandas would normally give birth every other year rather than every year as is encouraged by the captive set-up. While pooling captive cubs into a swooningly cute creche-type arrangement at the age of just six months might be good for the quantity of pandas, what does it do for their quality?

The Chengdu Base-Atlanta collaboration is beginning to gather evidence that these early years of mother-cub bonding are crucial for the development of well-rounded, well-adjusted adult pandas. For several years now, the researchers have been observing cubs reared in different situations, some whisked away from their mothers before reaching six months and others that stayed with them for more than a year. This is still work in progress but it has already emerged that mother-reared cubs are more active than cubs separated at six months; they spend longer fiddling with bamboo, perhaps picking up important feeding tips from their mothers, and they spend more time climbing and tumbling off objects, useful life skills for a creature that spends a lot of time lolling around in the forks of trees. The cubs separated before six months spent more time sitting still, which doesn't sound quite right. 'Mothers seem to be prodding the cubs into action,' says Rebecca Snyder, curator of mammals at Zoo Atlanta and lead author of this study. 'When the cubs find themselves in a creche amongst their peers, there are no mothers to provide this stimulation,' she says.

Snyder and her colleagues have also observed an interesting difference between the sexes. Amongst those cubs kept with their mothers for a full year, male youngsters spent more time play-fighting with their mothers than did females. There is a suspicion that denying males the opportunity to romp with their mothers might help account for the difficulty that captive-born males appear to have when it comes to breeding. As the researchers continue to monitor these pandas through their reproductive years, they should be able to work out if there are any long-term consequences of early weaning on sexual behaviour. This would help convince others of the importance of the pair bond. 'We would like to move towards a more natural arrangement for young pandas,' says Zhang Zhihe, director of the Chengdu Base.

The Chengdu-Atlanta collaboration has also produced other findings, most recently in the field of panda vocalisation. If you remember, Gustav Peters had made some early sound recordings from the Nixon pandas and the China-WWF project had documented these same calls in the wild. But by dissecting, manipulating and playing back these sounds, researchers have started to work out what sort of information they contain. Unsurprisingly perhaps, the acoustic structure of a call is highly distinctive from one panda to the next. More surprising is the observation that there appears to be a strongly heritable component to these calls, with more related pandas bleating out sounds with more similar physical features. 'So pandas could be using calls at close range to assess genetic relatedness,' says Ben Charlton, a sound expert brought in by Zoo Atlanta to lead this study.

In a series of experiments that mirrored those Ron Swaisgood and colleagues carried out on olfaction at Wolong, Charlton and friends confirmed that pandas should be able to infer information on sex, age, size and female fertility solely on the basis of these vocalisations. 'They are rich in information and more complex compared to most other mammals,' says Charlton. And although olfaction is probably the panda's main mode of communication, these jittery calls are perfect for short-range communication in a complex forest system. 'In the actual environment, even in quite dense bamboo, you can make out the frequency contour of these calls over distances of up to 40 metres,' he says. Not only are these discoveries profoundly interesting, but they could, at some stage, be used to further enrich the lives of captive pandas.

As we've examined panda smells and sounds, it's probably only fair to take a quick look at panda vision. The first work in this area was carried out on the pandas on loan to Zoo Atlanta. The keepers trained the pair to push on a system of plastic pipes in response to a range of variously coloured rectangles. Their reaction to these different stimuli indicates that pandas can see in some kind of colour, which tallies with the findings from Chi-Chi's right eyeball more than thirty years earlier.

A more ambitious study has been carried out on the pair of pandas at Schönbrunn Zoo in Vienna, Austria. For her PhD, zoologist Eveline Dungl had studied the portraits of scores of different pandas, working out (amongst other things) the shape and area of the black spot around each animal's eye. Not only did she find that there were considerable differences between the eyespots of different individuals, but she could distinguish between males and females on the basis of the angle between the two patches; males with their broader muzzles have a wider angle between their eyespots than do females. Were pandas able to do the same, with females maybe even assessing the fitness of potential mates? Using titbits to train her pandas to respond to eye-patch-like images, Dungl found that the pandas could discriminate between all manner of configurations and remember preferences for at least a year. 'The Schönbrunn pandas make it clear that panda vision could be far more important and that these animals are far smarter and appreciate mental stimulation more than most people had imagined,' says Dungl.

This foray into the world of panda research is just a taster but, hopefully, gives an idea of the intellectual gains that the study of captive pandas has yielded. It would be impossible to glean such insights from wild pandas alone, so this flood of insights has to be one of the most persuasive reasons for keeping pandas in captivity. There are plenty of others that might be put forward. It's an inescapable fact that people want to see pandas but that, owing to their rarity, their extreme environment and their talent for slipping out of sight, this is all but impossible in the wild, so is made feasible through zoos and dedicated institutions like the Chengdu Base and the Wolong CCRCGP. There, these amazing creatures can act as ambassadors, 'commanding emissaries for their wild counterparts and a tangible reminder of why so much effort needs to be directed at saving wild places'. Pandas, though they may not know it, are brilliant educational tools, connecting young and old alike with nature and perhaps even with science. All this human interest means that where there are captive pandas, there will be money. This has not always brought out the best in people, but if channelled into the right places it could do. The fact that the captive population is now self-sustaining may be seen as insurance against extinction in the wild. This, however, assumes that the reintroduction of giant pandas into the wild is possible. Currently, it is not. This is something for the future, and it is to the future that we now turn.

Into the future

Reintroduction has been on the horizon for as long as there have been captive pandas, but their successful return to the wild is still years, if not decades, away.

Reintroduction is more likely to succeed with some species than with others. Here are three simplified general rules. Plant-eaters are good as they don't have to chase down their prey; meat-eaters are not so good because it's a lot of work to get a captive up to predatory speed. That said, things can be difficult for a plant-eater that has lots of natural predators: the fewer the better. Finally, reintroduction of social animals is especially tricky because of the leap that captives must make as they move into a wild environment that is relatively complex; so solitary animals would seem more suitable candidates for returning to the wild.

On the face of it, then, the giant panda has a lot going for it. As long as it's released into good panda habitat, its bamboo food source should be everywhere. It does not need to seek out its prey, it just has to sit down and munch. The giant proportions and strong bite of the panda also mean that there are few creatures prepared to take it on. Furthermore, it's a solitary beast for most of the year. It seems likely that reintroducing the giant panda back into the wild has a greater chance of success than it does for many other captive species.

Ruth Harkness, remember, seems to have successfully returned her third and final panda to the forest after several months of captivity. During the China-WWF project in the 1980s, there were further anecdotal episodes suggesting that releasing pandas back to the wild might work. A male panda, which ended up being taken into captivity at Wolong to help fill the newly constructed enclosures, spent almost a year there before campaigning by George Schaller and others managed to secure his release. He survived in the wild, tracked by the China-WWF team for at least another eighteen months, and probably longer. Another panda, Zhen-Zhen, who paid regular, disruptive visits to the researchers' camp (coaxed in by treats laid by a mischievous field assistant) ended up being taken into captivity for several months. When released onto a slope some 10 miles from her old haunts above the camp, she seemed to settle back into her wild life with ease. But these examples all involve wild-born pandas and this probably makes quite a difference. How would captive-born pandas fare upon release?

The 1989 National Conservation Management Plan for the Giant Panda recommended several experimental trials, most of them on young pandas, that would pave the way for future reintroductions of captive-born individuals to the wild. But a report, published in 1991, concluded that 'it would be inappropriate to release captive pandas'. Further meetings convened in China in 1997 and San Diego in 2000 reached much the same conclusion, with the authors of the 2000 report pronouncing that 'a full-scale release program for giant pandas cannot be recommended at this time'.

This caution seems eminently sensible. The reintroduction of animals from captivity into the wild is a very young science, and one that has yet to prove itself. There have been hundreds of attempts to reintroduce species from captivity and most of them fail. There are many reasons for this, but there are three really important ingredients if reintroduction is to stand a chance of success. You must be sure that reintroduction makes biological sense; if it does, you can then begin training the animal for its return to the wild, but you should only do so if you have dealt with any threats to its existence in the wild. If you forget to tick any one of these boxes, you are virtually guaranteed to fail.

Let's start with the question of whether reintroduction makes biological sense. Though we have learned masses about wild pandas over the last thirty years, there are so many gaps in our knowledge that it would be a leap of faith to claim that investing in reintroduction is going to be money well spent. You might be surprised to learn, for example, that there is still great uncertainty over the total number of pandas in the wild and if you don't know what's out there, how are you going to judge the success or otherwise of an reintroduction effort?

How, after all this time and all this work, could this be? The answer, as those Westerners that came to hunt them discovered, is that pandas are incredibly elusive beasts. From 1968 to 1969, the Giant Panda Expedition began to count pandas but only in a few specific regions. The first attempt to put a figure on the giant panda population size as a whole began in 1974, in the throes of the Cultural Revolution. Incredibly, it's thought that some 3,000 people took part in this effort, with locally established teams wandering through suitable habitat estimating numbers as they went. They did this on the basis of footprints and the occasional sightings of actual animals. Officially, this First National Survey reported that there were around 1,000 to 1,100 pandas surviving, though this is almost certainly an underestimate. Yong Yange, a former director of the Panda Biodiversity Research Center in the Foping Nature Reserve in the Qinling Mountains, remembers the procedure in the 1970s. 'We were mainly trying to find out where pandas lived,' he told WWF China in an interview conducted a few years ago. 'So we went around with notepads and asked farmers and hunters where they had seen pandas. There wasn't much technology involved. Sometimes farmers would joke and tell us they saw eight pandas, but that for more money they could find 28!'

This flexible approach to numbers corresponds with the experience of John MacKinnon, who arrived in Beijing as WWF's chief scientific advisor in China in 1987 and is currently working as a technical expert on the EU-China Biodiversity Programme. One of the first things he did was to request the raw data from the 1970s survey and he found that, according to the county-by-county breakdown, there were almost 4,000 pandas in Sichuan alone, roughly four times the figure announced to the outside world. MacKinnon politely queried this discrepancy. 'They just looked at me like I was an idiot,' he says. One set of numbers was being used to show how important each province was in the panda programme and the other to alert the world to the species' plight. 'They were surprised that I was so naive as to imagine that numbers should add up.'

It made sense, therefore, to carry out a new, more rigorous survey and between 1985 and 1988, a joint China-WWF team of thirty-five people moved methodically from one county to the next. Their mission was to work out the distribution of pandas, estimate numbers but also to collect data on the forest, the bamboo and the people. The figure they came up with was 1,120 plus or minus 240. There was a slight problem here. A straight comparison from the first to the second survey would suggest that panda numbers were going up, whereas everything indicated the opposite. 'The range had shrunk and the bamboo area had shrunk and the number of bamboo patches had shrunk,' says MacKinnon. At the very least, however, the second survey would serve as a useful benchmark against which to measure future trends.

Wind forward another decade and it was time for another survey, carried out between 1998 and 2001 and also a collaboration between China's State Forestry Administration and WWF. Yet more data entered the picture. Using photographs taken from the air or from space, it was possible to get a much more reliable overview of panda habitat and its increasingly fragmented state. In addition, the survey teams began to collect faeces for subsequent laboratory analysis. In the China-WWF project in Wolong, researchers had discovered that they could distinguish between infants, sub-adults and adult pandas on the basis of the length of bamboo fragments in a faecal deposit; the bigger the fragment, the bigger the bite, the bigger the panda. In the Qinling Mountains, Pan Wenshi and colleagues had taken this further, using the length of faecal fragments to help infer population size. The survey team used this same approach in an effort to link individual poos to individual pandas. Though not an exact science, measuring the length of bamboo bits inside panda droppings could indicate whether several piles of faeces lying nearby had come from just one or more pandas. These are the sorts of dedicated lengths to which you must go when the species is as shifty as the giant panda. This Third National Survey managed to collect almost 3,800 scats, which were separated into 1,596 pandas. The apparent increase on the earlier surveys was thought to be down to this tighter methodology rather than a real boost in panda numbers.

Though this is the latest and most accurate estimate, the picture is likely to change once more as even newer technologies are brought to bear upon the population question. Since the late 1990s, the study of DNA contained in faeces – or molecular scatology as it's technically known – has proved a brilliant way to assess population numbers of rare and elusive creatures. It can also reveal the sex ratio of the population and, if the researchers chance upon more than one sample from the same animal, they can begin to build up a picture of the animal movement. As the cost of such genetic investigations continues to plummet, it seems increasingly likely that this technology will be used in the next survey of panda numbers. Indeed, an international team of researchers has already used molecular scatology to estimate the number of pandas in the Wanglang Nature Reserve in the north of Sichuan.

Here, the First National Survey had estimated a population size of 196 pandas. By the 1980s, when the Second National Survey came out, numbers had appeared to have crashed to just nineteen, rising slightly to twenty-seven in the Third National Survey. Just a few years later, however, analysis of DNA extracted from an exhaustive collection of panda faeces from Wanglang seemed to suggest that there were at least sixty-six animals out there, divided into roughly equal numbers of males and females. Importantly, they found that in many instances, neighbouring faeces that would have been evidence for one panda under the old 'bite-size technique' had in fact come from two different animals. It was not that the population of pandas had grown but that even the Third National Survey had underestimated numbers. If this was a systematic underestimate that applied to the giant panda's entire range, they concluded that 'there may be as many as 2,500–3,000 giant pandas in the wild'.

As is par for the panda course, this study caused a bit of a stink amongst other researchers uncomfortable with the notion that the findings in one reserve would necessarily apply to the entire population. 'This is a poor assumption,' wrote David Garshelis and colleagues in a stinging critique that laid into the methodology of the Wanglang study. The Wanglang authors fought back with a resolute defence of their methods and stressed again the potential of their approach to improve on existing estimates of panda numbers. The Third National Survey did not include babies, which should make up about 20 per cent of the population, says Wei Fuwen, director of the Key Lab of Animal Ecology and Conservation Biology at the Chinese Academy of Sciences' Institute of Zoology, and the senior author on the Wanglang paper. 'We think our prediction is reasonable,' he says.

So this, at the time of writing, is the somewhat unsatisfactory position we are in: we can't really make many concrete statements about how panda numbers have changed over the last forty years and we cannot yet be sure how many pandas we still have. If you don't know how many pandas there are in the wild, you can't be sure that you need to add more or whether the population is able to absorb another individual, and there is no way of gauging the impact of your noble intervention on the panda population. Under these uncertain circumstances, reintroduction of pandas is going to achieve very little. Worse still, it could be harmful: 'there is a potential danger to both wild populations and the animals released in the form of disease transmission and difficulties with social interaction,' noted the authors of the 2000 report. As you are about to discover, that turned out to be a pretty prescient statement.

Although there remain many questions about the very idea of reintroduction, the 2000 report acknowledged that there might nevertheless soon be enough pandas in captivity 'to use some individuals for an experimental release program that is designed to provide information needed for the planning of future reintroductions'. This would tick the box for the second of the three requirements for successful reintroduction: the appropriate preparation of an animal for release.

By the time the panel report was printed in 2004, the China Conservation and Research Center for the Giant Panda (CCRCGP) in Wolong had started making plans for just such a

35. There was great excitement surrounding the reintroduction of the first giant panda to the wild in 2006. Within a year, however, the male Xiang-Xiang was found dead, most probably attacked by a resident male into whose territory he wandered.

reintroduction. They identified an individual to receive training, a young male called Xiang-Xiang. He had been born at the centre in 2001 and appeared fit and healthy; from 2003 onwards, the Wolong staff began to prepare him for a life without humans, gradually increasing the size of his enclosures and his dependence on wild-growing bamboo as a food source. 'We thought that three years of training was enough for him,' says Zhou Xiaoping, assistant chief engineer of the CCRCGP.

So a date was set for Xiang-Xiang's release. On 28 April 2006, several dignitaries were present as the grille to his crate was lifted and he ambled off up the slope carrying a collar that would transmit his GPS coordinates to the researchers back at the Wolong CCRCGP. But in early 2007, his signal went dead. Some forty days later, on 19 February 2007, a team discovered his corpse lying in the snow. It's hard – indeed impossible – to know exactly what happened to Xiang-Xiang but the Wolong staff, after much soul-searching, reached the conclusion that it had not been enough to focus on Xiang-Xiang's foraging skills. His injuries – broken ribs and damaged organs – were consistent with him getting into a scrap with one or more other males, an experience that his captive lifestyle had not prepared him for. This story, though tragic, has resulted in a more cautious approach in the reintroduction ethic. 'Next time, we will consider many, many more factors,' says Zhou Xiaoping.

So when it comes, what will the next reintroduction look like? One lesson learned from the Xiang-Xiang episode is that the animal that's chosen should not be male. There is widespread agreement that a female is going to be subject to less aggression and be accepted more readily by wild pandas. There are several variants on this basic theme, which all stress the importance of a panda's early years for its development. One is to allow a mother to give birth in a large, naturalistic enclosure where her offspring has only rare encounters with humans and then, when the infant, providing it's a female, is old enough, set it free. Another is to release a female with her young cub, hoping that both will integrate well into the wild. There is even talk of releasing a pregnant female so that her offspring, when it's born, will have had no human contact at all. 'We will find a way,' says Zhou. 'We will make it happen.' A research programme currently underway at Wolong will bring in valuable data regarding the movements and behaviour of captive-born pandas as they are prepared for release into the wild.

All this sounds quite promising, except that we are a long, long way from meeting the third criterion for successful reintroduction: even with sound biological justification for going ahead and the methods for doing so perfected, reintroduction is unlikely to contribute much to panda conservation unless the pressures on the wild population can be eased. As the editors of *Giant Pandas: Biology and Conservation* concluded in 2004, the captive population plays 'at best a supportive role' to the overall conservation effort.

It is also true, however, that, reintroducing one or more of the hundreds of giant pandas in captivity is such a lovely idea and would have such immense popular appeal that it is an inevitable project. But it is hard to see it as anything other than a distraction from what really matters: protecting wild pandas. It is this rather tricky subject to which we must now devote most of what remains of this book.

There is no doubt that China has made extraordinary leaps and bounds since the creation of the Wanglang National Reserve in the 1960s, the first protected area dedicated to pandas. As we have already learned, the State Forestry Administration has added more than sixty panda reserves. Describing this transition in just two sentences makes it sound easy, but changing the pattern of land use in such a radical manner takes a lot of courage, money and problem-solving nous. The story of how one reserve came into existence will serve as a neat example of what is involved.

You'll recall that when Pan Wenshi set up his long-term research project in the Qinling Mountains in Shaanxi he received the cold shoulder from the local Ministry of Forestry and ended up working in forests controlled by a state-owned logging company, the Changqing Forest Bureau. This turned out to be something of a blessing, says Lü Zhi, Pan's first graduate student

36. Model mother Jiao-Jiao with one of many cubs she successfully reared in Changqing. Tragically, this star panda and her seventh offspring were both taken into captivity at the Louguantai Forest Park near the city of Xi'an in March 2001, where they died a few years later.

and his natural heir at the Center for Nature and Society at Peking University. 'It gave us the chance to observe the change in logging over time,' she says. 'If we had been in a Nature Reserve, we would not have seen with our own eyes what was going on.'

What *was* going on? In the early 1990s, the pressures on the forests began to change. Up until then, the researchers had managed to live amicably alongside those working for the state-owned Changqing Forestry Bureau. But as free-market reforms began to spread across China, the loggers suddenly had an incentive to scale up their operation, clear-cutting vast swathes of forest to realise ever greater profits. As the zoologists followed their star female Jiao-Jiao and other radio-tracked pandas, they became increasingly aware of the threat these changes were posing for the pandas and, of course, for their work. 'I had to negotiate with the timber company not to cut trees where Jiao-Jiao was about to give birth,' remembers Lü. She won a reprise for the panda, but it was only temporary. 'They said they'd be back the following year.'

Confronted with this impossible situation, the researchers began to voice their concerns to officials at various levels of government. At first, nobody listened. But at a panda conference in 1993, Pan's team penned a letter that spelt out the likely consequences of the ongoing logging for their pandas. Their recommendation, endorsed with the signatures of twenty-eight international scientists, was to create a new panda reserve and insist on a blanket logging ban within it. It was a bold proposal. Bolder still, they sent it to China's president Jiang Zemin and Premier Li Peng. To their surprise, the plan was approved and the central government allocated $8 million to relocate the several thousand employees of the Changqing Forestry Bureau and help find them work elsewhere. In 1995, with a further $4.5 million from the World Bank's Global Environmental Facility, the Changqing Nature Reserve was born. It was great news for Jiao-Jiao and her fellow pandas. 'We could not have asked for more,' wrote Pan.

When Lü returned several years later, she found that the logging camp that she'd lived in for more than a decade had been transformed into the field station for the new reserve. 'The logging roads in the side valleys were overgrown with vegetation. On land that had been clear-cut only a few years earlier, Chinese birch trees and bamboo had once again taken root, and pandas had begun to make occasional visits,' she wrote.

This transformation in Changqing was a sign of things to come, for China would soon set in motion two of the most ambitious ecological restoration projects ever attempted anywhere in the world. In 1997, the Yellow River basin experienced a devastating drought for more than half the year. Then, in the summer of 1998, massive rainfall caused devastating flooding of the Yangtze basin. Thousands of people died, and hundreds of thousands found themselves homeless, their world swept away by the waters. The damage and flood-control measures are thought to have cost tens of billions of dollars.

The finger of blame pointed firmly at decades of deforestation. Without trees to sponge up rainwater, the mountains channelled it directly into rivers. The Chinese government responded immediately with two initiatives of extraordinary scale: the Natural Forest Protection Program (NFPP), launched in 1998; and the Sloping Land Conversion Program (SLCP), started the following year. The NFPP aimed to put in place new and tougher measures for the protection of natural forests. One of its more specific aims was to put a stop to all commercial logging in the upper reaches of the Yellow and Yangzte Rivers by 2000. The SCLP, more commonly known as the 'Grain for Green' policy, aimed to convert crops located on steep slopes to grass and forest. In 1999, pilot projects started in Sichuan, Gansu and Shaanxi, the three provinces that still have wild pandas, and in 2003 the initiative was rolled out nationwide.

So how have they done? These are very big social changes to be taking on and they come at a price. From 1998 to 2000, the Chinese government invested $2.69 billion in the NFPP, committing an additional $11.63 billion to take the program up to 2010, much of this money spent on retiring, resettling and retraining forestry workers. One estimate suggests that the government will have sunk around $40 billion into Grain for Green over the same period, much of this money being used as direct compensation to farmers for the crops they would otherwise have produced.

As in the Changqing Reserve, there has been a dramatic change in direction, with the number of people employed in forest management surging in the space of a few years. Before the logging ban, those who relied upon logging for a living were reluctant to acknowledge that the forests they worked were home to pandas. It would have made their livelihoods difficult or impossible. With the logging ban, however, pandas suddenly became an asset, as the same workers looked for other sources of income. This helps explain how the number of protected areas dedicated to giant pandas leapt from around twenty before the logging ban to more than sixty today, with several more being added every year.

In 2006, UNESCO acknowledged the World Heritage Status of a huge swathe of panda habitat. The Sichuan Giant Panda Sanctuaries occupies almost 1 million hectares of forest in the Qionglai Mountains and nearby Jiajin Mountains. It includes seven nature reserves, nine scenic parks and is the largest contiguous area of panda habitat that remains, taking in around 30 per cent of the wild population. In just over half the area – the core zone – there is to be minimal human activity: 'Within this zone, no logging, hunting, burning, collection of medicinal plants, habitation, mines and industries will be permitted.' In the surrounding buffer zone, human activity is permitted but under strict limitations.

Of course, it is not just pandas that are protected here. With more than 5,000 plant species – about the same number as you'll find in France, a country some fifty times the area of this chunk of Chinese forest – the Sichuan Giant Panda Sanctuaries World

Heritage Site is the richest botanical treasure trove anywhere outside the tropics. That is not to mention the countless fascinating mammals, birds and other less conspicuous creatures that live there, many of them found nowhere else on earth.

The NFPP, Grain for Green and the Sichuan Giant Panda Sanctuaries World Heritage Site are all examples of China's increasingly green credentials. Indeed, for those in the West inclined to be critical of China, here are a few cautionary facts. With its absolutely massive population (1.33 billion or one-fifth of the world's population) it's obvious that China should have a massive impact on the world. Yet its one-child policy, for all the uncomfortable ethical questions it raises and the painful sacrifice made by millions of Chinese families, means that China's annual percentage growth rate is low relative to the global average (0.49 per cent versus 1.13 per cent). Even with a population more than four times that of the United States (1.3 billion versus 0.3 billion), China's ecological footprint is still less than that of the US (2,456 million global hectares versus 2,730 million global hectares). In 2009, China invested far more than any other country in the clean energy industry – $34.6 billion or 0.39 per cent of its gross domestic product compared to the United States' $18.6 billion or 0.13 per cent of GDP. When it comes to reforestation, China punches way above its numerical and geographical weight, with massive initiatives like the NFPP and SLCP helping seed some 4 million hectares of forest every year, which is probably more tree planting than the rest of the world put together.

That said, China's population is still on the increase and, as astute readers will have already clocked, 0.49 per cent of 1.3 billion is a fair few people – about 6 million, in fact, which is like China annexing a major capital city every year. What's more, China's economy is expanding at an extraordinary pace; since the 1970s it has been growing at around 10 per cent year-on-year. In the global GDP rankings, China still lags in second place behind the United States ($8,791 billion versus $14,260 billion in 2009) but if these economies continue to change at their current rates, China will have become top economic dog by 2014. If that happens, it is inevitable that its ecological footprint will also spread, placing ever greater pressure on the natural world.

Even if China is somehow able to protect its own natural resources, the pressure will just be felt elsewhere. The NFPP or logging ban illustrates this nicely. Through this policy, China may have been able to afford some protection for its forests, but it still has to get its wood from somewhere. Before the ban came into force in 1998, China was importing around 4 million square metres of timber every year. Since the logging ban, however, this figure has sky-rocketed. A 2004 report for WWF predicted that by 2010 China would be importing a staggering 125 million square metres of wood to meet its expanding development needs. While this may bring short-term economic benefits for other nations, notably Russia, Indonesia and Malaysia, you have to worry about the long-term future of their forests.

So what to do? Over the last twenty years, conservationists have come to the conclusion that if we are to contain the impact that humans have on nature, we need to study the relationship between humans and nature (rather than just nature itself). Only then can we arrive at sensible, evidence-based management decisions. One research group that understands this more than most is the Center for Systems Integration and Sustainability at Michigan State University. Since the 1990s, it has studied the relationship between humans, forests and pandas in the Wolong Nature Reserve and has made some very important and sometimes unsettling findings.

Of all China's reserves, Wolong has probably received more funds, stimulated more research effort and generated more data than any other. If the giant panda is a flagship for the zoological world, Wolong is a flagship for protected areas. As there are people living inside it, it's also a good place to study the impact of humans on nature. The Michigan State researchers have been pulling together many different streams of data, such as that on forest cover gleaned from aerial and satellite photos past and present; on-the-ground observations of bamboo distribution; evidence of pandas from faecal deposits; and government stats on human population size, one-to-one interviews and surveys of entire households within the reserve.

By studying aerial snapshots taken of the region in 1965, 1974 and 1997, it is possible to see what impact the formal creation of the reserve in 1975 had on panda habitat. Not only had the quality and quantity of panda habitat continued to decline between 1974 and 1997, but the rate of habitat loss and fragmentation had actually increased to levels that were similar or even higher than those outside the reserve. The reason for this appears to be the local human population, which increased by 70 per cent over that same period, and the number of households, which had more than doubled.

By collecting data on human demography and behaviour, the forest and its suitability for pandas, the researchers have been able to make several observations that should help the Chinese government make informed decisions about how to undertake conservation in such a tricky situation. The collection of wood for cooking and heating, for example, has a major impact on panda habitat in Wolong and in 1984, the reserve issued a set of regulations intended to minimise this impact. Unfortunately, although the awareness of these regulations was high (almost 70 per cent of households knew about at least one of the regulations), they had

had only a modest impact on behaviour (with over half of those who knew of the regulations going about their fuelwood collection business as normal). What's more, as villagers have to travel increasingly further afield to find their wood, they are cutting down trees in high-quality panda habitat more often than they used to.

One solution would be to encourage residents to switch from fuelwood to electricity as a source of energy, but they appear reluctant to do so. By exploring the reasons for this reluctance, the MSU researchers have evidence that there would be a greater uptake of electricity if it were subsidised and its quality improved by increasing voltage and reducing outage. Such changes will require support from central and provincial governments.

Another obvious way to reduce the human impact on panda habitat in Wolong is to reduce the population size. There are lots of ways in which this could be done. In the 1980s and early 1990s, the Chinese government attempted to relocate entire households but it didn't work too well, largely because the elderly were reluctant to move. Michigan State University research revealed that it would make more sense to focus on relocating young people rather than households. There are several reasons for this: young people tend to be more willing to relocate than their elderly relatives and, interestingly, would have the support of their seniors in making the move; as a bonus, a relatively aged population left on in the reserve is unlikely to expand in the same way as a relatively youthful one; and as it is the young who are responsible for harvesting firewood for cooking and heating, skewing the human demography in this way would reduce the degradation of panda habitat.

Another way to ease the tensions between humans and nature is to encourage local people into a lifestyle that is not so damaging to their immediate environment, such as away from agriculture

and into the tourism industry. Sichuan is a prime tourist destination. The region's five UNESCO World Heritage Sites, more
than twenty national nature reserves, half a dozen cities drenched
in historical and cultural significance, and a world-famous spicy
cuisine, among much else, mean that the Tourism Bureau of
Sichuan Province has been able to encourage rapid growth in
the tourism industry over the last decade. Between 2000 and
2007, Sichuan's annual tourism revenue increased fivefold from
25 billion to 125 billion Yuan or from 6.4 per cent to 11.6 per
cent of the province's total gross domestic product. That makes
tourism more important to Sichuan than it does to any other
province in China.

Over this same period, tourism to panda reserves has
undergone similar growth. In the Wolong Nature Reserve, for
example, annual tourist numbers grew from 130,000 in 2000 to
more than 200,000 in 2005. Surely, all the extra money these
visitors brought with them has been good for the people living
inside the reserve and taken some of the pressure off its pandas?
Not necessarily.

Ecotourism is frequently touted as a way to forge a sustain-
able link between the livelihoods of local people and the natural
resources around them: if tourists will pay good money to wander
through a relatively pristine forest (and they will), local people
have an incentive to protect it, or so the reasoning goes. Unfortunately, this attractive model has rarely realised its promise of
sustainability.

This is largely because the costs and benefits in ecotourism
are not distributed equally among everyone involved. Such a
business requires heavy initial investment and development and
this typically benefits outside contractors with no long-term
interest in the local community. Very few of the local people –
those who ought to be empowered by the ecotourism operation

– see a penny during this stage (and with all the disruption to their community, they probably end up paying a price). They are left with the infrastructure from which they may make a living, perhaps working in a hotel or restaurant or selling souvenirs to the steady stream of affluent visitors. However, these sectors tend to provide relatively few jobs, with many of them going to skilled outsiders rather than unskilled locals. Ecotourism development can therefore be counterproductive, cranking up the human footprint in a sensitive natural place and failing to draw in the local people whose involvement is crucial for long-term sustainability.

According to a study conducted by the MSU team and colleagues, the Wolong Nature Reserve's ecotourism industry may have suffered from some of these problems. 'Most investments were from external operators, most laborers were employed from outside, and most goods were purchased from outside cities,' they wrote in the journal *Environmental Management*. 'The benefits flowing to the rural residents were substantially minimal and even those realized were confined to a much smaller percentage of rural households, usually those far from panda habitat with potentially less impact on it,' they concluded.

Then, on 12 May 2008, a massive earthquake rocked Sichuan. It killed more than 90,000 people, injured hundreds of thousands and left at least 5 million without homes. In the Wolong Nature Reserve, not far from the epicentre, more than 100 people lost their lives and the impact was devastating. All the field stations, 98 per cent of houses in the villages and several schools either collapsed or became so unstable they could not be used. At the breeding centre, all thirty-two panda enclosures were either destroyed or damaged. More than sixty captive pandas then living there were moved to the safety of the Ya'an Bifengxia

Base of China Conservation and Research Center for the Giant Panda, a backup base established by the SFA in 2003. Beyond the Wolong Nature Reserve, more than thirty other panda reserves were seriously damaged by the quake. 'It virtually destroyed the entire conservation network built up over the last twenty years', says Wei Fuwen of the Chinese Academy of Sciences in Beijing.

The earthquake may not have done too much harm to the wild pandas themselves. One or two animals may have died, perhaps caught in a landslide, and it may have caused damage to a fair bit of panda habitat. In the short term, however, there's evidence that as humans have moved out, pandas are having a more relaxed time of it, moving into places formally frequented by tourists but not by pandas, says Wei Liu, a researcher at Michigan State University. In the long term, the earthquake could bring benefits to pandas, says John MacKinnon. 'It's left a lot of bare slopes and the bamboo gets in very quickly and will form 100 per cent carpets.'

The earthquake also presents an opportunity when it comes to rebuilding the region. In an article published in the journal *Conservation Biology*, Lü Zhi and colleagues at Peking University and the Shanshui Conservation Center made several key recommendations for the recovery: habitat restoration should be part of the overall plan, with every effort made to improve forest cover and encourage corridors between habitat fragments; new dams, roads and buildings should be subject to much tighter construction standards; and there is an opportunity to rethink where people live and how they use the land around them. 'Rebuilding after the earthquake provides an opportunity to jump start this revolutionary change,' they wrote.

This is going to be an immense challenge. When it comes to habitat restoration and building habitat corridors, the science, as with reintroduction biology, is in its infancy. A recent meta-analysis of seventy-eight experiments into the effectiveness of corridors confirms that, as a general rule, they do increase the movement of animals from one patch to another. But even with a species as well studied as the giant panda, there are several important pieces of information that are still required if conservationists are to construct a corridor that is going to lead animals from one isolated bamboo patch to another. For example, making generalisations about panda movements is still a dangerous game. What little concrete data we have presents a rather mixed picture, with differences in movement patterns from one panda region to the next. In the Qionglai Mountains, the China-WWF research headed by Hu Jinchu and George Schaller demonstrated that pandas spend most of the year at high elevations feeding predominantly on arrow bamboo, but migrate down the mountain in the summer months to profit from an abundance of umbrella bamboo. In the Qinling Mountains, by contrast, research in Changqing and a parallel study in the Foping Nature Reserve has revealed the precise opposite. There, pandas spend most of the year at low elevations feeding on one variety of bamboo and rapidly move uphill in the summer in search of another. In thinking about connecting up patches of habitat, it is obviously important to have a good idea where your pandas are going to move and when, and movement patterns clearly differ from place to place.

It would also be sensible to factor in data on more long-distance movements: such as how far do pandas move when they really want to, when do they go on such expeditions, and is one sex making more of these trips than the other. As yet, however, we don't have this information. In the Qionglai Mountains, for instance, it appeared to the China-WWF researchers that it was the males who were inclined to disperse: they had more wide-ranging movements and the occasional individual was observed going on an 'excursion'. Yet in the Qinling Mountains, Pan Wenshi's research found evidence of females going walkabout, moving tens of kilometres in a relatively short space of time. Just to complicate matters further, Wei Fuwen and colleagues used the DNA data they had collected from faeces in the Wanglang Nature Reserve and found evidence of dispersal for both sexes, with females tending to disperse further, possibly heading off in search of a suitable birthing den. If you are hoping to get pandas to use a corridor between two fragments of habitat, it's quite important to know how far the animals are prepared to move, and the Chinese government is currently supporting research to find out.

In addition, we will need concrete data on how best to build a corridor. 'If you build it, he will come' – that ghostly incantation from the 1989 Hollywood movie *Field of Dreams* – is somewhat optimistic when it comes to designing habitat corridors for pandas. 'You cannot just cover an area with bamboo and expect pandas to use it,' says Wang Dajun, one of Pan Wenshi's PhD students and now a senior researcher alongside Lü Zhi at Peking University's Center for Nature and Society. 'What looks like a corridor to us may not be a corridor for a panda.'

Assuming we can work out how to build a corridor that pandas will use, it will also be important to identify the best places to put them, and Wang and colleagues are working on this too. They are looking at a whole host of considerations, including topographical factors like the distance between two patches, biological parameters like the vegetation and its suitability for pandas, and human factors such as the size of the local population, the level of development and the pattern of land use. 'This should help prioritise those places where a corridor has the best chance of success,' says Wang.

The inevitable conclusion from this is that in some places,

where corridors don't stand much chance of success, we have to concede that the habitat is now fragmented, if not forever then at least for the foreseeable future. This kind of concession is important. Conservationists care about the natural world but they care about humans too. Most, for example, would agree with the broad aims of the Western China Development Plan, an initiative started in 2000 to bring the western half of China up to speed with the relatively affluent east. But they also hope that with the much-needed development of the transport, energy and communications infrastructure in the region, the aesthetic, cultural and biological richness of China's natural resources will not be lost forever.

Striking this kind of compromise between the need to improve living standards for millions of humans and the protection of the natural world has to be one of the toughest of vocations. Just as panda researchers strike a path along a precipitous ridge in search of their study species, so conservation biologists chart a precarious course as they strive to balance these two goals. The odds are stacked against them; when the terrain is unpredictable and the drop sheer, there are many ways to fall. With such a high chance of failure, what is it that motivates such people? For Lü Zhi, the answer is quite simple. 'It is,' she says, 'the right thing to do.'

Over the course of the last 150 years, the giant panda has suffered badly, losing vast swathes of its natural habitat, its wild population hit by collectors, poachers and our desire to see the animals in captivity. In spite of this troubled history, pandas now find themselves in a relatively good place. When the Wildlife Conservation Society's senior zoologist George Schaller wound up his relationship with the China-WWF panda project in the 1980s and came to write up his experiences for a popular audience, he had wanted 'to write not just a nostalgic book about the decline of yet another animal but to describe a painful past balanced in the end by a proclamation of hope, a parable of sin and redemption.' But in spite of looking, there was not much to be optimistic about and the *The Last Panda* reads like a beautiful but tragic eulogy. Had Schaller waited another decade, however, he might have found the glimmer of hope he had been looking for. Indeed, in a foreword to *Giant Pandas: Biology and Conservation* published just over a decade after *The Last Panda*, he had started to sound upbeat. 'In the 1980s, I was filled with creeping despair, as the panda seemed increasingly shadowed by fear of extinction. But now, in this new millennium,' he wrote, 'if the correct choices are soon made, the panda will surely endure as a living symbol of conservation and a luminous wonder of evolution.'

George Schaller is by no means alone in expressing hope for the giant panda. In their conclusion to the *Giant Pandas* volume, the editors Donald Lindburg (then at San Diego Zoo) and Karen Baragona (of WWF US) urged that 'the panda's day is now' and 'the prospects for saving giant pandas are today unequaled'. In 2009, several key panda experts (including Ron Swaisgood, David Wildt and Wei Fuwen) reached the following conclusion: 'The future of the panda should be bright, given the considerable public appeal, financial and institutional support from China and abroad and the apparent political will of China's State Forestry Administration to save the animal they refer to as their national treasure.'

Here are some of the achievements that lie behind this cautious optimism. The Chinese government has invested vast resources in the conservation of its 'national treasure', creating China's largest network of national parks, with more than sixty now dedicated to panda conservation that cover over 70 per cent of suitable habitat and an estimated 50 per cent of the wild population. Legislation introduced in the 1980s has dramatically reduced the incidence of panda poaching. The ban on logging in sensitive habitat has changed things immeasurably and the policy of Grain for Green has helped China to become the country doing more reforestation than the rest of the world put together. Simultaneously, scientists have begun to master the art of breeding pandas in captivity, so much so that the captive population is now self-sustaining. Very importantly, this means there should never be a need to remove another panda from the wild ever again.

During this journey, the Chinese people have suffered too, whether through the Opium Wars of the nineteenth century, the Japanese aggression in the 1930s, civil war in the 1940s, the backward Great Leap Forward in the 1960s or the Cultural Revolution that followed. But as with the giant panda, things are looking up for China too, with a dramatic rise in living standards over the last few decades, rapid and sustained growth of its economy and ongoing strengthening of its academic institutions. Somehow, the Chinese people have been able to bury the extraordinarily traumatic experiences they had to endure during the twentieth century to just get on with life in the twenty-first. It is my simple thesis that the parallels between pandas and China are not a coincidence.

It will be interesting – and informative – to monitor the way of the panda in years to come. It's worth, here, returning to Baoxing County in Sichuan, where this book began twelve chapters ago. If you make the journey from Ya'an City up the Baoxing River in the direction of the Dengchigou Valley Cathedral (of Armand David fame), you will find yourself passing through rural communities in the midst of an industrial revolution. There are workshops, factories, mines and hydroelectric dam after hydroelectric dam. Yet the mountains on both sides of this spoilt valley rise up into the Giant Panda Sanctuaries World Heritage Site, which boasts some of the highest standards of environmental protection on

37. The mining town of Baoxing sits on the polluted Baoxing River, but the mountains rising up on both sides are part of the Giant Panda Sanctuaries World Heritage Site.

offer. This tension between development and conservation so evident in Baoxing County is currently being played out right the way across the developing world. But Baoxing County and its pandas deserve particular attention because they are in China, a country with the numerical and economic might to shape the future – for better or for worse – of every living organism left on earth.

Epilogue

I hope you have enjoyed this trip along the way of the panda. As this black-and-white bear emerged from the obscurity of its bamboo hideaway, forging a new identity and coming to dominate the zoological world, so we have witnessed China wrestling free from colonial oppression, reconfiguring itself as the People's Republic and rising to become the formidable power that it is today.

As I stated at the outset, there is very little about the giant panda – apart from its colouration – that is black and white. In the space left to me, I would like to ponder what exactly it is we are thinking of when we think of a panda. Is it real or is it virtual? For those of you who have never seen a panda, you will have to lean entirely on cultural representations to help you, from a wildlife documentary at one extreme to Po the *Kung Fu Panda* at the other. If, like me, you have seen a giant panda in captivity, then the panda in your mind's eye might be a little more like the real thing. But even if you are one of the very, very few people in the world lucky enough to have seen a giant panda in the wild, it is unlikely that your imagined panda has not been tainted in some way by the absolutely immense presence of the giant panda in our global culture.

This presence has been growing ever since Armand David boxed up his pandas and sent them back to Paris. It is a presence that has advanced in fits and starts, punctuated by a surprising succession of firsts: taxonomists scrapped to be the first to put the giant panda in its rightful place; explorers set out to be the first to see then shoot one; collectors hoped to be the first to get one out of China alive; the public fought to be the first to see them; zoos strove to be the first to produce a baby; and zoologists vied for the opportunity to study them in the wild. Each of these steps helped turn the panda from a zoological to a cultural phenomenon. But if I were to highlight a single decade when the virtual panda made its greatest leap forward it would be the 1960s, and if I were to home in on just one panda it would be Chi-Chi.

As with the captive pandas before her, Chi-Chi found her image appearing in the guise of soft toys, on postcards and in newspapers and magazines. Unlike other pandas, however, she also found her way into millions of homes, courtesy of the groundbreaking television show *Zoo Time*. Chi-Chi's doomed relationship with An-An – the first really high-profile attempt to breed pandas in captivity – inspired columnists and cartoonists to fashion an anthropomorphised panda with even more appeal than Chi-Chi, one with political ambitions, a fussy diet and a dislike for sexual reproduction. This caricature has gone from strength to strength and, I believe, may account for the peculiar way in which the panda is simultaneously adored and ridiculed across much of the English-speaking world.

Most importantly, though, Chi-Chi became the face of global conservation in the shape of Sir Peter Scott's logo for the World Wildlife Fund, an act that did more than any other to turn the panda from a real to a virtual animal. As with the most successful brands, the WWF panda has become shorthand for a host of positive associations: beauty, wilderness, biodiversity, charity, protection, a happy future. It is also a brilliant brand in the sense that all these feel-good vibes can be used to generate a lot of hard cash for conservation projects around the world. But the flipside

38. The genre of panda satire, which really got going in the 1960s, is still very much alive.

of this explicitly commercial role was an explosion of virtual pandas as others followed WWF's lead, stamping the panda's form onto hundreds of different products, from radios to fizzy drinks, chocolate to biscuits, liquorice to cigarettes.

In the light of this commercialisation, it is entirely fitting that the Chinese government and WWF should have entered into a partnership in 1980 that saw the exchange of contracts and cash. It is true that this joint project helped to reveal something of the real panda for the very first time but it may also have strengthened the virtual panda in the public imagination. 'I am haunted by the realisation that the project may have harmed rather than helped the panda,' wrote zoologist George Schaller in *The Last Panda*. 'Many persons and several institutions have genuinely had the panda's interest at heart and their good intentions are unquestioned. But had the panda remained in the obscurity of its bamboo thickets, free from worldwide publicity and the greed this publicity helped to fuel, there might not now be so many captives, needlessly caught during and after the bamboo die-off, and not so many breeding stations.'

There can be no doubt that many of those breeding stations, notably the Wolong CCRCGP and the Chengdu Base, have done a great deal for pandas. They provide the opportunity to study this species in a manner that would be unthinkable in the wild; they have been instrumental in getting the captive population into a respectable, self-sustaining state; they present a unique opportunity to educate the public about pandas and about conservation more generally; and they have been able to raise plenty of conservation funds through ticket sales, merchandise and long-term loans to foreign zoos.

But captive pandas are deceptive creatures. They are easy to see; they get brought bundles of freshly cut bamboo, sometimes several times a day; they get state-of-the-art scientific input to help them breed; at the few institutions with enough pandas to produce more than one cub in a year, you may experience the extraordinary sight of a panda crèche and (if you're prepared to fork out a few hundred dollars) you can even have your photograph taken with one of its adorable inmates.

Wild pandas could not be more different: you will almost certainly never see one in the impenetrable pockets of bamboo that are still suitable habitat; they are solitary creatures, except for a few days a year when they have very productive sex; they have no need for artificial insemination, nor incubators, nor formula feed; you will never get to hold a wild cub and you can forget the photo. So, like the cuddly toys, the WWF logo and the satirical panda that thrives across much of the English-speaking world, the captive panda is more virtual than real.

Don't get me wrong: I am all in favour of virtual pandas. Since I set out researching this book, I – and my children – have received an extraordinary array of virtual pandas in the form of T-shirts, postcards, birthday cards, calendars, photographs, posters, soft toys, chopsticks and Playmobil figures (we now have three of the 'Panda Family' set). All of this instills a sense of familiarity, a feeling that we know and understand the panda. But here's the thing. We don't. Not even I do, and I have digested a very good proportion of the thousands upon thousands of websites, academic papers, magazine articles and books that have been dedicated to this one animal. It is very difficult to catch a glimpse of the real, wild panda when faced with a constant onslaught from these alluring virtual forms, particularly as it is only in the last few decades that research has begun to reveal the faint outline of the real, wild panda. It is my hope that this book may have redressed this balance in some small way, allowing you to recognise a virtual panda when you see one, and sense the wonder of the intangible wild panda. For unless we acknowledge

39. Visitors to the Chengdu Zoo pay homage to the virtual panda.

the considerable difference between them, there is a danger that all we will do is conserve the virtual rather than the real giant panda.

And there are lots of reasons why wild pandas matter. For a start, the continued existence of real, wild pandas (even if nobody can actually see them) gives a peculiar legitimacy to virtual pandas in all their forms. To illustrate what I mean, imagine for a moment a world without wild pandas: the soft toy panda is not quite so cuddly; the WWF logo is no longer a rousing emblem but signifies loss; and with all hope of reintroduction essentially extinguished, the captive population suddenly has little purpose beyond being there for our amusement. Then there is the pure and simple beauty – and the undeniable mystery – of wild pandas themselves. The continued existence of wild pandas, and the opportunity to study them, just makes the world a more interesting place in which to live. Giant panda habitat also embraces one of the most biodiverse regions on the planet, so protecting it protects a lot more than just the panda. But conservation of the giant panda in the wild is about much more than these stunning animals or even about the thousands of other endangered species that benefit from its protection. The conservation of wild pandas has also become a test of ourselves as a species.

I have very mixed feelings about *Homo sapiens*. Much of human behaviour – the corruption, the greed, the fraud, the theft, the murder, the war, the rape – is so typical of the evolutionary struggle to survive and reproduce that I cannot help but see us as animals heading along our own predictable path towards ultimate extinction. Many of these traits are – even now – pressing the giant panda into ever tighter, more isolated fragments of forest. Yet much of human behaviour – the empathy, the resolve, the ingenuity, the creativity – also tells me we are right to imagine that we are not like other animals. We have the unique ability to imagine how, given certain actions, the world will pan out for ourselves and for other species that have to share planet earth. Is there room for wild pandas as the way of the panda continues to unfold? I hope so. Because of the two worlds I am now imagining – one with wild pandas and one without – I know which one I'd rather be in.

Notes

Prologue

ix 'a book entitled'. Desmond Morris and Ramona Morris, *Men and Pandas* (New York: McGraw-Hill, 1966), pp. 124–30.

x 'as Chris Catton noted'. Chris Catton, *Pandas* (New York: Facts on File Publications, 1990), p. 65.

xi 'here's a species'. Chris Packham, 'Let pandas die', *Radio Times*, 22 November 2009.

Chapter 1

4 'resembling either a tiger or a bear'. Translated in Peh T'i Wei, 'Through historical records and ancient writings in search of the giant panda', *Journal of the Hong Kong Branch of the Royal Asiatic Society*, 28 (1988), pp. 34–43, p. 38.

5 'the tapir and the giant panda'. Elena E. Songster, 'A Natural Place for Nationalism: The Wanglang Nature Reserve and the Emergence of the Giant Panda as a National Icon' (San Diego: University of California, San Diego, 2004), p. 27; see also Songster, *Panda Nation: Nature, Science, and Nationalism in the People's Republic of China* (forthcoming).

5 'famous for its docility'. Gathorne Gathorne-Hardy, email to author, 12 September 2009.

5 'a sense of trustworthiness'. Translated in Wei, p. 40.

5 'with rewarding frequency'. George B. Schaller and others, *The Giant Pandas of Wolong* (University of Chicago Press, 1985), pp. 5–7.

7 'it was my ambition'. Armand David, *Abbé David's Diary: Being an Account of the French Naturalist's Journeys and Observations in China*

in the Years 1866 to 1869, trans. by H. Fox (Harvard University Press, 1949), p. 3.

7 'all science is dedicated'. David, p. xv.

8 'mountains to the west of Beijing'. David, p. 4.

9 'the striking, wiry skin'. David, p. 276. David described it as a *'fameux ours blanc et noir'*, which is usually translated as 'famous black-and-white bear'. As George Schaller points out in *The Last Panda*, however, *'fameux'* can also mean 'first-rate'. Since this is the first time David referred to this animal in his writing, and there is no evidence he had actually heard of it before, I have gone with 'most excellent' here.

9 'an interesting novelty'. David, p. 276.

10 'left the mission at dawn'. For the description of David's trip to the mountain above the Dengchigou Valley Cathedral, see David, pp. 278–82.

10 'with David still breathing'. David, p. 283.

11 'most significant discoveries'. Fa-ti Fan, *British Naturalists in Qing China: Science, Empire and Cultural Encounter* (Harvard University Press, 2004), p. 80.

12 'augment our national collections'. David, p. 166.

13 'increasingly wretched'. David, p. 46.

13 'the nauseous smell'. David, p. 167.

13 'an intrepid opium smoker'. David, pp. 208–9.

14 'a sudden shock of realisation'. Jonathan D. Spence, *The Search for Modern China*, first edn (New York: Norton, 1991), p. 171.

15 'jumped ship at Jiujiang'. David, p. 170.

15 'he had been philosophical'. David, p. 6.

15 'large-scale unrest'. David, p. 253.

16 'he drew his revolver'. David, p. 7.

16 'dozens of hair-raising encounters'. David, pp. 7–8.

16 'exterminate all Christians'. David, p. 278.

17 'evil-minded pagans'. David, pp. 174–5.

18 'hills turned to mountains'. For a description of David's journey from Chengdu to the Dengchigou Valley Cathedral, see David, pp. 266–72.

20 '*Ursus melanoleucus*'. David, '*Voyage en Chine fait sous les auspices de S. Exc. le Ministre de l'Instruction publique*', *Nouv. Arch. Mus. Hist. Nat. Paris*, 5 (1869), pp. 3–13.

Chapter 2

21 'its colours are exactly like'. David, p. 283.
21 'it is these two specimens'. David also collected a further two panda specimens that are also in the Paris museum, though they do not appear in Milne-Edwards' description.
23 'Endersby has drawn attention'. Jim Endersby, 'From having no Herbarium'; local knowledge versus metropolitan expertise: Joseph Hooker's Australasian correspondence with William Colenso and Ronald Gunn', *Pacific Science*, 55 (2001), pp. 343–58.
23 'Hooker asserting his authority'. Jim Endersby, *Imperial Nature* (Chicago: University of Chicago Press, 2008), p. 137.
24 'I propose for the generic name'. Quoted in Morris and Morris, p. 1.
24 'from its exterior form'. Alphonse Milne-Edwards, '*Note sur quelques mammifères du Thibet oriental*', *Ann. Sci. Nat., Zool.*, 5 (1870), art. 10. Quoted in Morris and Morris, p. 19.
24 'another interesting new animal'. Armand David, '*Rapport adressé à MM. les professeurs administrateurs du Muséum d'histoire naturelle*', *Nouv. Arch. Mus. Hist. Nat. Paris*, 7 (1872), pp. 75–100.
25 'quite different conclusions'. Dwight D. Davis, 'The giant panda: a morphological study of evolutionary mechanisms', *Fieldiana Zoology Memoirs*, 3 (1964), pp. 1–337, p. 16.
26 '*Ailuropoda* is a bear'. Davis, p. 11.
29 'for the collection, preservation and study'. 'Serological Museum of Rutgers University,' *Nature* 161, no. 4090 (1948), p. 428.
29 'quite reasonable prediction'. C. A. Leone and A. L. Wiens, 'Comparative serology of carnivores', *Journal of Mammalogy*, 37 (1956), pp. 11–23.
30 'is clear and unequivocal'. Vincent M. Sarich, '"Chi-Chi": Transferrin', *Trans. Zool. Soc. Lond.* 33 (1976), pp.165–71.
30 'just forty-two chromosomes'. R. E. Newnham and W. M. Davidson, 'Comparative Study of the Karyotypes of Several Species

in Carnivora Including the Giant Panda (*Ailuropoda melanoleuca*),' *Cytogenetic and Genome Research* 5, no. 3–4 (1966), pp. 152–63.

30 'molecular method for ordering species'. Stephen J. O'Brien, *Tears of the Cheetah: and Other Tales from the Genetic Frontier*, first edn (New York: Thomas Dunne Books/St Martin's Press, 2003).

31 'once we had the photographs'. Interview with the author, 24 October 2009.

32 'giant panda chromosomes'. Stephen J. O'Brien and others, 'A molecular solution to the riddle of the giant panda's phylogeny', *Nature*, 317 (1985), pp. 140–44, p. 142.

32 'most subsequent research'. Li Yu and others, 'Analysis of complete mitochondrial genome sequences increases phylogenetic resolution of bears (Ursidae), a mammalian family that experienced rapid speciation', *BMC Evolutionary Biology*, 7 (2007), 198; Johannes Krause and others, 'Mitochondrial genomes reveal an explosive radiation of extinct and extant bears near the Miocene-Pliocene boundary', *BMC Evolutionary Biology*, 8, (2008), 220. This study estimates the giant panda split away from the rest of the bear lineage around 20 million years ago.

32 'if O'Brien hoped his evidence'. A study of carnivore haemoglobins (the protein that makes red-blood cells red and captures oxygen for distribution around the body) revealed that the lesser and giant panda haemoglobin had a surprisingly similar structure (D. A. Tagle and others, *Naturwissenschaften*, 73 (1986), pp. 512–14). Soon afterwards, the first comparison of DNA from the mitochondria, the tiny structures responsible for powering each cell seemed to pull the giant towards the lesser panda once more (Y. Zhang and L. Shi, *Nature*, 352 (1991), p. 573).

34 'I knew then what I was up against'. O'Brien, interview, 24 October 2009.

34 'the panda is a panda'. George B. Schaller, *The Last Panda* (The University of Chicago Press, 1993), pp. 261–7.

34 'unnecessarily overdramatised the issue'. Ernst Mayr, 'Uncertainty in science: is the giant panda a bear or a raccoon?', *Nature*, 323 (1986), pp. 769–71.

35 'a detailed description'. Ya-ping Zhang and Oliver A. Ryder, 'Mitochondrial DNA sequence evolution in the Arctoidea', *Proceedings of the National Academy of Sciences of the United States of America*, 90 (1993), pp. 9557–61.

35 'there is now so much DNA data'. See, for example, Zhi Lü and others, 'Patterns of genetic diversity in remaining giant panda populations', *Conservation Biology* 15 (2001), 1596–1607; Baowei Zhang and others, 'Genetic viability and population history of the giant panda, putting an end to the "evolutionary dead end"?', *Molecular Biology and Evolution* 24 (2007), pp. 1801–10.

35 'this has even led some researchers'. Qiu-Hong Wan and others, 'Genetic differentiation and subspecies development of the giant panda as revealed by DNA fingerprinting, *Electrophoresis* 24, (2003), pp. 1353–9; Qui-Hong Wan and others, 'A new subspecies of giant panda (*Ailuropoda melanoleuca*) from Shaanxi, China', *Journal of Mammalogy* 86, (2005), pp. 397–402.

37 'complete sequence of its entire genome'. Ruiqiang Li and others, 'The sequence and de novo assembly of the giant panda genome', *Nature* 463 (2010), pp. 311–17.

37 'the giant panda is a bear'. See, for example, Li Yu and Ya-ping Zhang, 'Phylogeny of the caniform carnivora: evidence from multiple genes', *Genetica*, 2006, pp. 1–3; Rui Peng and others, 'The complete mitochondrial genome and phylogenetic analysis of the giant panda (*Ailuropoda melanoleuca*)', *Gene*, 397 (2007), pp. 1–2.

Chapter 3

38 'revive the Qing, destroy the foreign'. Spence, *The Search for Modern China*, p. 232.

39 'the object of the journey'. Quoted in Ernest Wilson, 'Aristocrats of the Garden' (Doubleday, Page & Co., 1917), p. 274.

40 'it is the sportsman's prize'. Ernest Wilson, 'A Naturalist in Western China', Vol. 2 (Methuen, 1913), pp. 182–4.

41 'the expedition leader'. In most popular accounts, Hugo Weigold is credited with being the first Westerner to see a living giant panda. But historian Alexis Schwarzenbach has unearthed Walter Stötzner's

travel diary, which suggests that Stötzner may be the one who deserves this peculiar claim to fame. See Alexis Schwarzenbach, 'WWF – A Biography', Collection Rolf Heyne (forthcoming).

41 'I saw an animal asleep'. J. Huston Edgar, 'Giant panda and wild dogs on the Tibetan border', *The China Journal of Science and Arts*, (1924), p. 270–71.

42 'waiting for the Panda'. J. Huston Edgar, 'Waiting for the Panda', *Journal of the West China Border Research Society*, 8 (1936), pp. 10–12. Muping is the old name for Baoxing.

45 'these population depredations'. Mary Anne Andrei, 'The accidental conservationist: William T. Hornaday, the Smithsonian bison expeditions and the US National Zoo', *Endeavour*, 29 (2005), pp. 109–13.

46 'a carpet of "bleaching skeletons"'. Quoted in Andrei.

46 'we killed very nearly all we saw'. William T. Hornaday to Spencer F. Baird, 21 December 1886.

47 'must be sound of body and firm of mind'. Quoted in Roderick Nash, *Wilderness and the American Mind*, 4th edn (Yale University Press, 2001), p. 152.

47 'Roosevelt felt that men of his class'. Gregg Mitman, *Reel-Nature* (Harvard University Press, 1999), p. 15.

48 'any duffer with a good check-book'. Quoted in Mitman, p. 16.

48 'the Golden Fleece'. Theodore Roosevelt and Kermit Roosevelt, *Trailing the Giant Panda* (Scribner, 1929), p. 3.

49 'without seeing a wild animal of any sort'. Quoted in Catton, *Pandas*, p. 12.

50 'rankest folly'. Quoted in Michael Kiefer, *Chasing the Panda: How an Unlikely Pair of Adventurers Won the Race to Capture the Mythical 'White Bear'* (New York: Four Walls Eight Windows, 2002), p. 37.

50 'unexpectedly close I heard a clicking chirp'. Quoted in Morris and Morris (1966), p. 29.

50 'have extraordinary luck'. Quoted in Kiefer, p. 39.

50 'in the United States'. For more on the great dinosaur rush see Tom Rea, *Bone Wars: The Excavation and Celebrity of Andrew Carnegie's Dinosaur* (University of Pittsburgh Press, 2001).

51 'a few feet ahead'. T. Donald Carter, 'The giant panda', *Bulletin of the New York Zoological Society*, Jan–Feb (1937), pp. 6–14.

55 'from his vantage point'. Dean Sage, 'In quest of the giant panda', *Natural History*, 35 (1935), pp. 309–20.

57 'unusually large panda'. 'Giant panda shot', *The Sydney Morning Herald*, 22 August 1935.

Chapter 4

58 'I am highly expectant'. Quoted in Vicki Croke, *The Lady and the Panda : The True Adventures of the First American Explorer to Bring Back China's Most Exotic Animal* (New York: Random House Trade Paperbacks, 2006), p. 314.

58 'the unluckiest or most incompetent'. Croke, p. 45.

59 'haggard and luckless adventurer'. Croke, p. 47–8.

59 'flat sprawly city'. Ruth Harkness, *The Lady and the Panda* (London: Nicholson & Watson, 1938), p. 14.

59 'at the Chinese clubs'. Croke, p. 34.

60 'anything but well'. Quoted in Croke, p. 48.

60 'VRYENGLISH GENTLEMAN'. Quoted in Croke, p. 71–2.

61 'riddled with bullets'. Harkness, p. 90.

62 'hideous and disgustingly obscene'. Ernest Wilson, *A Naturalist in Western China*, Vol. 1 (London: Methuen & Co. Ltd, 1913), p. 168.

64 'one dog, $20.00'. Croke, p. 155.

64 'staking out the den'. Croke, p. 157.

64 'mounting my own son'. Harkness, p. 231.

64 'completely captivated'. Harkness, p. 232.

65 'huge media attention'. Douglas Deuchler and Carla W. Owens, *Brookfield Zoo and the Chicago Zoological Society* (Arcadia Publishing, 2009), p. 38.

66 'the explosions were deafening'. Croke, p. 190.

67 'a rather cozy feeling'. Quoted in Croke, p. 192.

67 'a period of terror'. Spence, p. 448.

68 'of her countless mourners'. 'Su-Lin, America's favorite animal, dies of quinsy in Chicago Zoo', *Life Magazine*, 11 April 1938.

70 'the conditions of his captive pandas'. Quoted in Croke, p. 265.

70 'in a letter to *The Field*'. Rosa Loseby, 'Five giant pandas,' *The Field*, 24 December, 1938.

71 'vigil for several days'. Ruth Harkness, *Pangoan Diary* (Creative Age Press, Inc., 1942), p. 6.

71 'surge in panda extraction'. Arthur de Carle Sowerby, 'Live giant pandas leave Hongkong for London', *China Journal*, December (1938), p. 334.

72 'One old gentleman'. Yee Chiang, *Chin-Pao and the Giant Pandas* (Country Life, 1939), p. 83.

72 'Ming is a true representative of China'. Yee Chiang, *The Story of Ming* (Penguin Books, 1945).

73 'through the United China Relief'. Quoted in John Tee-Van, 'Two Pandas – China's Gift to America', *Bulletin of the New York Zoological Society*, 45 (1942), pp. 2–18.

Chapter 5

79 'a modern zoo'. T'an Pang Chieh, 'Rare animals of the Peking Zoo', *Science and Nature*, trans. by C. Radt, 1958. At that time Beijing Zoo was known as the Peking Zoological Gardens, or Peking Zoo.

80 'welcomed the foreigners'. Heini Demmer, 'The first giant panda since the war has reached the Western world', *International Zoo News*, 5 (1958), pp. 99–101.

80 'her soul was sick'. Interview with Demmer, broadcast in 'Chi-Chi the panda' (BBC, 1992).

81 'another would-be emigrant'. 'The panda from Peking', *The Times*, 8 May 1958, p. 10.

81 'the same export controls'. Translated in Shu Guang Zhang, *Economic Cold War: America's Embargo Against China and the Sino-Soviet Alliance, 1949–1963* (Stanford University Press, 2001), p. 24.

81 'let them besiege us!'. Translated in Shu Zhang, p. 70.

83 COCOM and CHINCOM: for more detail, see Zhang, *Economic Cold War*; and Jacqueline McGlade, 'The US-led trade Embargo on China: The origins of CHINCOM, 1947–52,' in *East-West Trade and the Cold War* (2005), pp. 47–63.

83 'some high person'. Demmer, *International Zoo News*, p. 101.

84 'a very large compound'. Demmer, p. 100.

84 'needless to say'. Demmer, p. 101.

84 'where an absolutely magnificent large cage'. Demmer, p. 101.

85 'a few days later'. See, for example, 'Visitor to zoo hurt by panda', *The Times*, 8 September 1958.

86 'the hope that the programmes'. Solly Zuckerman, *Monkeys, Men, and Missiles : An Autobiography, 1946–88* (Collins, 1988), p. 60.

86 'I was green'. Desmond Morris, interview with Christopher Parsons, 6 September 2000 (www.wildfilmhistory.org).

86 'lifeblood of the zoo'. Quoted in Mitman, *Reel Nature*, p. 132.

86 'attendance at the Lincoln Park Zoo'. Mitman, p. 133.

87 'so many animal programmes'. Desmond Morris, *Zoo Time* (Rupert Hart-Davis Ltd, 1966), introduction.

87 'things often go wrong'. Morris, *Zoo Time*, introduction.

88 'luckily of course'. Morris, interview with Parsons.

88 'ZSL went public'. 'Giant panda to stay in London', *The Times*, 24 September 1958.

88 'man must conquer nature'. Judith Shapiro, *Mao's War Against Nature: Politics and the Environment in Revolutionary China* (Cambridge University Press, 2001), p. 67; the idea of conquering nature also appears frequently in Sigrid Schmalzer, *The People's Peking Man: Popular Science and Human Identity in Twentieth-Century China* (The University of Chicago Press, 2008).

89 'its defining characteristic'. Shapiro, p. 71.

90 'in some cases, furrows ten feet deep'. Shapiro, p. 78.

90 'he was dressed in black leather gear'. Desmond Morris, interview in 'Chi-Chi the panda' (BBC, 1992).

91 'Comrade Chi-Chi'. Ronald Carl Giles, *Daily Express*, 25 September 1958.

92 'An elderly gentleman'. Mike Kerris, interview with the author, 1 October 2009.

92 'Chi-Chi's diet'. Michael R. Brambell, 'The giant panda (*Ailuropoda melanoleuca*)', *Trans. Zool. Soc. Lond.*, 33 (1976), pp. 85–92.

93 'Chi-Chi, we soon found'. Denis Forman, interview in 'Chi-Chi the Panda' (BBC 1992).

Chapter 6

94 'how to save the world's wildlife'. E. Max Nicholson, 'How to save the world's wildlife,' 6 April 1961, Nicholson Archive, The Linnean Society of London, EMN 4/3/1.

96 'a series of three articles'. Julian Huxley, 'The wild riches of Africa', *The Observer*, 13 November 1960; 'The wild protein', *The Observer*, 20 November 1960; 'Wild life as a world asset', *The Observer*, 27 November 1960. The quotation comes from the first of the three articles.

96 'a hotel owner called Victor'. Victor A. Stolan to Julian Huxley, 6 December 1960, EMN 4/2.

97 'seriously interested'. Nicholson to Stolan, 16 December 1960, EMN 4/2.

97 'two ideas in particular'. Stolan to Nicholson, 3 January 1961, EMN 4/2.

97 'Nicholson proceeded cautiously'. Nicholson to Huxley, 9 January 1961, EMN 4/2.

97 'had the response'. Max Nicholson, 'Earliest planning of World Wildlife Fund', 1977, EMN 4/1.

98 'the Morges Manifesto'. Max Nicholson, 'The Morges Manifesto', 29 April 1961, EMN 4/3/1.

98 'with IUCN backing'. The name was agreed on at the third meeting of the 'participatory committee' (16 May 1961); there was a discussion of a logo at the fourth meeting (30 May 1961); and everyone settled for the panda at the sixth meeting (6 July 1961), EMN 4/3/1.

99 'most valuable trademark'. Quoted in Raymond Bonner, *At the Hand of Man: Peril and Hope for Africa's Wildlife* (Simon & Schuster, 1993), p.64.

99 'by the 1960s'. Songster, 'A Natural Place for Nationalism', p. 178.

99 'The "panda" is China's most famous precious animal'. Translated in Songster, p. 179.

100 'have propelled this emerging icon'. Songster, p. 178.

101 'a panda-based logo'. *World Wildlife Fund Twentieth Anniversary Review*, EMN 4/19/1, 2. This is the first time that Watterson's

sketches and his role in creating the panda logo received a public airing. Lady Philippa Scott remembered Watterson's visit to her home and the drawing of pandas in the studio (interview with the author, 9 October 2008); historian Alexis Schwarzenbach, in researching his forthcoming book *WWF – A Biography*, has located some of Watterson's early panda sketches in the basement of WWF International in Gland but it remains uncertain whether these are the originals.

102   'is there a chance'. Peter Scott to Michael Adeane, 17 July 1961, EMN 4/3/1.

102   'Adeane, in reply, was polite but firm'. Adeane to Scott, 18 July 1961, EMN 4/3/1.

103   'not overly optimistic'. Mervyn Cowie to Max Nicholson, 3 November 1961, EMN 4/1.

103   'the Arusha Manifesto'. Nicholson and Ian S. MacPhail, The Arusha Manifesto, EMN 4/3/2.

104   'I, personally, am not very interested'. Quoted in Nash, *Wilderness and the American Mind*, p. 342.

104   'more than willing to lend'. C. I. Meek to Gerald G. Watterson, 8 August 1961, EMN 4/3/2.

104   'why a Panda at a meeting'. MacPhail, 'Meeting at Royal Society of Arts on 28th., September. Proposed arrangements and programme', September 1961, EMN 4/3/2.

105   'Doomed'. *Daily Mirror*, 9 October 1961.

106   'a massive response'. 'To the rescue!', *Daily Mirror*, 13 October 1961.

106   'good confirmation of our diagnosis'. Memo issued by Nicholson to the heads of national campaigns, 11 October 1961, EMN 8/7.

106   'I find it increasingly difficult'. Nicholson to Jean G. Baer, 25 October 1961, EMN 4/3/2.

107   'blueprint for setting'. 'The Launching of a New Ark,' in *First Report of the President and Trustees of the World Wildlife Fund. An International Foundation for Saving the World's Wildlife and Wild Places 1961–1964* (Collins, 1965), pp. 15–207.

108   'owes its survival to the sort of'. 'This is the symbol of the World Wildlife Fund', EMN 8/7.

109 'since you have a panda as a symbol'. Quoted in George Schaller, *The Last Panda*, p. 11. I have reconstructed these events from Schaller's book and interviews with Nancy Nash and Wang Menghu.

109 'I can get us into China'. Nancy Nash, interview with the author, 11 December 2009.

110 'productive force'. Quoted in Schmalzer, *The People's Peking Man*, p. 169.

112 'China and wildlife group agree'. 'China and wildlife group agree on help for endangered species', *New York Times*, 24 September 1979.

112 'bad move'. Nash, interview with author, 3 March 2010.

112 'the crucial issue'. Spence, *The Search for Modern China*, p. 667.

112 'that says Taiwan'. Nash, 3 March 2010.

113 'it was the height of the Cultural Revolution'. George Schaller, interview with the author, 16 December 2009.

114 'his quiet project was being invaded'. Schaller, interview.

114 'you have been invited'. Inferred from Schaller, *The Last Panda*, p. 4.

114 'suddenly Hu signalled'. Schaller's foreword to Zhi Lü and Elizabeth Kemf, *Wanted Alive! Giant Pandas in the Wild. A WWF Species Status Report* (WWF, 2001).

115 'This facility'. Schaller, *The Last Panda*, p. 12.

115 'we were stunned'. Schaller, interview.

115 'without her the project never would have happened'. Schaller, interview.

116 'Sir Peter's panda looked like a panda'. Nash, interview, 11 December 2009.

117 'WWF was no longer the small organisation'. David Hughes-Evans and James L. Aldrich, '20th anniversary – World Wildlife Fund', *The Environmentalist*, 1 (1981), pp. 91–3.

117 'WWF's largest national branch'. Data taken from WWF-US website (http://bit.ly/9x59O; accessed 16 July 2010).

117 'a tremendous amount of good'. Schaller, interview.

Chapter 7

118 'Chi-Chi's mood suddenly changed'. Oliver Graham-Jones, *First Catch your Tiger* (Collins, 1970), p. 167.

119 'the preservation and breeding'. William T. Hornday quoted in Mary Anne Andrei, *Endeavour*.

119 'International Zoo Yearbook'. Peter J. S. Olney, 'International Zoo Yearbook: past, present and future', *International Zoo Yearbook* 38 (2003), 34–42.

121 'his mother at first held him'. Quoted in Morris and Morris (1966), p. 87.

122 'the pressures upon me'. Graham-Jones, interview in 'Chi-Chi the panda' (BBC, 1992).

122 'defying him to calculate the correct dosage'. Morris and Morris (1966), p. 83.

122 'bringing the two giant pandas together'. Quoted in 'Zoo flirts with Reds for frustrated panda', *Palm Beach Post*, 17 September 1964.

122 'these animals were not just animals'. Desmond Morris, interview in 'Chi-Chi the panda' (BBC, 1992).

123 'I am not sure that the proposal'. All the quoted correspondence between the Zoological Society of London, the Ministry of Defence and the Foreign and Commonwealth Office is featured in 'Chi-Chi the panda' (BBC, 1992).

123 'I have always suspected'. This letter also appears in the 'Chi-Chi the panda' documentary.

124 'the Russians took it'. Desmond Morris, interview in 'Chi-Chi the panda'.

124 'an avuncular, friendly old bloke'. Morris, interview with Parsons, 6 September 2000.

124 'they bugged my room'. Morris, interview with Parsons.

124 'but when the animal is the cynosure'. Graham-Jones, *First Catch Your Tiger*, p. 175.

125 'transported at various altitudes'. Graham-Jones, p. 176.

125 'state-of-the-art box'. Graham-Jones, p. 176.

125 'a general air of carnival'. Graham-Jones, p. 179.

125 'whisked unceremoniously away'. Graham-Jones, p. 181.

126 'it was dark by then'. Graham Jones, p. 183.

126 'Chi-Chi did not calm down'. See, for example, Ylva Brandt and others, 'Effects of continuous elevated cortisol concentrations during oestrus on concentrations and patterns of progesterone, oestradiol and LH in the sow', *Animal Reproduction Science*, 110 (2009), pp. 172–85.

127 'panda romance doubtful'. 'Panda romance doubtful', *The Montreal Gazette*, 4 April 1966.

128 'the panda frollicked'. 'Panda-monium – Chi-Chi plays hard to get', *Birmingham Mail*, 6 October 1966.

128 'the pandas were reunited'. 'One hug, no more, says Chi-Chi', *Leicester Mercury*, 7 October 1966.

129 'Chi-Chi is playing'. 'Chi-Chi is playing hard to get', *Oldham Evening Chronicle*, 7 October 1966; 'Chi-Chi gives An-An a cuff', *Swindon Advertiser*, 7 October 1966; 'Chi-Chi's right hook for the suitor', *Newcastle Evening Chronicle*, 7 October 1966.

129 'two pandas spend night'. 'Two pandas spend night together', *Gloucester Echo*, 8 October 1966; 'Pandas' night of promise', *Shields Gazette*, 8 October 1966; 'Strangers in the night', *Birmingham Mail*, 8 October 1966.

129 'time runs out'. 'Time runs out for Chi-Chi', *Hull Daily Mail*, 11 October 1966; 'Chi-Chi has only three nights left', *The Citizen*, 11 October 1966; 'From Russia – without love', *Bath and Wiltshire Chronicle*, 11 October 1966.

129 'Chi-Chi, An-An'. 'Chi-Chi, An-An, say ta-ta', *Staffordshire Evening Sentinel*, 17 October 1966; 'Bride who never was flies home', *Press and Journal*, 18 October 1966; 'Return of the virgin panda', *Morning Star*, 18 October 1966.

129 'frankly, George'. David Myers, 'Frankly, George, I reckon you'll cause a big enough sensation there without the gimmicks', *Evening News*, 18 November 1966.

129 'happy to oblige'. Stanley Franklin, 'USA will put two animals into space orbit lasting a year', *Daily Mirror*, 18 October 1966.

130 'I'm afraid that we've been had'. 'Why pandas are becoming', *Daily Mail*, 26 October 1966.

130 'a return match. 'A return 'match' for An-An', *Yorkshire Evening Press*, 25 February 1967; 'Another date for Chi-Chi?', *Northern Daily Mail*, 24 February 1967; 'Another marriage proposal for Chi-Chi?', *Lincolnshire Echo*, 25 February 1967.

130 'An-An is sick.' 'An-An is sick, so Chi-Chi's spring honeymoon is off', *Bournemouth Evening Echo*, 27 February 1967.

131 'may be love'. 'May be love at second sight for Chi Chi', *Daily Mail*, 3 August 1968; 'A new romance?', *Sunderland Echo*, 3 August 1968; 'Another date?', *Bolton Evening News*, 3 August 1968.

131 'we have no reason to believe'. 'Crisis will not stop An-An', *Sunday Express*, 25 August 1968.

131 'to his intense embarrassment'. Graham-Jones, p. 196.

131 'Chi-Chi's long isolation'. Quoted in Graham-Jones, p. 197.

132 'sort of consciousness'. Konrad Lorenz, 'The companion in the bird's world', *Auk*, 54 (1937), pp. 245–73.

132 'subsequent researchers'. Sabine Oetting and others, 'Sexual imprinting as a two-stage process: mechanisms of information storage and stabilisation', *Animal Behaviour*, 50 (1995), pp. 393–403.

133 'females were not so easily fooled'. Keith M. Kendrick and others, 'Mothers determine sexual preferences', *Nature*, 395 (1998), pp. 229–30.

133 'this man wasn't brilliant'. Morris, interview with Parsons.

133 'Chi-Chi was humanised'. Ramona Morris and Desmond Morris, *The Giant Panda*, revised by Jonathan Barzdo (Penguin, 1982), p. 104.

133 'in the constant company of humans'. J. Randall, 'Uniform for An-An', *The Guardian*, 4 September 1968.

134 'isn't it possible'. Catherine Storr, 'Peculiar panda?', *The Guardian*, 26 August 1968.

134 'reunion was hardly rapturous'. 'Reunion was hardly rapturous', *Yorkshire Post*, 3 September 1968; 'Chi-Chi plays it cool', *Morning Advertiser*, 3 September 1968; 'An-An snores as Chi-Chi love calls', *South Wales Evening Argus*, 3 September 1968.

134 'hello Moscow'. 'Hello Moscow, this is An-An', *The Sunday Telegraph*, 10 November 1968.

135 'Chi-Chi did not present herself'. Michael R. Brambell and others, 'An-An and Chi-Chi', *Nature*, 222 (1969), pp. 1125–6.

136 'An-An goes home'. 'An-An goes home, mission unfulfilled', *Daily Telegraph*, 8 May 1969; 'The panda love-in is over', *Western Mail*, 8 May 1969; 'An-An gets back to the USSR', *The Journal*, 8 May 1969.

136 'gosh, I feel so sexy today'. Raymond Jackson, 'Gosh, I feel so sexy today!', *Evening Standard*, 22 May 1969.

Chapter 8

138 'when we last went to look'. J. Anthony Dale, interviewed on *Nationwide* (BBC, April 1972).

138 'embalmed and injected body'. Davis, *Fieldiana Zoology Memoirs*, p. 13.

139 'the end was nigh'. Michael Brambell, interviewed in 'Chi-Chi the panda' (BBC, 1992).

139 'newspapers mourned the passing'. 'British panda Chi-Chi dies', *Star-News*, 23 July 1972.

139 'fixed in twenty minutes'. Brambell in 'Chi-Chi the panda'.

140 'here was an indication'. Herbert J. A. Dartnall, 'Visual pigment of the giant panda *Ailuropoda melanoleuca*', *Nature*, 244 (1973), pp. 47–9.

141 'the zoological museum is nearly full'. Charles Darwin to John S. Henslow, 30 October 1836, Darwin Correspondence Database (letter no. 317; accessed 18 June 2010).

142 'mounted and put on display'. G. Frank Claringbull, 'Chi-Chi at the Natural History Museum', 27 July 1972, Natural History Museum Archives, DF 700/106.

142 'a diminutive Scotsman'. Richard Fortey, *Dry Store Room No. 1: The Secret Life of the Natural History Museum* (HarperPress, 2008), p. 203.

142 'fielding calls from the media'. A. Clarke to Michael Belcher, 7 August 1972, DF 700/106.

143 'a couple of crucial changes'. Claringbull, 'Chi-Chi at the Natural History Museum', 5 October 1972, DF 700/106.

143 'interested to learn'. J. Anthony Dale to Belcher, 9 October 1972, DF 700/106.

144 'carpenter, metalworker, seamstress'. Quoted in Joanna Lyall, *Kensington News & Post*, 12 October 1972.

144 'most helpful'. Georgina Wilson to Belcher, 1972, DF 700/106.

144 'I cannot refrain'. William Henry Flower, *Essays on museums and other subjects connected with natural history* (Ayer Publishing, 1972), p. 17.

145 'fit over the model like a glove'. Quoted in Lyall.

146 'pleased about his orchestration'. Belcher to Dale, 13 October 1972, DF 700/106.

146 'an opportunity for satire'. Ann Godden, 'Jean Rook, the First Lady of Fleet Street', 1991 (http://bit.ly/bB4edw).

146 'Rook championed Chi-Chi'. Jean Rook, *Daily Express*, 12 October 1972.

146 'Dale responded'. Dale to Belcher, 17 October 1972, DF 700/106.

146 'back at the museum'. Belcher to J. Gordon Sheals, 20 September 1972, DF 700/106.

148 'before the public opening'. Claringbull, *Chi-Chi at the Natural History Museum*, 8 December 1972, DF 700/106.

148 'Blue Peter'. Belcher to Claringbull, 23 November 1972, DF 700/106.

149 'lots of people were rather sad'. Peter Purves, *Blue Peter*, 11 December 1972.

149 'representing the sublime'. Robin Tucker to Zoological Society of London, undated, NHM Archives, PH/219.

150 'typing furiously'. Anthony Chaplin to Ronald H. Hedley, 6 November 1978, PH/219.

150 'Guy was almost human'. Colin Rawlins to Roger S. Miles, 26 June 1978, PH/219.

150 'the situation was so delicate'. Sue Runyard to Hedley, 12 November 1980, PH/219.

151 'a pelt is spoilt'. Arthur G. Hayward, 'Report', 23 July 1981, PH/219.

151 'this method ... is absolutely brilliant'. Pat Morris, interview with the author, 25 September 2009.

152 'a lovely job'. Hedley to Hayward, 4 November 1982, PH/219.

152 'first day of purgatory'. Tony Samstag, 'To Guy, with gratitude', *The Times*, 5 November 1982.

153 'on Chinese soil'. Alec Douglas-Home, BBC interview in November 1972.

154 'in spite of this change in leadership'. David Bonavia, 'Mr Heath given a boisterous welcome by Chinese girls waving Union Jacks', *The Times*, 25 May 1974.

154 'Heath had three days of talks'. John Campbell, *Edward Heath: A Biography* (Jonathan Cape, 1993), p. 635.

154 'conspiracy theories began to circulate'. PHS, 'The Times Diary', *The Times*, 7 August 1974.

155 'a pretty expensive business'. Quotations in Ollie Stone-Lee, 'Pandas "sparked diplomatic fears"', *BBC*, 29 December 2005 (http://bit.ly/cuBdGd; accessed 18 June 2010.

155 'a deliberate rebuff'. Goronwy O. Goronwy-Roberts to James Callaghan, 'Lord Zuckerman', 14 November 1974. National Archives FCO 21/1246.

Chapter 9

160 'there can be no stable and enduring peace'. Richard Nixon, 15 July 1971.

161 'it's gonna be a hell of a story'. Richard Nixon to Pat Nixon, 13 March 1972, Nixon Library, conversation no. 21–56.

162 'a Miss G. D. Shepherd'. G. D. Shepherd to NZP, 17 March 1972, Smithsonian Institution Archives.

163 'I think this is just perfect'. Emery Molnar to NZP, 9 April 1972, Smithsonian Institution Archives.

163 'for example, we have a little girl'. Wen-Tsuen Lee to Richard Nixon, 30 March 1972, Smithsonian Institution Archives.

163 'although we do not'. Sibyl E. Hamlet, draft letter, Smithsonian Institution Archives.

163 'from our vantage point'. Carl W. Larsen to Hamlet, 29 March 1972, Smithsonian Institution Archives.

164 '9-point plan'. Theodore H. Reed, 'Plans for the Pandas, if we Receive them', 1972, Smithsonian Institution Archives.

164 'there were an awful lot of people'. Pat Nixon to Richard Nixon, 20 April 1972, Nixon Library, conversation no. 714–11A.

165 'the menageries that have existed'. Quoted in Richard W. Burkhardt, 'A Man and His Menagerie', *Natural History*, February 2001.

166 'nothing has been written'. Also quoted in Burkhardt's excellent article.

166 'at the time Hsing-Hsing'. Devra G. Kleiman, interview with the author, 27 February 2009.

167 'pandas in zoo'. 'Pandas in zoo make lazy lovers, keepers find', *The Palm Beach Post*, 21 April 1974.

167 'the low taste'. Reed to Ripley, 8 May 1974, Smithsonian Institution Archives, RU365, Box 24, Folder 8.

168 'our organization believes'. Joshua H. Batchelder to J. Perry, 29 May 1974, Smithsonian Institution Archives.

168 'they offered to give us'. Reed, 'Water bed for the pandas', 29 May 1975, Smithsonian Institution Archives.

168 'this caught me (and I think, others)'. Devra Kleiman to Reed, 8 May 1974, Smithsonian Institution Archives, RU 365, Box 24, Folder 8.

169 'the receptive period'. Rosemary C. Bonney and others, 'Endocrine correlates of behavioural oestrus in the female giant panda (*Ailuropoda melanoleuca*) and associated hormonal changes in the male', *Journal of Reproduction and Fertility*, 64 (1982), pp. 209–15.

170 'she was so vocal'. Morris and Morris, *Men and Pandas*, (1966), p. 120.

170 'it was an exciting opportunity'. Gustav Peters, email to author, 3 March 2009.

170 'he came away with the first insight'. Peters, 'A note on the vocal behavior of the giant panda, *Ailuropoda melanoleuca* (David, 1869)', *Z. Säugetierkunde*, 47 (1982), 236–45.

170 'when we would put them together'. Kleiman, interview, 27 February 2009.

172 'we are often talking about species'. David Wildt, email to author, 1 June 2010.

173 'standard electroejaculation procedures'. Carol Platz and others, 'Electroejaculation and semen analysis and freezing in the giant panda (*Ailuropoda melanoleuca*)', *J. Reprod. Fertil.* 67, (1983), pp. 9–12.

174 'totally incompatible'. Devra G. Kleiman, 'Successes in 1983 panda breeding outweigh death of cub', *Tigertalk* (July 1983), Smithsonian Institution Archives, RU 365, Box 24, Folder 12.

175 'if implantation does occur'. See Hemin Zhang and others. 'Delayed implantation in giant pandas: the first comprehensive empirical evidence.' *Reproduction* 138 (2009), pp. 979–86.

176 'the early morning hours'. 'Keeping up with the Zoo's most popular celebrities', Smithsonian Institution Archives, RU 371, Box 3, Folder April 1981.

176 'Great expectations can lead'. Smithsonian Institution Archives.

177 'the panda's thumb'. Stephen J. Gould, 'The panda's peculiar thumb', *Natural History* 87 (1978), pp. 20–30.

Chapter 10

178 'virtually all aspects of an animal's existence'. George B. Schaller and others, *The Giant Pandas of Wolong*, (University of Chicago Press, 1985), p. xv.

180 'scent posts.' *The Giant Pandas of Wolong*, p.172–8.

181 'secretive mode of communication'. Schaller, *The Last Panda*, p. 99.

181 'chanced upon a news story'. Howard Quigley, interview with the author, 12 February 2010.

182 'have a taste for meat'. Armand David, '*Rapport adressé à MM. les professeurs administrateurs du Muséum d'histoire naturelle*', *Nouv. Arch. Mus. Hist. Nat. Paris*, 7 (1872), pp. 75–100.

182 'villagers reported to the researchers.' Quoted in *The Giant Pandas of Wolong*, p. 49.

183 'the panda sits crouched'. *The Last Panda*, p. 53.

183 'a real, live panda'. Quigley, interview.

183 'a rare one, a national treasure.' *The Last Panda*, p. 53.

184 'truly a unique experience'. Quigley, interview.

184 'the team went on to capture'. The findings of the China-WWF research are all taken from *The Giant Pandas of Wolong*. In 1984, the China-WWF collaboration set up a second research site in the Tangjiahe Nature Reserve, where they radiocollared several more pandas (see *The Last Panda*, pp. 169–99).

185 'to witness its lonely winter sport'. *The Last Panda*, p. 52.

186 'early and active national attention'. Songster, *A Natural Place for Nationalism*, p. 249.

187 'I don't buy it at all'. Alan H. Taylor, interview with the author, 1 March 2010.

188 'survive the bamboo die-off'. *The Last Panda*, pp. 204, 210–11.

189 'that genetic clock didn't go off'. Taylor, interview. Alan H. Taylor and others, 'Spatial patterns and environmental associates of bamboo (*Bashania fangiana* Yi) after mass-flowering in Southwestern China', *Bulletin of the Torrey Botanical Club*, 118 (1991), pp. 247–54.

189 'the arrow bamboo began to run out'. Kenneth Johnson and others, 'Responses of giant pandas to a bamboo die-off', *National Geographic Research*, 4 (1988), pp. 161–77; Donald G. Reid and others, 'Giant panda *Ailuropoda melanoleuca* behaviour and carrying capacity following a bamboo die-off', *Biological Conservation*, 49 (1989), pp. 85–104.

189 'catching free-ranging animals'. Wenshi Pan in Zhi Lü, *Giant Pandas in the Wild: Saving an Endangered Species* (Aperture, 2002), p. 14.

189 'pennies for pandas'. 'Nancy Regan starts fund-raiser to benefit starving pandas', *Lakeland Ledger*, 27 March 1984.

190 'an inept species at an evolutionary dead end'. Pan in Lü, p. 14.

190 'one of our nation's greatest riches.' Translated in Songster, p. 95.

191 'For these animals'. Translated in Songster, p. 108.

191 'the formation of dedicated panda reserves'. Jianghong Ran and others, 'Conservation of the endangered giant panda *Ailuropoda melanoleuca* in China: successes and challenges', *Oryx*, 43 (2009), pp. 176–8.

192 'into an extinction vortex'. Franck Courchamp and others, 'Rarity value and species extinction: the anthropogenic Allee effect', *PLoS Biology*, 4 (2006), e415.

192 'Chinese authorities confiscated fifty-two panda skins'. Yi-Ming Li and others, 'Illegal wildlife trade in the Himalayan region of China', *Biodiversity and Conservation*, 9 (2000), pp. 901–18.

192 'China's need for agricultural land'. Spence, p. 687. According to Spence, China and the US occupy 960 and 930 million hectares and in the late 1970s had 99 and 186 million hectares of agricultural land respectively.

193 'the Dazhai Road'. Judith Shapiro, *Mao's War Against Nature*, (Cambridge University Press, 2001), p. 96.

193 'terraces were built and grain was planted'. Shapiro, p. 100.

194 'I remember vividly'. Quoted in Shapiro, pp. 108–9.

194 'suffered and declined in numbers'. *The Last Panda*, pp. 233.

194 'the Giant Panda and its Habitat'. Ministry of Forestry of the People's Republic of China and WWF – World Wide Fund For Nature, *National Conservation Management Plan for the Giant Panda and its Habitat*, 1989.

194 'it took about three months'. John MacKinnon, interview with the author, 15 March 2010.

195 'widening WWF involvement'. For excerpts from the Phillipson Report, see *The Coming Fall of the House of Windsor*, ed. by N. Hamarman, Executive Intelligence Review, 1994.

195 'the panda experiment has been "very disappointing"'. *Sunday Express*, 29 July 1990.

195 'it had made swift academic strides'. Spence, pp. 696–711. Spence gives figures of $910 million for direct foreign investment and $1.05 billion for the international loans.

196 'Occidental Petroleum'. John S. Dermott and Jamie Florcruz, 'Mining China', *Time*, 14 May 1984.

196 'this commercial gesture'. *The Last Panda*, pp. 235–6.

198 'to produce top quality research'. Wenshi Pan and others, *The Giant Panda's Natural Refuge in the Qinling Mountains* (Peking University

Press, 1988); Wenshi Pan and others, *A Chance for Lasting Survival* (Peking University Press, 2001).

199 'poisoned by the fumes'. Lü, *Giant Pandas in the Wild*, p. 61.

199 'close enough to study one'. *Giant Pandas in the Wild*, p. 60.

199 'the small male comes near'. *The Last Panda*, p. 67.

200 'wild panda pair-bonding and cub-raising'. Wenshi Pan and others, 'Future survival of giant pandas in the Qinling Mountains of China', in *Giant Pandas: Biology and Conservation*, ed. by D. Lindburg and K. Baragona (University of California Press, 2004), pp. 81–7.

200 'Jiao Jiao lifted up her head'. *Giant Pandas in the Wild*, p. 66.

201 'rescuing abandoned cubs'. Zhi Lü and others, 'Mother-cub relationships in giant pandas in the Qinling Mountains, China, with comment on rescuing abandoned cubs', *Zoo Biology*, 13 (1994), pp. 567–8.

203 'a miniature video camera'. Xiaojian Zhu and others, 'The reproductive strategy of giant pandas (*Ailuropoda melanoleuca*): infant growth and development and mother–infant relationships', *Journal of Zoology*, 253 (2001), pp. 141–55.

203 'the population in Qinling is self-sustaining'. Wenshi Pan and others, in *Giant Pandas: Biology and Conservation*, pp. 81–7.

Chapter 11

204 'the potential for panda breeding'. Zhihe Zhang and others, 'Historical perspective of breeding giant pandas ex situ in China and high priorities for the future', in *Giant Pandas: Biology, Veterinary Medicine and Management*, ed. by D. E. Wildt and others (Cambridge University Press, 2006), pp. 455–68.

205 'had reached reproductive age'. David E. Wildt and others, 'The Giant Panda Biomedical Survey: how it began and the value of people working together across cultures and disciplines', in *Giant Pandas: Biology, Veterinary Medicine and Management*, pp. 17–36.

205 'the artificial insemination technology'. Zhihe Zhang, interview with the author, 11 March 2010.

205 'cold and drafty conference room'. For details of this meeting see
     Wildt and others, pp. 17–36.

208 'the semen of the giant panda'. JoGayle Howard and others, 'Male
     reproductive biology in giant pandas in breeding programmes
     in China', in *Giant Pandas: Biology, Veterinary Medicine and
     Management*, pp. 159–97.

209 'some people even accused'. Zhihe Zhang, interview.

210 'the case of the Florida panther'. US Fish and Wildlife Service,
     Florida Panther and the Genetic Restoration Program, 1993.

211 'DNA profiling or fingerprinting'. Stephen O'Brien and others,
     'Giant panda paternity', *Science*, 223 (1984), pp. 1127–8.

212 'to maintain the genetic fitness'. Jonathan D. Ballou and others,
     'Analysis of demographic and genetic trends for developing a
     captive breeding masterplan for the giant panda', in *Giant Pandas:
     Biology, Veterinary Medicine and Management*, pp. 495–519, p. 514.

213 'there are bureaucratic obstacles'. Victor A. David and others,
     'Parentage assessment among captive giant pandas in China', in
     Giant Pandas: Biology, Veterinary Medicine and Management, pp.
     245–73, p. 246.

213 'a vial of sperm'. David E. Wildt, interview with the author, 12
     February 2010.

213 'we are happy to work'. Zhihe Zhang, interview.

214 'we intend to cooperate'. Xiaoping Zhou, interview with the
     author, 12 March 2010.

214 'seek giant panda quantity while neglecting their quality'. Zhihe
     Zhang, *2009 Working Report of the Giant Panda Breeding Technology
     Committee of China*, 10 November 2009.

216 'standardised faecal grading'. For the standardised faecal grading
     system, see Mark Edwards and others, 'Nutrition and dietary
     husbandry', in *Giant Pandas: Biology Veterinary Medicine and
     Management*, pp. 101–58.

217 'at Schönbrunn Zoo in Vienna'. Eveline Dungl, interview with the
     author, 2008.

218 'we encouraged and helped to keep'. Mark Edwards, interview with
     the author, 31 March 2010.

218 'in parallel with all this work'. This was pieced together from
interviews with Ronald R. Swaisgood (10 February 2010) and
Donald Lindburg (24 March 2010).

220 'environmental enrichment'. Kathy Carlstead and David
Shepherdson, 'Effects of environmental enrichment on
reproduction', *Zoo Biology*, 13 (1994), pp. 447–58.

220 'pandas got larger enclosures'. Swaisgood and others, 'A quantitative
assessment of the efficacy of an environmental enrichment
programme for giant pandas', *Animal Behaviour*, 61 (2001), pp.
447–57.

221 'distinguish between odours of different individuals'. Swaisgood
and others, 'Giant pandas discriminate individual differences in
conspecific scent', *Animal Behaviour*, 57 (1999), pp. 1045–53.

222 'chemical communication'. Swaisgood and others, 'The effects
of sex, reproductive condition and context on discrimination of
conspecific odours by giant pandas', *Animal Behaviour*, 60 (2000),
pp. 227–37.

223 'less than a third'. Swaisgood, interview.

223 'Wolong's captive population'. Swaisgood and others, 'Application
of behavioral knowledge to conservation in the giant panda', *Int. J.
Comp. Psychol.*, 16 (2003), pp. 12–31.

223 'get the pandas to breed'. Xiaoping Zhou, interview.

224 'very cunning experiments'. Angela M. White and others,
'Chemical communication in the giant panda (*Ailuropoda
melanoleuca*): the role of age in the signaller and assessor', *Journal of
Zoology*, 259 (2003), pp. 171–8.

225 'smells coming to the fore'. Lee R. A. Hagey and Edith A.
MacDonald, 'Chemical cues identify gender and individuality in
giant pandas (*Ailuropoda melanoleuca*)', *Journal of Chemical Ecology*,
29 (2003), pp. 1479–88.

225 'a panda's forearms'. Lee Hagey, email to author, 23 November
2009.

226 'a kaleidoscope of scent patches'. Lee R. Hagey and Edith A.
MacDonald, 'Chemical composition of giant panda scent and its
use in communication', in *Giant pandas: biology and conservation*,

ed. by D. Lindburg and K. Baragona (Berkeley: University of California Press, 2004), pp. 121–4.

226 'cubs reared in different situations'. Rebecca J. Snyder and others, 'Behavioral and developmental consequences of early rearing experience for captive giant pandas (*Ailuropoda melanoleuca*)', *Journal of Comparative Psychology*, 117 (2003), pp. 235–45.

227 'in a creche amongst their peers'. Rebecca J. Snyder, interview with the author, 16 February 2010.

227 'we would like to move'. Zhihe Zhang, interview.

228 'using calls at close range'. Ben D. Charlton and others, 'Vocal cues to identity and relatedness in giant pandas (*Ailuropoda melanoleuca*)', *The Journal of the Acoustical Society of America*, 126 (2009), pp. 2721–32; Charlton, interview with the author, 10 February 2010.

228 'a series of experiments that mirrored'. Charlton and others, 'The information content of giant panda, *Ailuropoda melanoleuca*, bleats: acoustic cues to sex, age and size', *Animal Behaviour*, 78 (2009), pp. 893–98; Charlton and others, 'Female giant panda (*Ailuropoda melanoleuca*) chirps advertise the caller's fertile phase', *Proceedings of the Royal Society B: Biological Sciences*, 2009.

228 'they are rich in information'. Charlton, interview.

228 'Chi-Chi's right eyeball'. Angela S. Kelling and others, 'Color vision in the giant panda (*Ailuropoda melanoleuca*)', *Learning & Behavior: A Psychonomic Society Publication*, 34 (2006), pp. 154–61.

228 'a more ambitious study'. Eveline Dungl, 'Große Pandas (*Ailuropoda melanoleuca*) konnen Augenflecken und andere visuelle Formen unterscheiden lernen' (PhD thesis, University of Vienna, 2007).

229 'the fitness of potential mates'. Dungl and others, 'Discrimination of face-like patterns in the giant panda (*Ailuropoda melanoleuca*)', *Journal of Comparative Psychology*, 122 (2008), 335–343.

229 'the Schönbrunn pandas'. Eveline Dungl, email to the author, 29 March 2010.

229 'the world of panda research'. Susie Ellis and others, 'The giant panda as a social, biological and conservation phenomenon', in

Giant Pandas: Biology, Veterinary Medicine and Management, ed.
D. E. Wildt and others (Cambridge University Press, 2006), pp.
1–16, p. 11.

Chapter 12

232 'managed to secure his release'. Donald G. Reid and others, pp.
85–104, p. 90.

232 'settle back into her wild life'. Schaller, *The Last Panda*, pp. 162–3.

232 'wild-born pandas'. Kristen R. Jule and others, 'The effects of
captive experience on reintroduction survival in carnivores: A
review and analysis', *Biological Conservation,* 141 (2008), pp. 355–63.

232 'it would be inappropriate to release captive pandas': cited in the
2000 report by Sue Mainka and others.

232 'a full-scale release program'. Mainka and others, 'Reintroduction
of giant pandas', in *Giant pandas: biology and conservation,* ed.
by D. Lindburg and K. Baragona (University of California Press,
2004), pp. 246–49.

233 'to find out where pandas lived'. Caroline Liou, 'China's
Third National Panda Survey helps create a new generation of
conservationists' (http://bit.ly/d3UqmZ, accessed 21 June 2010).

234 'they just looked at me'. MacKinnon, interview.

236 'there may be as many'. Xiangjiang Zhan and others, 'Molecular
censusing doubles giant panda population estimate in a key nature
reserve', *Current Biology,* 16 (2006), R451-R452.

236 'this is a poor assumption'. David L. Garshelis and others, 'Do
revised giant panda population estimates aid in their conservation',
Ursus, 19 (2008), pp. 168–176.

236 'the Wanglang authors'. Xiangjiang Zhan and others, 'Accurate
population size estimates are vital parameters for conserving the
giant panda', *Ursus,* 20 (2009), pp. 56–62.

237 'our prediction is reasonable'. Fuwen Wei, interview with the
author, 8 March 2010.

237 'a potential danger'. Mainka and others.

238 'three years of training was enough'. Xiaoping Zhou, interview.

240 'at best a supportive role'. Donald G. Lindburg and Karen Baragona, 'Consensus and challenge: the giant panda's day is now', in *Giant Pandas: Biology and Conservation*, pp. 271–6, p. 274.

241 'the change in logging'. Zhi Lü, interview with the author, 9 March 2010.

242 'we could not have asked for more'. Wenshi Pan's foreword in Lü, *Giant Pandas in the Wild*, p. 17.

242 'overgrown with vegetation'. Lü, *Giant Pandas in the Wild*, p. 89.

244 'Grain for Green'. Jintao Xu and others, 'China's ecological rehabilitation: Unprecedented efforts, dramatic impacts, and requisite policies', *Ecological Economics*, 57 (2006), pp. 595–607.

244 'within this zone'. 'Sichuan Giant Panda Sanctuaries – Wolong, Mt Siguniang and Jiajin Mountains – UNESCO World Heritage Centre', Annex 4, p. 28.

245 'annual percentage growth rate'. 'CIA – The World Factbook – Country Comparison: Population growth rate', estimated 2010 (http://bit.ly/4avCkQ, accessed 21 June 2010).

245 'China's ecological footprint'. Calculated from 'Footprint for Nations' (http://bit.ly/asH1Ey, accessed 21 June 2010).

245 'China invested far more than any country'. Calculation based on China and the US investing 34.6 billion and 18.6 billion, respectively (see *Who's winning the green energy race?* The Pew Charitable Trusts (http://bit.ly/bN1XXz, accessed 21 June 2010); China and the US estimates of GDP from 2009 are $8,789 billion and $14,260 billion, respectively, taken from 'CIA – The World Factbook – Country Comparison: National product' (http://bit. ly/19QwIo, accessed 21 June 2010).

245 'when it comes to reforestation'. John MacKinnon and Haibin Wang, *The Green Gold of China* (EU-China Biodiversity Programme, 2008), p. 278.

245 'China's economy is expanding'. 'China – Country Overview', The World Bank, (http://bit.ly/bLrD5H, accessed 21 June 2010).

246 'a 2004 report'. Chunquan Zhu and others, *China's Wood Market, Trade and the Environment* (WWF, 2004).

247 'the rate of habitat loss'. Jianguo Liu and others, 'Ecological degradation in protected areas: the case of Wolong Nature Reserve for giant pandas', *Science*, 292 (2001), pp. 98–101.

247 'the number of households'. Zhi Lü and others, 'A framework for evaluating the effectiveness of protected areas: the case of Wolong Biosphere Reserve', *Landscape and Urban Planning*, 63 (2003), pp. 213–23.

248 'a modest impact'. Guangming He and others, 'Spatial and temporal patterns of fuelwood collection in Wolong Nature Reserve: Implications for panda conservation', *Landscape and Urban Planning*, 92 (2009), pp. 1–9.

248 'to switch from fuelwood to electricity'. Li An and others, 'Modeling the choice to switch from fuelwood to electricity. Implications for giant panda habitat conservation', *Ecological Economics*, 42 (2002), pp. 445–57.

248 'to reduce the population size'. Liu and others, 'A framework for evaluating the effects of human factors on wildlife habitat: the case of giant pandas', *Conservation Biology*, 13 (1999), pp. 1360–70; Liu, 'Integrating ecology with human demography, behavior, and socioeconomics: needs and approaches', *Ecological Modelling*, 140 (2001), pp. 1–8.

249 'Tourism Bureau of Sichuan Province'. Weiqiong Yang and others, 'Impact of the Wenchuan Earthquake on tourism in Sichuan, China', *Journal of Mountain Science*, 5 (2008), pp. 194–208.

250 'most investments were from external operators'. He and others, 'Distribution of economic benefits from ecotourism: a case study of Wolong Nature Reserve for Giant Pandas in China', *Environmental Management*, 42 (2008), pp. 1017–25.

250 'a massive earthquake'. Alexandra Witze, 'The sleeping dragon', *Nature* 457 (2009), pp. 153–7; Dajun Wang and others, 'Turning earthquake disaster into long-term benefits for the panda', *Conservation Biology*, 22 (2008), pp. 1356–60.

251 'it virtually destroyed'. Fuwen Wei, interview.

251 'in the short term, however'. Liu Wei, email to the author, 9 May 2010.

251 'it's left a lot of bare slopes'. MacKinnon, interview.

251 'an opportunity to jump start'. Wang and others.

251 'an immense challenge'. Lynne Gilbert-Norton and others, 'A meta-analytic review of corridor effectiveness', *Conservation Biology*, 24 (2010), pp. 660–68.

252 'migrate down the mountain'. *The Giant Pandas of Wolong*.

252 'revealed the precise opposite'. Wenshi Pan and others, *A Chance for Lasting Survival*; Xuehua Liu and others, 'Giant panda movements in Foping Nature Reserve, China', *Journal of Wildlife Management*, 66 (2002), pp. 1179–88.

253 'faeces in the Wanglang'. Xiangjiang Zhan and others, 'Molecular analysis of dispersal in giant pandas', *Molecular Ecology*, 16 (2007), pp. 3792–800.

253 'designing habitat corridors'. Dajun Wang, interview with the author, 7 March 2010.

254 'it is the right thing to do'. Zhi Lü, interview.

254 'a nostalgic book'. *The Last Panda*, p. 251.

255 'in the 1980s'. George B. Schaller, 'Foreword', in *Giant Pandas: Biology and Conservation*, p. xii.

255 'the panda's day is now'. Donald G. Lindburg and Karen Baragona, 'Consensus and challenge: the giant panda's day is now', in *Giant Pandas: Biology and Conservation*, pp. 271–6.

255 'the future of the panda'. Swaisgood and others, 'Giant panda conservation science: how far we have come', *Biology Letters* 6 (2010), 143–5.

Epilogue

261 'I am haunted'. Schaller, *The Last Panda*, p. 251

List of Illustrations

*Indicates author's own photograph.

While every effort has been made to contact copyright-holders of illustrations, the author and publishers would be grateful for information about any illustrations where they have been unable to trace them, and would be glad to make amendments in further editions.

Acknowledgements

I would like to thank everyone at Profile Books for all the support and attention to detail they have invested in *The Way of the Panda*, especially my editor, Peter Carson and managing editor, Penny Daniel, also Rukhsana Yasmin and Rebecca Gray. Thanks too to James Pullen at the Wiley Agency Ltd.

I am immensely grateful to the following for giving up their valuable time to be interviewed at length: Desmond Morris, Eveline Dungl, Wang Tiejun, George B. Schaller, Stephen O'Brien, Ben Charlton, Rebecca Snyder, Alan Taylor, Ronald Swaisgood, Donald Lindburg, David Wildt, Howard Quigley, Wang Dajun, Lü Zhi, Zhu Xiaojian, Xie Yan, Wang Menghu, Nancy Nash, Sarah Bexell, Zhang Zhihe, John MacKinnon, Wei Fuwen, Mark Edwards, Zhou Xiaoping and, in particular, Devra Kleiman who was able to read through and comment on much of my manuscript before she sadly passed away in April 2010. There are, of course, many more key protagonists in the panda's story that I might have spoken to and it was only time that prevented me; this book rests heavily on their written work.

On top of these key interviews, I contacted dozens of others, who happily spoke to me or emailed me answers to my questions. Thank you Carla Nappi, Sujit Sivasundaram, Jim Endersby, Geraint Hughes, Peter Ho, Mary Anne Andrei, Pat Morris, Gregg Mitman, Judith Shapiro, Blair Hedges, Gustav Peters, Ri-Cheng Chian, Lee Hagey, Lord Cranbrook, Stephen Nott, Mike Kerris, Matt Gage, Tim Birkhead, Bill Holt, Philippa Scott, Michael Bruford, Melinda Hill, Gordon Corbet, Wei Liu, Yadira Galindo, Sun Shan, Lan Zheng, Lu Zhang, John Hannon, Vicki Croke and Phil McKenna. In particular, I would like to express special gratitude to Elena Songster and Alexis Schwarzenbach; in spite of working on similar projects – Dr Songster on the symbolism of the panda in China and Dr

Schwarzenbach on a history of the World Wildlife Fund – both have been incredibly open and willing to read through and comment on bits of my text. One chapter ('Life after death') was improved by comments from Sam Alberti and part of it will appear in a collection of essays on *The Afterlives of Animals* to be published by the University of Virginia Press in 2011. I have been blogging as I've been writing, which has helped me to get ideas down and also to embrace feedback from others, especially Chet Chin, Dee Ganna, Andrei Kotkin, Andi McLean and Jérôme Pouille.

I spent quite a bit of time in libraries poring over obscure articles and archives at the Natural History Museum in London (thanks Polly Parry, James Hatton and Richard Sabin); the Linnean Society of London (Gina Douglas and Lynda Brooks); the Zoological Society of London (Michael Palmer and James Goodwin); and the Smithsonian Institution Archives (Pamela Henson). I have also been helped by several people at the Muséum National d'Histoire Naturelle (Cécile Callou); the Museum für Naturkunde in Berlin (Saskia Jancke); and the excellent British Cartoon Archive (Nicholas Hiley).

I hope you like the collection of images as much as I do and I owe an absolutely massive debt to everyone who let me to reproduce their artwork or photographs for free. Thank you Macmillan for the images from *Nature* magazine, the Smithsonian Institution for the panda skull, Barbara Chiang for the wonderful paintings by Chiang Yee, Nancy Nash for the panda at Beijing Zoo, Desmond Morris for the photo at Moscow Zoo, Luke Hayes and the Design Museum for the photograph of Panda Eyes, Jessie Cohen and the Smithsonian National Zoo for the image of Ling-Ling and Dr Kleiman, George B. Schaller for the slides from Wolong in the 1980s, Lü Zhi for her super photos from Changqing in the 1990s, Mark Edwards for the bottle-feeding panda and Anne Belov for her satirical panda cartoon. Without their support, the book would not look half as good as it does. Thanks also to Martin Lubikowski for the very superior line drawings.

My research trip to China was funded by an award from the Society of Author's K. Blundell Trust and the British Council kindly invited me to give a lecture with Dr Wang Dajun at the Tianjin Natural History Museum. In planning my itinerary, I received excellent advice from many people, but particularly from Alex Witze, Dora Duan and Li Rengui. In addition to all those who gave me an interview, I was welcomed openly by everyone else at the Shansui Conservation Center, the Center for Nature and Society at Peking University, the Wildlife Conservation Society, the Institute of Zoology at the Chinese Academy of Sciences, the EU-China Biodiversity Programme, the Chengdu Research Base of Giant Panda Breeding and the China Conservation and Research Center for the Giant Panda at Bifengxia.

I have leaned on friends and family along the way, including my parents John and Stella, siblings Tom and Mary, Mark Ruddy, Hugh and Sheila Stirling, Zaid Al-Zaidy, Matthew Lea, Marisa Chan, Kate Moorcroft, John Taylor, John Whitfield, Sara Abdulla, Camille Roux, Adam Rutherford, Tom Gillmor and the Celeriac XI. At the heart of it all, as ever, are Charlotte, Harry and Edward.

If you would like to find out about aspects of writing this book or keep abreast future events, please subscribe to my blog thewayofthepanda/blogspot.com, show that you 'like' the book on Facebook http://www.facebook.com/WayOfThePanda or follow me on Twitter @ WayOfThePanda.

Further reading

General

Desmond Morris and Ramona Morris, *Men and Pandas* (New York: McGraw-Hill, 1966).

Chris Catton, *Pandas* (New York: Facts on File Publications, 1990).

Elena E. Songster *Panda Nation: Nature, Science, and Nationalism in the People's Republic of China* (forthcoming).

George B. Schaller, *The Last Panda* (Chicago:University of Chicago Press, 1993).

Jonathan D. Spence, *The Search for Modern China*, first edn (New York: Norton, 1991).

Will Hutton, *The Writing on the Wall: China and the West in the 21st Century,* (Abacus, 2008).

PART I. EXTRACTION

Armand David, *Abbe David's Diary: Being an Account of the French Naturalist's Journeys and Observations in China in the Years 1866 to 1869*, trans. by H. Fox (Boston: Harvard University Press, 1949).

Fa-ti Fan, *British Naturalists in Qing China: Science, Empire and Cultural Encounter* (Boston: Harvard University Press, 2004)

Dwight D. Davis, 'The giant panda: a morphological study of evolutionary mechanisms', *Fieldiana Zoology Memoirs*, 3 (1964).

Stephen J. O'Brien *et al*, 'A molecular solution to the riddle of the giant panda's phylogeny', *Nature*, 317 (1985).

Gregg Mitman, *Reel-Nature* (Boston: Harvard University Press, 1999).

Theodore Roosevelt and Kermit Roosevelt, *Trailing the Giant Panda* (New York: Scribner, 1929).

Michael Kiefer, *Chasing the Panda: How an Unlikely Pair of Adventurers Won the Race to Capture the Mythical 'White Bear'* (New York: Four Walls Eight Windows, 2002).

Vicki Croke, *The Lady and the Panda: The True Adventures of the First American Explorer to Bring Back China's Most Exotic Animal* (New York: Random House, 2006).

Ruth Harkness, *The Lady and the Panda* (London: Nicholson & Watson, 1938).

Yee Chiang, *The Story of Ming* (Penguin Books, 1945).

Shuyun Sun, *The Long March* (London: Harper Perennial, 2007).

PART II. ABSTRACTION

Shu Guang Zhang, *Economic Cold War: America's Embargo Against China and the Sino-Soviet Alliance, 1949–1963* (CA. Stanford University Press, 2001).

Judith Shapiro, *Mao's War Against Nature: Politics and the Environment in Revolutionary China* (Cambridge: Cambridge University Press, 2001).

Sigrid Schmalzer, *The People's Peking Man: Popular Science and Human Identity in Twentieth-Century China* (Chicago: University of Chicago Press, 2008).

Alexis Schwarzenbach, 'WWF – A Biography', Collection Rolf Heyne (forthcoming).

Max Nicholson, *The New Environmental Age* (Cambridge: Cambridge University Press, 1989).

Elspeth Huxley, *Peter Scott: Painter and Naturalist* (Faber and Faber, 1993).

'The Launching of a New Ark,' in *First Report of the President and Trustees of the World Wildlife Fund. An International Foundation for Saving the World's Wildlife and Wild Places 1961–64*, (London: Collins, 1965).

Bob Mullan and Garry Marvin, *Zoo Culture*. 2nd edn, (IL:University of Illinois Press, 1999).

Oliver Graham-Jones, *First Catch your Tiger* (London: Collins, 1970).

Roderick Nash, *Wilderness and the American mind*, fourth edn (CT: Yale UniversityPress, 2001).

Zuckerman, Solly. 'What went wrong', *Sunday Times*, 10 November 1968.

Ramona Morris and Desmond Morris, *The Giant Panda*, revised by Jonathan Barzdo (London: Penguin, 1982).

Michael R. Brambell *et al*, 'An-An and Chi-Chi', *Nature*, 222 (1969).

'Chi-Chi the panda' (BBC, 1992).

William T. Stearn, *The Natural History Museum at South Kensington. A History of the British Museum (Natural History) 1753–1980* (Heinemann, 1981).

Lorraine Daston and Gregg Mitman, eds, *Thinking with Animals: New Perspectives on Anthropomorphism* (New York: Columbia University Press, 2005).

Sam Alberti, ed., *Afterlives of Animals*, (University of Virginia Press, forthcoming).

PART III. PROTECTION

George B. Schaller and others, *TheGiant Pandas of Wolong* (Chicago: University of Chicago Press, 1985)

Zhi Lü, *Giant Pandas in the Wild: Saving an Endangered Species* (CA: Aperture, 2002).

Ministry of Forestry of the People's Republic of China and WWF – World Wide Fund For Nature, *National Conservation Management Plan for the Giant Panda and its Habitat*, 1989.

Wenshi Pan *et al*, *The Giant Panda's Natural Refuge in the Qinling Mountains* (Peking University Press, 1988).

Wenshi Pan and others, *A Chance for Lasting Survival* (Peking University Press, 2001).

Donald Lindburg and Karen Baragona (eds.) *Giant Pandas: Biology and Conservation* (CA: University of California Press, 2004).

David E. Wildt *et al*, *Giant Pandas: Biology, Veterinary Medicine and Management* (Cambridge: Cambridge University Press, 2006).

Xiangjiang Zhan *et al*, 'Molecular censusing doubles giant panda population estimate in a key nature reserve', *Current Biology*, 16 (2006).

Baowei Zhang *et al*, 'Genetic viability and population history of the giant panda, putting an end to the "evolutionary dead end"?', *Molecular Biology and Evolution* 24 (2007): 1801–10.

Sichuan Giant Panda Sanctuaries – Wolong, Mt Siguniang and Jiajin
   Mountains – UNESCO World Heritage Centre.
John MacKinnon and Haibin Wang, *The Green Gold of China*
   (EU-China Biodiversity Programme, 2008).
Jianguo Liu *et al*, 'A framework for evaluating the effects of human
   factors on wildlife habitat: the case of giant pandas', *Conservation
   Biology*, 13 (1999).
Jianguo Liu *et al*, 'Ecological degradation in protected areas: the case of
   Wolong Nature Reserve for giant pandas', *Science*, 292 (2001).
Dajun Wang *et al*, 'Turning earthquake disaster into long-term benefits
   for the panda', *Conservation Biology*, 22 (2008).
Swaisgood *et al*, 'Giant panda conservation science: how far we have
   come', Biology Letters 6 (2010), 143–5.

Index

M

MacKinnon, John 194, 234, 251
Macmillan, Harold 129
MacPhail, Ian 98, 103, 104–5,
    106–8
Maltsev, Terentsy 90
Mao Zedong
    civil war 74, 75
    Dazhai 192
    Great Leap Forward 88–9,
        90
    and Heath 154
    Long March 56
    and Nixon 160, *160*
    Panda Electronics 99
    and Soviet Union 81–2, *82*, 83
    and US 81
Margaret, Princess 71–2, 102
Mastroianni, Marcello 84
Mayr, Ernest 34–5
Mei-Lan 79
Mei-Mei 68
Mei-Xiang 215
Memphis Zoo 215
Merlini, Marisa 84
Mexico 161
Michigan State University (MSU)
    246–50
Milne, A. A. 141
Milne, Christopher Robin 141
Milne-Edwards, Alphonse 19–20,
    21, *22*, 23, 24, 25, 37
Min Mountains 186, 187
Ming *69*, 71–2
Ming-Ming 121, 173

Ministry of Construction (China)
    205, 206, 210, 212
Ministry of Forestry (China)
    cubs 201, 203
    Pan Wenshi 189, 198, 240
    panda deaths investigation 186,
        187
    protection 188, 190–91
    and San Diego Zoo 215
    Wolong pandas 213
    and WWF 113, 115
    see also State Forestry
        Administration
missionaries 11–12
    see also David, Armand
Mitman, Gregg 47, 86–7
mo 5
Molnar, Mrs Emery 163
Morges Manifesto 98
Morris, Desmond ix
    Chi-Chi 90, 93, 169–70
    Chi-Chi and An-An 122, 123,
        124, 128, *128*, 133, 224
    Zoo Time 86, 87, 88
Morris, Pat 151–2
Morris, Ramona vii
Morton, Sam 125
Moscow Zoo
    An-An 118, 161
    Chi-Chi 83–4
    Chi-Chi and An-An 119, 122,
        124–9, 131
    Ping-Ping 83, 84, 118,
        161
Mountfort, Guy 95, 97–8